The
Mind of a
Murderer

The Mind of a Murderer

Privileged Access to the
Demons That Drive
Extreme Violence

Katherine Ramsland

Foreword by Dr. Michael Stone

 PRAEGER

AN IMPRINT OF ABC-CLIO, LLC
Santa Barbara, California • Denver, Colorado • Oxford, England

Copyright 2011 by Katherine Ramsland

Library of Congress Cataloging-in-Publication Data

Ramsland, Katherine M., 1953–
   The mind of a murderer : privileged access to the demons that drive extreme violence / Katherine Ramsland ; foreword by Michael Stone.
      p. cm.
   Includes bibliographical references and index.
   ISBN 978-0-313-38672-5 (hard copy : alk. paper)—ISBN 978-0-313-38673-2 (ebook)
 1. Murder. 2. Murderers. 3. Violence. I. Title.
   HV6515.R2534   2011
   364.152′3019—dc22   2010040760

ISBN: 978-0-313-38672-5
EISBN: 978-0-313-38673-2

15 14 13   2 3 4 5

This book is also available on the World Wide Web as an eBook.
Visit www.abc-clio.com for details.

Praeger
An Imprint of ABC-CLIO, LLC

ABC-CLIO, LLC
130 Cremona Drive, P.O. Box 1911
Santa Barbara, California 93116-1911

This book is printed on acid-free paper ∞

Manufactured in the United States of America

For Alexandre Lacassagne,
who started it all and who would understand

Contents

Foreword

Katherine Ramsland, the doyenne of forensic psychology and one of the most prolific writers on the topic of murder and other forms of violent crime, has in her newest book created something unique in the literature on multiple murder. In *The Mind of a Murderer*, Dr. Ramsland provides biographical sketches of a dozen and a half notorious murderers, spanning over a century—from Joseph Vacher in the 1890s to Tommy Lynn Sells of the 1990s. Each killer was responsible for a number of deaths—ranging from four to more than forty.

But the cases were chosen specifically because each killer had been the subject of an intense, and often prolonged, examination, most often by a psychiatrist or psychologist. In a few cases, the expert was a sociologist or a minister. Since each expert offered opinions about the "causes" and prime motives of the murderer's actions, we are treated to a century's worth of speculation about what prompts someone to commit multiple murder. About two thirds of the cases involve serial sexual homicide (the most common form of "serial killer"), but we also learn about two mass murderers, two spree killers (whose murders were spread out over a couple of weeks), a familicide, and an infanticidal woman who killed her five children.

The vignettes are arranged in chronological order, allowing the reader to progress from the rather simplistic and often quaint ideas put forward by the experts in the early 1900s to the more sophisticated and scientifically grounded theories of the last generation. To embark on this scientific journey is a humbling experience. It is pretty clear that the notions about cause that we currently find so compelling—so much more *convincing* than what the psychiatrists were thinking in the era between the two world wars—are destined to strike readers fifty years hence as, well, simplistic and quaint.

As always, Dr. Ramsland writes with a clarity of prose and elegance of style that make her the envy of forensic commentators and establish her as a genuine authority in her field. That, however, is not the main reason this books belongs on your shelf. The main reason is this: with every vignette you will learn something about a famous murderer that you did not know before. Even in the chapter on Tommy Lynn Sells, who is currently counting the days till his execution on Texas's Death Row—where

I interviewed him and where he receives letters from me as we continue to exchange them—Dr. Ramsland's probing research unearthed things about this man that I did not know. I didn't know, for example, that he had a tombstone tattoo on his arm with the name of his dead twin sister (they both contracted meningitis at age two, which she did not survive). I also didn't know that, when he was seventeen, he tried to have sex with his mother, who then kicked him out.

The opinions of the experts reflect, as is always the case, the zeitgeist and corpus of knowledge of their time. The French physician and forensic investigator Alexandre Lacassagne worked in the last quarter of the nineteenth century, when fingerprinting was just in its infancy. He relied, instead, on the astute and thorough questioning of medical and law enforcement personnel to learn all he could about the characteristics of killers and about the specifics of their methods. He learned how the grooves etched into bullets when fired from a particular gun could aid in identifying a killer. But his main interest was not so much in the method as in the *mind* of the killer. To that end, he interviewed the sadistic killer Joseph Vacher over an extended period, building up a picture of which risk factors were at work (childhood cruelty and bullying, rage, and callousness) and which were not (hereditary "taint," brain damage, and epilepsy). Lacassagne's insights stand up well even in our day.

The search for cause and effect regarding the mind of the murderer continued and took a curious detour in the mid-twentieth century. Psychoanalysis was now the fashionable source of explanation, and correlation was king. If, as children, killers had suffered parental neglect or cruelty (as was usually the case), then bad parenting (the correlation) was determined to be the "cause" of their actions. One somehow forgot that, for each killer, there were probably a hundred persons who emerged from similarly dreadful homes and were never even assaultive. Think also of Jeffrey Dahmer's brother: they were raised in the same household, but the brother turned out normal. Or the three brothers of killer Gary Gilmore (the subject of Norman Mailer's *Executioner's Song*), all raised by the same abusive alcoholic father, but all decent and productive citizens—unlike Gary.

As for the various correlations, they were then given catchy titles from biblical or Greek mythology, along the lines of Freud's Oedipus complex. Thus, as Dr. Ramsland tells it, a young girl who killed her siblings suffered from what psychiatrist Paul de River called a "Cain complex"; because she also killed a parent, this meant she also had an "Electra complex." The new terms did lend an air of erudition to the speaker—but, alas, had no explanatory value.

The experts from the last quarter of the twentieth century, as Dr. Ramsland makes clear, were more open to the multiplicity of risk factors that nudge certain men and women to commit murder. The recognition of inherited tendencies, long ignored at midcentury, made a comeback. Sometimes an expert went overboard, as when psychiatrist Helen Morrison claimed that "there is something in the genes that leads a person to become a serial killer. In other words, he is a serial killer before he is born." Not true. Though genes are occasionally a major factor, there is no baby resting in the obstetrics ward of whom we can say, "*That* one will be a serial killer!"

Dr. Ramsland, carrying forward the scientific spirit of Lacassagne, shows us how expert opinion about the mind of the murderer has evolved over the past hundred years—passing through a long period of one-size-fits-all theories, and back to the open-minded, multifactorial approach of Lacassagne. We can at this stage of our knowledge speak about *patterns* in the lives of certain types of killers. We can speak about the *pathways*—including the unpredictable bumps in the road that lead one person with a risky pattern to "actualize" the pattern and commit murder, while another person in a similar pattern, moving along a similar pathway, leads a peaceful and productive life. In the past hundred years, our knowledge about patterns and pathways has improved significantly. But we are still a long way from being able to speak *prescriptively*. We cannot say, for example, that a young person showing risk factors *X, Y,* and *Z* (such as parental cruelty, genes for a "callous-unemotional personality," and serious injury to the brain's frontal lobe) is *destined* to become a murderer. All we can say is that such a person is many times more likely to pursue a violent path than someone showing none of those factors.

If I may add my own allusion to Greek mythology, Dr. Ramsland offers us a double odyssey. Like Odysseus confronting all manner of monsters and scary figures—such as the Cyclops and the seductive Circe—we are given the chance to travel alongside some of the most "high-profile" killers of the past hundred years. Then we become acquainted with the experts who studied each of them the most extensively. We end up coming as close as we can get to the *mind of the murderer* in this second decade of the twenty-first century. This makes Dr. Ramsland's book doubly rewarding, doubly interesting, and doubly important.

Michael H. Stone, MD
Professor of Clinical Psychiatry, Columbia University
Author of *The Anatomy of Evil*

Acknowledgments

In many ways, this book is the result of years of interaction with many people, as well as opportunities to research and write about individual cases of serial killers. Therefore, I'm sure I can't name everyone who should be acknowledged, but among those with whom I discussed portions of this book and from whom I received significant feedback are the following:

- Marilyn Bardsley, my editor and friend at the Crime Library, and my most encouraging friends, Ruth Osborne, Kelly Martin, Detective Joe Pochron, Zachary Lysek, Pelli Wheaton, and Marie Gallagher;
- The FBI profilers and detectives who have taught me a great deal about serial killer investigations: Gregg McCrary, Robert Ressler, Robert Keppel, and John Douglas;
- The psychologists and psychiatrists who have taught me about clinical and forensic practice: Lou Schlesinger, Michael Stone, Phillip Resnick, and Al Carlisle;
- Robert Hare, who provided great resources for understanding psychopaths;
- The psychologists, psychiatrists, and counselors who undertook to get closer to these offenders with compassion, curiosity, and clinical scrutiny;
- The serial killer who first inspired me to become interested in this field of research;
- Karen Walton at DeSales University, along with students in my Dangerous Minds course, whose interest inspires me to keep learning;
- Michael Wilt, my editor, for his guidance and enthusiasm for this project; and
- John Silbersack, my agent and trusted friend, whose vision, support, and encouragement have kept me going for over two decades.

CHAPTER 1

Introduction: The Criminal Type

Life is not a series of gig lamps symmetrically arranged, but a luminous halo, a semi-transparent envelope surrounding us from the beginning of consciousness to the end.

—Virginia Woolf

When I first received Karl Berg's book *The Sadist*, I opened it at once. It's one of the earliest detailed clinical examinations of a brutal, blood-starved serial killer. Since Berg had also created a rudimentary profile from crimes he'd linked, as well as performed the victims' autopsies, when he finally came face-to-face with the sadistic offender, Peter Kürten, his perspective was unique. In this narrative, we first see Berg's experience as the bodies turn up, stabbed, bludgeoned, or choked, which prepares us for the "monster." When the police make an arrest, we know what's next: Kürten speaks. He was among the worst of the worst, and as a clever, calculating psychopath he freely described to Berg what he'd done to each victim.

There's a clear difference between the recorded facts of a case and the way a killer tells his or her own story. The raw quality of such confessions makes us feel as if we're in the same room. It's disturbing yet titillating, grotesque, and wondrous. How, we ask, can a person get this way?

That's the reason for this book. As I've written about the psychology of extreme offenders, I've noticed that over the past century, several mental health professionals have ventured closer than usual to a killer's soul to learn its secrets. Sure, there have been journalists and crime writers who befriended killers for this same purpose, but this book includes only the work of professionals educated in the principles and techniques of criminology, psychiatry, psychology, or counseling. Presumably, their background not only guides them in gathering psychologically relevant information but also reminds them of the need for theories and treatment plans. While some were merely curious, others believed they could shed significant light on the intimate nature of extreme violence. A few even tried to become a therapist or a friend.

Progress in the field of criminal psychology builds on prior work. Each mental health expert evaluates offenders according to the context and explanatory codes of his or her times. But despite assessments of countless offenders over the past century, only a few clinicians have ventured beyond the typical evaluation period to thoroughly explore a specific criminal's mind. As we examine these singular in-depth studies, we discover that the nineteenth-century "criminal autobiographies" provided some tools and techniques that are still in use today. We also see how certain notions have shaped and even limited analyses, so as we've learned more we've discarded some theories and strengthened others.

No one is better positioned to offer intimate details than someone with expertise on the abnormal mind. Thanks to their training, the clinicians in these pages have used their privileged access to provide productive ideas about what makes the most perverse murderers tick. These tales offer a map of the past century, almost decade by decade, in terms of how the psychiatric profession has approached mass and serial murder. Some accounts are amusingly naïve, while others provide genuine clarity and direction. All of them, collectively, have helped us to better see where we've been and where we might now go as we ponder the most violent of criminal minds.

Overview

Since the earliest days of psychiatry, "alienists" have tried to understand the motives and acts of the criminally insane. Initially they believed that anyone who acted contrary to reason must be psychotic, but then a certain type of rational criminal stood out. In 1809, hospital director Philippe Pinel was among the first to note this "mania without delirium," thereby acknowledging the disturbing behavior of what we now call a psychopath. (He treated a missionary who had coldly murdered his family to send their souls to heaven.) Following Pinel, other wardens of psychiatric asylums studied what they called "moral insanity" to learn how the faculty for socially appropriate behavior could fail. Such offenders, they observed, had no conscience about their cruel or destructive acts, and yet delusional mental illness was absent. They seemed to know what they were doing but to care little about harm done to others or even themselves.[1]

Since around 1830, the enthusiasm for scientific methods influenced physicians with a specialty in mental disease to clarify and systematize their knowledge about violent offenders. They focused on defining a context that made sense of dangerous aggression, based on cause-and-effect ideas about disease. Isaac Ray was a founder of the discipline of forensic psychiatry, with his publication in 1838 of the authoritative text *A Treatise on the Medical Jurisprudence of Insanity*. He was a superintendant for several psychiatric hospitals, and his ideas influenced the defense team during the 1843 English trial of Daniel M'Naghten, a case that inspired the wording for the insanity defense still in use today. Ever a defender of the rights of the mentally ill, Ray helped lead the way for medical professionals to treat such people humanely. In his treatise, he distinguished different types of murderers (e.g., the homicidal monomaniac versus the criminal murderer). The former commits murder for its own sake, whereas the latter usually does it for selfish gain. The monomaniac makes no plan and has little concern about consequences, and peculiarities of character usually precede his conduct.[2]

As Darwin's theory of evolution created an early form of environmental criminology, physicians created diagnostic texts with which to foster professional communication and disease codification. This model inspired psychiatrists and heads of asylums to do likewise.[3]

Psychiatrists believed that mental illness had a biological cause, and as it was passed to each successive generation, it degenerated. Their notions endured throughout the nineteenth century until Emil Kraepelin began to systematically collect data on his cases. His study revealed patterns that he turned into a typology of mental illness. By the early twentieth century, he had upended erroneous theories about biological psychiatry.

Then nervous disorders, especially of the upper classes, brought in hypnotherapists and psychoanalysis, with psychotherapy aimed toward getting at the heart of psychological disorders—unhappiness, stress, and unresolved conflicts. A psychiatrist or alienist was a person who worked in asylums, while a neurologist was trained in pathology and medicine, usually ran a private office, and attended to "nervous disorders." They saw that psychological influences played a role in a patient's condition as well as in his or her treatment. The use of suggestion in treatment was particularly prominent.[4]

During the decade prior to World War I, psychotherapy became popular with members of middle-class society, who apparently enjoyed being the center of a specialist's attention. Sigmund Freud led the way to the couch, becoming world famous for his controversial theories about sexuality, repressed unconscious conflicts, and the deep roots of neuroses.

By the 1950s, genuine science began to displace the idea of unconscious conflicts with research on the brain. Medications had made significant inroads into the treatment of major mental illness, and within two decades, psychoanalysis had become more of a parenthesis between two forms of biological psychiatry than the light of truth it had purported to be. "In retrospect," says social historian Edward Shorter, "Freud's psycho-analysis appears as a pause in the evolution of biological approaches to brain and mind rather than as the culminating event in the history of psychiatry."[5] He admits that psychoanalysis was of enormous conse-quence, however, because it took psychiatry out of the asylum and gave it prestige as an office-based specialty.

But let's back up to the nineteenth century, where the idea of the crim-inal mind would lead to the earliest form of intimate case analysis.

Preparations

Richard von Krafft-Ebing was among the nineteenth-century alienists who believed in the degeneracy of mental illness. The theory held that a weak strain that began with an acquired characteristic such as alcohol-ism or compulsive theft would become genetically transmittable (a pro-cess that was unclear). Alienists studied the progress (or regress) of these influences within families. Thus, they recorded detailed case histories.

Born and educated in Germany, by the 1860s Krafft-Ebing was a staff psychiatrist in Baden, Germany, when he first preached the notion that criminality was the result of degeneration. Psychosis was but a link in a genetic chain. He thought that degeneration most commonly affected the sex drive, producing an undersexed, oversexed, or sexually deviant condi-tion. He then began the ambitious enterprise of using cases to identify and categorize sexual pathologies. As director of the Feldhof Asylum, he was often a consultant to the courts regarding psychological issues, and this gave him access to the most extreme offenders. He also became a pro-fessor, teaching medicine and psychiatry at the University of Strasburg, as well as at universities in Graz and Vienna. Because he had his feet in both worlds, he assisted in moving psychiatry from the asylum to the more learned communities. In addition, he had his own private practice.[6] To his credit, Krafft-Ebing began the ambitious process of learning what he could about these unique and often quite brutal people.

His goal was to make the diagnosis of mental disorders more uniform with a classification system, which he published as *A Textbook of Insan-ity* and *Psychopathia Sexualis with Especial Reference to the Antipathic Sexual Instinct: A Medico-Forensic Study*. Clarifying such terms as "necro-philia," "masochism," and "fetishism," he helped to define the differences between what was considered normal and abnormal. Among the cases he described were many recidivating offenders, including sexually sadistic serial killers. He took the details of some of them from the work of a con-temporary, the Italian anthropologist Cesare Lombroso.[7]

Lombroso had ascended quickly in the field of criminology with his "confirmation" of what he called "the criminal type." In 1876, he published a book about criminal anthropology, focusing largely on his own prodigious studies, which grew through successive editions into the multivolume study *L'uomo delinquente* (*The Criminal Man*). Lombroso had made systematic measurements of the skulls and bodies of numerous offenders, developing a theory that not only was criminality inherited but also its propensity was visible in certain features of the physical body. The "born criminal," he and his colleagues concluded, was genetically defective. In fact, it seemed likely that such people were primitive throwbacks who, due to their lack of intellectual sophistication, were compelled toward crime. The born criminal, Lombroso insisted, had a diminished sensibility to pain, no sense of right and wrong, and no remorse.

Due to his growing influence, Lombroso managed to shift the study of criminal behavior into what he viewed as the realm of science. It was all about measuring, observing, calculating, and comparing. During his prime, he founded the Italian School of Positivist Criminology, developed a rudimentary lie detector, and warned the courts to be cautious about capital punishment. He took a dim view of how crimes were often solved with little evidence. Although Lombroso's interest in criminals originated in a study of tattoos, he soon began collecting skulls, preserved brains, and objects made or used by lunatics and criminals. He worked in an asylum during the 1870s, where he was able to make anthropometric measurements on numerous inmates and assemble a portfolio of illustrations. Later, Lombroso took a position at the University of Pavia, and it was during this time that his publications drew the attention of professionals across Europe. Many sent him crime-related items from their own institutions or studies, in the hope that a large-scale collaboration would provide more proof for the theories.

According to Lombroso, what set criminals apart were certain physical abnormalities, which he called "stigmata." Among them were overly long arms, bulging brows, asymmetrical facial features, a broad nose, dusky skin, bushy eyebrows that often appeared as one, thick necks, and large jowls. As he added to his studies, Lombroso began to separate such people into criminal types, such as "criminaloids" who infrequently committed crimes and offenders inspired by passion or a compelling situation. His passion grew into examining genetic factors that predisposed a person to habitual crime. He believed that one day he and his anthropological colleagues would be instrumental in improving risk assessment and helping society to curb and control crime.

Lombroso's disciples, in Italy and elsewhere, launched a movement to make anthropology into the ultimate and most fundamental science. "Our theories," Lombroso wrote, "are based on a mass of facts that are there for all to see; it has proved that despite the opposition from distinguished men, our school has attracted and convinced the best scientists in Europe who did not disdain to send us . . . the most valuable documents in their collection."[8] However, because he failed to use control groups and did not adequately examine alternative theories, he fell short. Lombroso was too eager to be correct, and because he suffered few challenges, his notions had a strong influence on psychiatry and criminology.

When he was professor of forensic medicine at the University of Turin, Lombroso established the Archive for Psychiatry, Anthropology and Criminal Science. He allowed the public to see it in 1884. Thereafter, he set up conferences among his growing body of colleagues, and in 1892, his years of collecting exhibits paid off with the opening of the Museum of Psychiatry and Criminology.[9] It was the first of its kind, and others grew up around Europe based on his model.

Key to his success was his access to the criminally insane, and among Lombroso's patients was twenty-two-year-old Vincenz Verzeni. This patient was accused of two murders, including the shocking mutilation of a girl whose intestines had been torn out. A third woman had survived a similar assault and had identified Verzeni as the perpetrator. Since the attacks were so violent, and since pieces were missing from the corpses, Lombroso examined Verzeni's skull. No one was surprised to learn that his cranium was asymmetrical or that his ears were defective and the right one was smaller. More interesting, he had oversized genitals. This man was clearly depraved.

Verzeni admitted to the crimes and offered lurid details: the murders and mutilations, he said, had aroused him. In fact, he'd been fantasizing about such assaults for a while. He especially enjoyed putting his hands around someone's neck, he said, and sometimes he played a dangerous game: he would throttle and rape a woman or girl, and if he had an orgasm before she died, he let her live. If not, she died. He also participated in certain postmortem activities, such as drinking blood or ripping parts off a corpse to keep or consume. He declared that, for him, the impulse to maim and kill was irresistible.[10]

Lombroso studied Verzeni closely and concluded that there were signs of degeneracy in the arrested development of the right frontal bone in the skull. There were also indicators for degenerate behavior from Verzeni's ancestry. He was a classic born criminal. The *Washington Post* ran an article in 1907 that described this case and noted that European sociologists and penologists considered crime to be a disease. They expected surgeons, "remedies," and hospitals to eventually replace prisons and the gallows.

In other words, at this time, society perceived psychiatrists as educated professionals with an accurate interpretation of human behavior.

Yet it was a French pathologist, Alexandre Lacassagne, who first urged offenders to tell their stories, instigating what he called "criminal autobiographies" and developing a theory about social criminality that undermined Lombroso's body-based notions. No one followed up on Lacassagne's work until decades later, when Karl Berg interviewed Peter Kürten.

During the early twentieth century, there were few extended analyses of extreme offenders, and they were considered quite bold. Besides Berg's work on Kürten, serial killer Carl Panzram analyzed himself in a book-length autobiography, drawing the interest of psychiatrist Karl Menninger, but the sensational case of Albert Fish in the 1930s truly demanded the sustained evaluation of a competent professional. Dr. Fredric Wertham took up the challenge. Fish was a demented deviant with an amazing number of paraphilias who cannibalized a child and described the erotic experience to the dead girl's mother. Given his numerous oddities, including self-flagellation, he was a natural subject for study. Wertham applied a Freudian interpretation, which was in vogue at the time.

This psychodynamic approach to criminal behavior, based on blaming the mother (or the most involved caretaker), remained widely accepted into the 1960s, when Marvin Ziporyn befriended mass murderer Richard Speck, who'd killed eight nurses in Chicago in a single night. While Ziporyn, too, thought Speck's upbringing was overly maternal, he also considered research in brain disorders. This was a unique angle for criminal assessment.

Yet the concept of psychopathy—the remorseless manipulator with no particular motive—had been evolving according to changing fashions in the professional community. In 1941, Dr. Hervey Cleckley published *The Mask of Sanity* to lay out the basic traits and behaviors of a psychopath, including manipulativeness, irresponsibility, self-centeredness, and a lack of empathy or anxiety. The psychopath was also more violent, more likely to recidivate, and less likely to respond to treatment. This was not a mental illness; it was a character disorder, showing up in varying degrees in many of these extreme offenders. By the mid-twentieth century, they seemed to be getting either bolder or more numerous.

With rising murder rates during the 1960s, the FBI expanded its jurisdiction. At the FBI Academy, founded in 1972, several agents taught ideas from psychology and sociology. Special Agent Howard Teten offered a course in abnormal psychology and applied criminology, which became the basis for founding the FBI's Behavioral Sciences Unit and its method of behavioral profiling in cases of serial murder. Interviews with convicted murderers were entered into the Violent Criminal Apprehension Program database, and to reinforce their investigative analysis with science, the agents utilized the work of criminal psychologists who had applied theories to serial offenders. Among them were Donald Lunde, James Brussel, and James Melvin Reinhardt, all of whom appear in the following chapters. The FBI also utilized the Psychopathy Checklist, a diagnostic instrument developed during the 1970s by prison psychologist Robert Hare.

Recognizing the need for a systematic approach that also acknowledged the uniqueness of individuals, mental health experts continued to study extreme offenders. For a better handle on assessment, Dr. Michael Stone devised a Scale of Evil with which he assigned a hierarchy of scores to progressively evil acts, while other experts balanced their interviews with the latest findings from brain research.

Collectively, psychologists and psychiatrists who have used their training and skills to probe the minds of the most extreme murderers have retrieved important information about motives, pre- and postcrime behavior, fatal fantasies, mental rehearsal, compartmentalized personalities, and the role of mental disorders. At times, their theories thwarted their goals, but with a set of offenders whose behaviors have been consistent from one case to another, it's been possible to isolate recurring conditions and factors. From the first person who believed a criminal had insights to offer to today's technological approach, much has been learned about how and why some people commit shocking acts of violence. Collecting this type of research in one place can assist us to refine our approach for the future. So, let's return to Alexandre Lacassagne.

CHAPTER 2

Joseph Vacher and Alexandre Lacassagne

1

The violated body of a young shepherd named Victor Portalier lay naked in a field on August 31, 1895, his belly ripped open. Those who discovered him thought it was a wolf attack, the bane of sheep herders there in southern France, but his unclothed state startled them. Within moments, the police had fanned out to search the area. A gendarme on a bicycle spotted a young man in tattered clothing walking along the road, so he ordered him to produce identification. Upon learning with delight that this wanderer had once been in his own former military regiment, the gendarme relaxed and asked if he'd seen any suspicious characters; another military man, he thought, would certainly be alert to unusual behavior. The young man readily described a figure fleeing across a field a mile to the north. The gendarme thanked him and left, inadvertently allowing the charming killer to continue on his way.

An examination of the murdered shepherd revealed wounds from both a knife and a razor, while bruises on his neck indicated that he'd been strangled. There was also evidence of sexual violation. Although the police in this area did not yet know it, this attack was but one more in a string of similar such murders around the French countryside over the past year. Because the murders were in different districts, no one had yet linked them. Most had been in rural areas, targeting young men or women herding sheep, although the marquis of Villeplaine had been killed while walking in his park, his throat slit open. Because his coat and pocketbook were missing, it was presumed that a thief had targeted him. However, there were no leads for running down a suspect. Some journalists offered a disturbing idea: only seven years earlier in London, Jack the Ripper had gutted half a dozen prostitutes, and he'd never been caught. England was just over the channel. Perhaps "Jack" had traveled.

The series of murders in France seemed to have begun on November 20, 1884, when a killer strangled, stabbed, and mutilated a thirteen-year-old girl. The same thing happened the following May to a young woman.

9

In August—the same month as the shepherd boy murder—an elderly woman had been strangled and ravaged, and in September, a sixteen-year-old girl had sustained similar treatment, although her abdomen was also ripped open—just like the Ripper murders. Then a fifteen-year-old boy was strangled, stabbed, raped, and disemboweled, including genital castration. The killer lay low or traveled for about six months, then a girl reported fighting off a man who had attempted to rape her. Police in the area chased him off. During that fall, there were two more murders with bodily mutilation, including genital removal on a fourteen-year-old female victim. In 1897, three more people were killed in brutal fashion before a woman in the town of Adrèche fought off her attacker with screams so loud she attracted her husband and sons. They subdued the man and took him to the police.

His name was Joseph Vacher, and he was twenty-nine years old. He'd tramped around the countryside with an accordion and bagpipe, earning a few sous at village fairs from his performances or from begging. A former soldier who'd been discharged for "psychic disturbances," he confessed to killing five shepherds—three girls and two older women. Later he added more, some as yet undiscovered. He even directed the police to a male victim he'd thrown down a well and a female he'd placed in a thicket. To mitigate his crimes, Vacher claimed that he suffered from temporary insanity that irresistibly compelled him. He called himself a "scourge sent by providence to afflict humanity" and offered a diagnosis: a rabid dog had bitten him when he was young, and he'd been treated with herbs that had poisoned his blood. This, he insisted, had made him lust for fresh blood. This was the reason that, as his victims died, he'd lapped blood from their wounds. Head wounds were especially productive. However, the clarity of his memory and his efforts to avoid capture undermined his hope to be declared mad. Clearly, he was not psychotic. Still, his mental state remained an issue, so doctors for both the prosecution and defense examined him.[1]

Among them was Dr. Jean Alexandre Eugène Lacassagne, a medical professor from the University of Lyon. He would gain renown from this case, but it would also inspire in him a groundbreaking idea for the study of criminology.

2

By this time, Lacassagne had become a significant figure in the emerging field of forensic science. Born in 1843, he'd studied medicine at a military school and worked at a military hospital in Paris. His prior experience as a military doctor in North Africa had inspired an interest in pathology, violence, and wound analysis. In 1878, when he was thirty-five, Lacassagne published *Précis de médicine*, after which he was offered a position at the university's Institute of Medicine. He also founded the journal *Archives d'Anthropologie Criminelle*. Thus, he established himself as an expert in the field of medical jurisprudence, and his primary expertise was in toxicology.

Lacassagne quickly learned how important it was to observe the small details of a crime scene and to gather as much information as possible before making a judgment. In the case of an apparent suicide, he questioned nurses about how often victims of suicide are discovered with their eyes closed, as was the case with this one. They said they'd noticed it in only natural deaths. This information made Lacassagne dig deeper, and he soon helped the police to recognize a homicide and to bring the killer (who'd staged the scene) to justice.[2]

In his day, Lacassagne became a celebrity investigator. He read in a wide variety of fields, yet he remained aware of the limitations of medicine. Thus, he was careful to exercise doubt in order to keep his mind and observation skills active. Because he was both careful and knowledgeable, Lacassagne made contributions to several areas of investigation, such as ballistics. He removed the bullet from a murder victim in 1889 and noticed seven longitudinal grooves on its surface. This gave him an idea. He examined the insides of the barrels of pistols that belonged to the suspects and found one that had exactly seven grooves. He showed this to the arresting officers, and it helped to convict the gun's owner.

Lacassagne made his most significant contributions to the field of criminology. He'd been a student of Cesare Lombroso, who believed that criminal types could be recognized via bodily "maps" (see Chapter 1 for more on Lombroso's theories), but eventually he decided that Lombroso had underestimated the influence on criminal development of sociological factors. "Societies have the criminals they deserve," he once said.[3] In a speech he gave in 1881, he stated that physicians had a social responsibility to educate others about criminality. It was up to experts, not attorneys, he insisted, to demonstrate such truths to judges and juries.

Lacassagne's "Lyon school" was influential across France for nearly three decades, from 1885 until 1914. He viewed the social arena as the primary breeding ground for crime: in other words, even if a person has the seeds of crime in his or her soul, nothing will grow without something else fertilizing the soil. To organize his ideas, Lacassagne described three zones for the human brain: occipital (animal instinct), parietal (social), and frontal (superior faculties). Similarly, society produced "instinctual criminals," "act criminals," and "thought criminals."

In addition, Lacassagne instigated the earliest criminal autobiographies.[4] He believed that solid data came not just from scientific observers but also from the subjects themselves. To this point, Lacassagne had gained data from interviews, but he came up with what he viewed as a more productive idea that would benefit the prisoner as well as the theorist. He identified prisoners who wished to express themselves, either in writing or with drawings, and he encouraged them to do so. He supplied the instruments they needed and asked them to ponder their lives. They were to address their writings to him, as if speaking to him. He hoped they would thereby gain some insight about why they had become social offenders. Each week Lacassagne came to the prison to check their notebooks, correcting the writing and sometimes guiding the authors into productive directions. If they filled a notebook, he gave them another, and sometimes he would publish their work in his professional journal. Occasionally, he paid them. If he thought a manuscript was not acceptable, he made the prisoner rewrite it, but he usually left the choice of material to the subject. A few participants in his experiment came to view Lacassagne as a friend or father figure, especially those who felt improved by the experience. Many were keen to work with a scientist to try to understand themselves.

As his theory suggested, Lacassagne found that many prisoners had violence, tension, poverty, and disease throughout their family histories. Several of the men had never had a relationship with a woman. They often had little education and only a precarious means of supporting themselves or their families. Their marginality contributed to their impulse to commit crimes and most had started young, earning numerous short prison sentences. Writing this all down, some attested, made them feel slightly less anonymous, as if they might actually have something important to say. A few made observations about other prisoners they had met.

Lacassagne collected more than sixty such manuscripts from both male and female prisoners, averaging about twenty-five pages, although one man, set for execution, had filled six notebooks. Scholars who have studied these autobiographies suggest that this offender had deliberately blackened his character or mentioned a background that supported Lacassagne's theory simply to capture the doctor's attention.[5] This is, indeed, a primary concern with the scientific study of criminal personalities via personal contact. Examiners have difficulty veiling their interests as they listen, and astute subjects who want to impress them figure out what to say. Despite the oft-repeated desire to "assist science," either party can become more interested in his or her own needs or goals.

As is often the case today, a few offenders sought to be viewed as experts in crime or at least in their particular variety of crime. Some of Lacassagne's subjects believed that the experts were wrong: they relied on distorted theories because they wanted the crimes to make sense (i.e., to have an understandable motive). One killer of four claimed that while the professionals who evaluated him attributed his offenses to greed, *he* saw the influence of a childhood head injury, lifetime substance abuse, and the sudden blinding sensibility that preceded each stabbing event. Who would know himself better than him, but none of the doctors had even considered these items. In this, said the offender, they were remiss. (From what we now know, he was probably closer to the mark than the alienists in his day.)

These same charges can be leveled at criminologists even today, as theory often precedes and molds analysis, influencing conclusions. Professionals are ever alert to cases that support their ideas, especially if they have a passionate agenda, and Lacassagne was no different.

3

Lacassagne exhaustively examined Joseph Vacher for five months. In addition to interviews with Vacher, Lacassagne talked with his relatives and associates. In keeping with the criminological theories of the day, he performed a thorough physical examination of the notorious offender. He also spoke with him at length. Lacassagne discovered no physical evidence of degeneration, merely a difficult temperament: Vacher was prone to self-centered rages, based on entitlement, and showed no remorse for any of his crimes. He frequently mentioned that he should be sent to an insane asylum.

Lacassagne found that Vacher's family was mentally sound and free of evidence of cerebral trauma or epilepsy, but from earliest infancy Vacher had been vicious and cruel. He'd mistreated animals and bullied other children. Sent to a strict Catholic school at Saint-Genis-Laval, he'd heard about the consequences of sin, but it had little effect: he'd been expelled for sexual contact with other boys. He'd gone on to acquire a history of sexual transgressions, having assaulted a child when he was twenty and been kicked out of a monastery when he inappropriately touched other young men there. Known to be lazy, Vacher had not lasted long in any occupation. During his military stint in the Zouaves regiment, he became a noncommissioned officer but proved irascible. He'd fly into violent rages, threaten other soldiers, and even scream out in his sleep. His bunkmates believed that Vacher, who'd told them how he often dreamed about murder, might kill them in the night. He was finally discharged.

Upon his release, Vacher approached a young woman, Louise Barrant, whom he had long adored, but she refused to marry him. In fact, she mocked his efforts to court her, so in 1893 he shot her four times and then shot himself twice through the right ear. Rather than die, he went partially deaf. (Louise survived as well.) The bullet remained in his brain, paralyzing the right side of his face, which helped to make life even more difficult (as well as later give him a possible "cause" for his rages). His incessant paranoia (or, one source says, his sexual contact with a corpse) got him a brief stint in an insane asylum. Although some psychiatrists there considered him dangerous, in 1894 Vacher was pronounced cured and released. Far from being cured, though, he was ready for much worse.

After Vacher's final arrest, he claimed that the lack of a motive for the murders he'd committed established his inability to control himself. In addition, he had not really "hurt" anyone. "My victims never suffered," he claimed, "for while I throttled them with one hand, I simply took their lives with a sharp instrument with the other." Afterward, he said, he'd experienced "an exquisite feeling of consolidation."[6]

Motiveless murder was nearly unknown in the late nineteenth century, so the defense experts agreed with him: his murderous acts had been outside his control. Sheer bloodthirst, while rare, had been the supposed motive of the prostitute murders in London, and scarcely a journalist could cover the Vacher case without reference to Jack the Ripper. One *New York Times* reporter alluded to the failed romance that had unhinged Vacher's mind, although his troubles had clearly begun long before this attempted homicide and suicide.

The egotistical Vacher wanted his story published in French newspapers. He also demanded to be tried separately for each of his crimes, with the trials to take place in the districts in which they'd been committed. Possibly he sought to spread out and thus increase the amount of press coverage he could receive. When he beat the warden, nearly killing him before guards arrived to save the man, reporters surmised that Vacher had done this to prove to the public (and potential jurors) how unstable he was.

However, the prosecution identified self-enrichment motives in some of the murders: to steal a shirt, food, or money. For this side, Lacassagne concluded that Vacher had "inverted tendencies" and was feigning a mental illness. With another expert, he wrote a report to the effect that Vacher was not subject to any known impulse disorder. Rather, he was an "immoral, passionate man, who once terribly suffered from a depressing persecution mania coupled with an impulse to suicide. Of this he was cured and therefore became responsible for his actions. His crimes are those of an antisocial, sadistic, bloodthirsty being, who considers himself privileged to commit these atrocities because he was once treated in an asylum for insanity, and thereby escaped well-merited punishment. He is a common criminal and there are no ameliorating circumstances to be found in his favor."[7]

Richard von Krafft-Ebing included Vacher as a case history in his *Psychopathia Sexualis*, adding that it was not uncommon to find an appetite for human flesh.[8] What Vacher did with the parts he'd removed is not clear, but there was an assumption that he might have committed acts of cannibalism.

For the court, Lacassagne demonstrated Vacher's "simulated insanity," showing how he had planned and carried out his murders, covering his trail. He impressed even Vacher, who murmured, "He's very good." Several witnesses who had escaped the "ugly tramp" testified about his calm approach: no one had noticed that he was out of control. Those who knew him described his excessive paranoia and his unfounded rages. The jury found him guilty of eleven murders. Journalists wrote that he remained a suspect in a dozen more.

Despite his braggadocio during his imprisonment, Vacher had to be dragged to the guillotine. He professed his innocence and insanity the entire way. The "French Ripper" was executed at Bourgh-en-Bresse on December 31, 1898.

After his execution, anatomists acquired his dissected parts and studied his brain. A certain Dr. Laborde made a plaster cast of it, using this exhibit to demonstrate to members of the French Academy of Medicine how the "frontal convolutions" were well developed, similar to the brain of León Gambetta, a prominent French statesman. Laborde concluded from this "evidence" that Vacher had been a neglected genius. In different surroundings, he claimed, each man might well have turned out like the other. Laborde's audience remained unconvinced. It did not seem possible that a criminal of Vacher's ilk could ever have amounted to much, let alone been highly intelligent. Instead, the French played up the potential danger of wandering vagrants, as if they represented the true criminal type. Vacher's skull ended up in one of the criminological museums that was gaining popularity around Europe at this time.

It was nearly three decades before another expert in criminal psychology made such a prolonged study of a sadistic murderer. He, too, examined the criminal from a sociological perspective, but by this time, psychoanalysis had become a social force of its own.

CHAPTER 3

Peter Kürten and Karl Berg

1

It was a cold winter morning on February 9, 1929, when men on their way to work noticed something under a hedge in the Flingern district of Düsseldorf, Germany. They knelt down on the sloping ground for a better look, noticed a strong smell of petroleum, and discovered a dead girl, partially burned. They fetched the police, who pulled out the fully clothed, frozen corpse for examination. Her dark hair was completely charred, and it was difficult to tell from her bloated face how old she was, but they guessed between seven and ten. Her chest was covered with blood, and she appeared to have been stabbed to death. When she was taken for autopsy, Dr. Karl Berg, an expert in forensic medicine and the official consultant to the Düsseldorf Police Department, also noticed bloodstains on her underwear near her genitals. He placed the material under a microscope and found seminal fluid. Since she had not been raped, Berg surmised that the killer had used a finger to forcefully push his semen against the outside of her vagina, bruising her in the process.

There were also thirteen parallel stab wounds to her left breast, grouped together, five of which had penetrated the heart. They appeared to be from a weapon shaped like scissor blades. Berg believed that the victim had been on the ground at the time, probably unconscious and dying. She'd been stabbed numerous more times in various places, as well as strangled, but despite a lot of blood on her head, the scene was oddly free of it.

This girl was soon identified as eight-year-old Rosa Ohlinger. Last seen at 6:00 P.M. the previous evening, those who knew her believed she had taken a shortcut from a public footpath. It was clear from her undigested stomach contents that she'd met her killer within the hour, just after dark.

It reminded Berg of the stabbing of an elderly woman, Frau Kühn, six days earlier. Since it had occurred in roughly the same area, Berg wondered if the same person had perpetrated both. Frau Kühn had told the police that a man had walked straight up to her, greeting her with "Good evening," and had then grabbed the lapels of her coat and threatened, "No row. Don't scream." Then he'd stabbed her over and over, fast, until he'd cut her two dozen times, but her screams had finally scared him off. Berg had examined her that day, finding mostly flesh wounds on her head, trunk, and arms, and now that he thought of it, those wounds, too, had been shaped like those of scissor blades.

Five days after the Ohlinger murder, an intoxicated mechanic named Scheer was fatally attacked around midnight as he left a tavern. Forty-five years old, he had sustained about twenty wounds, and these also appeared to be inflicted with scissors. Sixteen thrusts, all but one horizontal, had been to the back of his neck. A stab to his temple had caused a hemorrhage into the brain, and a stab to his back had caused bleeding in his lung. A lack of defensive wounds indicated that the killer had approached him from behind.

Despite three attacks in quick succession, the police developed no leads. Frau Kühn's description matched no known criminals. Since the victims were so different, the police did not believe these crimes were linked. Berg disagreed. He started a rudimentary profile, noting the blitz approach, the geographic location, the stabbing modus operandi (MO), the time of day, and the absence of a motive that made sense, like robbery. He noted that each victim had been stabbed in the temple, an odd place to aim. He was certain that one man was behind all three incidents.

About six weeks later, a man attacked two women in separate incidents. Erna Penning was walking home on the evening of April 2 when she heard steps come up fast behind her. She pulled up her coat collar in time to stave off a noose that was thrown over her head. Because her hands were under the cord, she blocked it from being drawn tight. She struggled and felt her attacker try to strangle her with his free hand, so she grabbed his nose and pinched hard, managing to throw him off, and she ran. Thus, she survived. The next night, another woman described something similar, and only the fortuitous approach of a couple had saved her. They told police a man had been dragging her along the ground with a rope.

Thanks to their description, the police arrested someone, who became the primary suspect in all five attacks. In fact, this man told police many details from these attacks and confessed to everything. However, he was mentally unstable and some of his statements contradicted the facts. Thus, while they had someone in custody, they weren't certain he was the man they were after. They did believe the attacks would now cease, and they did . . . until the end of that summer.

On the night of August 21, someone stabbed three different people. Each received only one wound, and all survived. Berg thought the weapon was different from the one used in the February murders, so either they now had another stabber in the area or their suspect had changed his choice of weapon. Still, this man had killed no one.

Then, on a Saturday evening not long afterward, two sisters, ages five and fourteen, disappeared on their way home from a market in Flehe. A thorough search of the route they should have taken turned up nothing, but it was dark. With morning's first light, a searcher discovered them not far from their home. They'd been killed and tossed into a garden, close to a public path. Both were face down, with their clothing in disorder. The autopsy revealed that they'd been strangled and their throats were cut, but they had not been sexually penetrated. An adult man's footprints were mingled with theirs, and a witness claimed that just after 9:00 the evening before, she'd heard a child scream, "Mama! Mama!"

Berg found that the youngest child, nearly beheaded, had bled to death from a severed artery, while the older one had stab wounds to her back. The lack of defensive wounds indicated that both children had been unconscious when stabbed. Berg figured that the youngest one had been dispatched first, quickly, giving the older one time to call out. He thought she'd managed to run a short way before loss of blood overcame her. From the wound dimensions, he deduced that the weapon had been a specific type of dagger.

Berg believed they had a serial sadist on their hands, a lust killer who stabbed people to death for the sheer thrill of it. In fact, later on the same day as the child murders, a young woman who had resisted a rape was also stabbed, but people had rescued her before she'd died. She described a man in his mid-thirties named "Baumgart" who had flirted with her for several hours before forcing himself on her, and had then stabbed her several times. His attack was so fierce that he'd broken his knife in her back. Significantly, he had stabbed her in the head three times, as well as twice in the throat. When Berg examined the broken piece from the knife, he found that it was the very type of dagger he'd expected.

What disturbed him was the theory that a sadist would have satisfied his appetite that morning with the double homicide and thus should not have been inclined to attack another person so soon. He knew it could have been a different offender, since the victim had not been strangled, but he also surmised that the offender was driven by a need that sent him out for blood, no matter how he got it. Berg expected to hear of more murders in short order.

Many locals believed they had a vampire, because this attacker was elusive and operated at night. From the appearance of some of the neck and face wounds, he also seemed to be taking blood from his victims. Townspeople were in a panic.

On September 29, the body of Ida Reuter, a servant, was discovered. She had been raped and sexually posed, with a circle of bludgeon-type wounds around the crown of her head. The autopsy indicated that the weapon had been a square-faced hammer. Within two weeks, another girl was similarly assaulted on October 12, and the imprints of fingernails were found in her vagina. Both victims had been similarly dragged about 100 feet away from where they'd been hit and felled. Anger was evident in these attacks.

Later that same month, a woman was walking in this district when a man approached her and asked if she was afraid, since "quite a lot of things have happened here already." She attempted to ignore him, but he fell into step with her and quickly hit her with a blunt instrument. She fell to the ground but survived. On the same evening, a prostitute was similarly assaulted, but neither description proved helpful for an identification.

November brought more such crimes. On the seventh, a five-year-old girl named Gertrude disappeared. Two days later, her body was found lying in a patch of stinging nettles against the wall of an isolated house. She'd been dumped face down, with her legs parted and her underwear torn. Berg's autopsy indicated that she'd been stabbed thirty-six times and strangled. Two wounds were on the left side of the skull, and nine had pierced the heart. Her body was horribly mutilated, with wounds to her kidneys, anus, and vagina. This told Berg that the attacker was truly out of control.

Just hours after this grim discovery, a letter arrived to a local Communist newspaper. It gave directions to Gertrude's body, as well as to another corpse: that of a young woman who'd been missing for several months. She'd been buried in the woods. In fact, the police had received a similar letter in October, but they hadn't located the site. With this map, they dug in the designated location and found the preserved remains. Maria Hahn, the deceased, had been battered, stabbed, and hacked up. There were three successive stabs to the left temple and seven parallel stabs to the neck, which appeared to have been made by something small and sharp (determined later to be scissors).

The local newspapers were in a flurry, asking when the police would nab this man. People were scared to go out, and parents watched their children with greater care. It seemed impossible that someone could attack so many people and then just melt into the night. Berg believed that they could not point unequivocally at a single offender. The victim types differed, as did the weapons, and at times even the MO. All had been committed outside during the evening hours and in the same general area, but this was not sufficient to narrow down the search to only one man. While there were surviving victims who offered descriptions, these incidents differed from the fatal attacks.

Berg compared the spree with one that had occurred in Eschweiler, in which six women had been attacked. The offender had hit them all with a hammer in order to carry out a sexual assault while they were unconscious. Although not suspected in Düsseldorf, his method gave police the idea that they were looking for at least two different offenders. In addition, they believed their suspect was deranged, not ordinary. Thus, he'd stand out.

But then, murders of this nature appeared to end. The "Düsseldorf Murderer" was lying low, or perhaps he'd been arrested for something else. As winter passed into spring, it seemed possible that the stabber had died or moved on. But then everything changed.

On May 14, 1930, a man approached a girl at a railroad station and got her to walk away from the crowds. Neither was aware of a man following them. They walked together along several streets, but near a park, the man made an advance and the girl resisted. This drew the man shadowing them into a protective confrontation.

"What do you mean to do with this girl?" he asked.

The first man was startled, but he had a response: "She has no place to sleep, so I'm taking her to my sister's."

When the girl asked her rescuer whether the street in question was nearby, she learned that it was all a lie: that street was in the opposite direction. She stepped to her rescuer's side, and the other man quickly left. Her rescuer took her to his own home, #71 Mettmanner Strasse. But he was not quite the hero he'd seemed. She began to suspect that he'd rescued her merely to have her to himself for the same purpose as the other man. She asked if he would take her elsewhere. He agreed and took her on the tram. When they got off, he walked her toward the Grafenberger Wald. There, in an isolated place, he seized the young woman by the neck and forced her to kiss him. He insisted she allow him to have sex with her, and she thought it would be better to give in. He then took her back to the tram and left her to find her own way elsewhere.

The girl confided this incident to a woman she knew in Düsseldorf, who took the matter to the police. Ernst August Ferdinand Gennat had been director of the Berlin Criminal Police since shortly after a separate homicide division had been created in 1902. He had developed a homicide squad, the Zentrale Mordinspektion, which he'd led to an impressive record of success. By this time, they were solving nearly 95 percent of the crimes, and it was Gennat who'd first suggested the phrase "serien-mörder" (serial killer) in reference to this series of unsolved slayings.

Patiently, investigators helped the girl retrace her steps from that night a week before, and soon she was leading them to her rapist's house—the home of Peter Kürten. He recognized the girl as she approached, star-tled that she'd managed to find him again, and ran to get his wife. He explained to her that he could be arrested for an attempted rape. Then he fled, leaving her to talk to the police. They took her into custody and searched the apartment. But their prey had eluded them.

Later, Mrs. Kürten found her husband and suggested that they both commit suicide, whereupon he confessed to her that he was the Düssel-dorf killer. She was astonished and asked how it was possible. According to her statement later, he responded, "It just came over me." He also cried, which he later said was the first time he had ever done so in his life.

Kürten would tell Berg that he'd urged his wife to turn him in and col-lect the reward, but she would say that he'd instructed her *not* to give him away. Either way, she decided to do the right thing, and on May 24, two days before Kürten's forty-sixth birthday, she lured him to a church square. There, the police closed in and placed him under arrest.

Kürten readily confessed to detectives. He repeated everything he'd told his wife about his crimes, adding stories that he'd made up, or, as Berg put it, "he lengthened the chain with some imaginary links."[1] Later Kürten would tell Berg that his lies were an imitation of his father, who had always enjoyed being the center of attention.

Defense psychiatrists believed he was insane, but Kürten claimed that he could master his urge but just had not done so, in which case he was guilty. He did not attempt to excuse himself, despite a compulsion that drove him night after night to seek victims. However, as he awaited his trial, he changed his mind several times, sometimes hoping for execution and sometimes for a finding of manslaughter or "legal irresponsibility," with hope of a pardon. Berg concurred that Kürten, while driven by lust, did not have an "irresistible urgency." He had known what he was doing, and he'd carefully avoided the danger of discovery, going home unsatis-fied rather than taking too great a risk. He was not insane.

Yet Berg remained suspicious. Kürten had confessed too readily, offer-ing too many stories, and soon his game was clear: in court, the offender declared he'd made it all up, based on newspaper accounts, and he was not really the Düsseldorf Murderer. The jury didn't buy it, and they con-victed him.

In fact, Berg knew the case of the buried woman had not made the papers, and Kürten's confession had perfectly fit the facts, so after being confronted Kürten admitted that, in essence, his confession had been true. He told Berg he had no conscience. "Never have I felt misgivings in my soul; never did I think to myself that what I did was bad."[2] He blamed the "torture" he'd received during stints in prison and added, "I derived the sort of pleasure from these visions [of harm to others] that other people would get from thinking about a naked woman."[3] He even went so far as to say that since he had avenged injustice, God would approve of everything he'd done.

After his conviction for nine counts of murder and seven counts of attempted murder, Kürten gave a speech. He admitted he had no excuse for his ghastly deeds, and yet he attempted to place the blame on the press, the victims, and the conditions of his household growing up. He said he'd never tortured a victim, although throttling someone for five minutes as she fights for her life is a form of torture. He admitted to a "psychic collapse," claiming that all criminals reach a threshold beyond which they cannot go. He also asked for forgiveness.

About his impending execution in 1931, Kürten said that if he could hear his blood bubbling forth from his neck stump right afterward, he'd die a happy man. "That would be the pleasure to end all pleasures," he announced.

He saw a confessor and wrote thirteen letters to the relatives of his victims, asking for their pardon and their prayers. He was pleased to see that his wife had received a reward for turning him in. His last meal was Wiener schnitzel, baked potatoes, and a bottle of wine. Then he asked for a second helping. The next morning, Kürten was executed on July 2, 1931, at the Klingelputz Prison in Cologne.

2

After Kürten's conviction in 1930, Dr. Karl Berg went to his prison cell to study him—initiating one of the earliest attempts to thoroughly understand the abnormal mind of a repeat offender. He wanted the full story as Kürten would tell it, so he kept him under observation for a year. Kürten confessed freely to Berg in shocking detail, which became the basis for Berg's now classic book, *The Sadist*, later translated into English for the Library of Abnormal Psychological Types. Berg had already heard many of the details, but he got Kürten to reveal even more.

By this time, Berg was a part-time professor of forensic medicine at the Düsseldorf Medical Academy and the medical director of the Düsseldorf Institute of Legal and Social Medicine, which he had founded. In addition, he was a medico-legal officer of the Düsseldorf Criminal Court. This put him in prime position to evaluate Kürten, but Berg also recognized the opportunity he had to thoroughly study a rare type of criminal. Not only was Kürten a psychopathic serial killer, but he also had a peculiar paraphilia: he grew aroused from drinking his victims' blood. Like most psychiatrists of his era, Berg was thoroughly acquainted with Richard von Krafft-Ebing's work, so he knew how unlikely it was that he would see another such criminal during the course of his career. Thus, Berg sought to probe the soul of this strange and enigmatic man. He found his task, distasteful as it was, quite absorbing.

He organized the material with the facts of Kürten's crimes placed first, and the prison interviews second. He finished by analyzing Kürten's character in light of what was then known about the paraphilic character disorder of sadism.

Although at trial Kürten had pled not guilty by reason of insanity, claiming he had a compulsive blood lust, he'd provided clearheaded details of his long life of crime. For those aspects of the crime in which Kürten had taken great pleasure, his memory was quite accurate. He began with the first and reeled them off in chronological order until he was finished. Whenever his audience had looked horrified, he'd leered, clearly enjoying the effect he was having on them. For the court, Kürten described crimes for which he had not even been accused, culminating in seventy-nine different criminal incidents (including thirteen murders).

As Berg listened, he knew he had his work cut out for him. He wanted to figure out how such an ordinary-looking person had grown into a true monster. In their sessions together, he collected as many facts as he could.

Kürten was born on May 26, 1883, into a family in Köln-Mülheim in the Rhine River Valley. Kürten's entire family of thirteen had lived in a one-bedroom apartment, and his father was a violent man who abused alcohol, so he'd witnessed his father repeatedly assaulting his mother, including raping her. Thus, he'd learned from this role model how to treat a woman. It was only after his father had been arrested for assaulting his thirteen-year-old daughter that his father was removed from the home.

In school, Kürten had proved to be a good student and offered his teachers no documented trouble, but he'd made friends with a dogcatcher who lived in his building. This man had taught the boy how to torture animals. It wasn't long before this activity had become erotic, as the two masturbated together while the dogs suffered. Kürten had then visited farms to rape the larger animals. Often, he'd stabbed them to draw blood, which further excited him to the point where he was growing addicted to the combination of blood, struggle, and arousal. This is now known as "orgasmic conditioning."

His first attempted murder, of a teenage girl, occurred when he was sixteen and had been apprenticed to a sand molder, which had been his father's trade. The attempt was, he said, the result of a sudden impulse. He throttled the girl as they went for a walk, and he believed she was dead. He did not check later to make sure. His second attempt to strangle a girl ended with her surviving, and she recalled him saying, "That's what love's like." (This young woman actually testified at Kürten's murder trial, describing how he had alternated between kindness and violent cruelty.)

That same year, Kürten was arrested for theft and sent to prison. He stayed there for four years. Once out, he started setting fires to local barns, to which he would masturbate. He supported himself with frequent burglaries and moved on from this to openly assaulting women. Arrested again, Kürten received several sentences.

Out of prison around age thirty, one Sunday evening Kürten crept into the room of an inn to steal whatever he could find. Inside, he spotted a young girl in bed, under a feather quilt. He stepped over to her. She remained asleep. He breathed in, growing aroused. It was risky, but he wanted her. Reaching down, Kürten strangled her, holding her by the throat as she woke up and struggled. She scratched at his hands, but it didn't take long before she went unconscious. As he sexually assaulted her by penetrating her genitals with his fingers, he sliced her throat, left to right, with a pocketknife. Her blood spurted as her heart pounded, and he leaned into it, catching the blood in his mouth. At that moment, he ejaculated. The power of his orgasm was intoxicating. But he knew he could not tarry. He made his way out and fled.

The police found two small incisions on the victim's throat, one shallow and one deep, with an indication on the deeper cut that it had been made after several efforts, not with a single smooth stroke. Next to the bed, the mat had absorbed a large amount of blood, but there was little on the bedclothes. Bruising around the victim's genitals indicated forced digital penetration, but no semen was found. Her tongue was bitten through, and her body was pallid and without lividity. Found in the room was a handkerchief with the initials "P.K.," which matched those of the girl's father, but he claimed not to own the item. There were no other suspects, and the murder went unsolved until Kürten confessed years later.

Kürten claimed he'd also bludgeoned a man, woman, and sleeping girl with an axe during this period; set fires; and tried to strangle another woman. He also said he was responsible for the unsolved murder of a young woman in her bed (possibly referring to the incident at the inn described above). Out less than a year, he was arrested again and locked away for eight years. Emerging in 1921, he moved to another town and met a woman, whom he married. Yet domestic bliss failed to dampen the appetites he'd developed, so he found ways to continue to set fires and assault women. He also moved to Düsseldorf.

Kürten was soon convicted of raping two servants, getting a few months in jail; once free, he became more secretive. He tried killing several girls he'd seduced, but they managed to get away. Using the name "Fritz Ketteler," he looked for females in subservient positions who appeared to be easy. Then, on February 8, 1929, he killed a child—Rosa Ohlinger.

First he led her along in a kindly way, as if to help her find her way home. He used a pair of scissors on her, stabbing two dozen times until it was clear that she was dead. To his surprise, when he returned home (about five minutes away) to clean up, there were no bloodstains on him, so he went out to the movies. After that, he grew worried, so he returned with petroleum to set the body on fire. He'd meant only to cause a stir among the townspeople, he insisted, and had not touched the girl sexually.

By this time Kürten was forty-five, the age at which sexual aggression begins to decline, but in his case, it revved up. His next victims were Frau Kühn, whom he stabbed with scissors, and then the mechanic, before he went on a violent spree, stabbing, assaulting, and even bludgeoning women with a hammer. Sometimes he would search for a victim for hours, always aware of the need to be home before his wife returned from work. He seemed to have killed Scheer because the man had given him some trouble. As Kürten stabbed him, Scheer clung to him, making him panic. In less than ten minutes, the man was dead and disposed of.

Kürten said he had stabbed the five-year-old child, Gertrude, three dozen times, in part because he enjoyed reading the newspaper accounts afterward. He'd revealed where to find her because he'd grown impatient. Seeing his black deeds in print made him feel powerful.

He also talked in detail about a sadistic murder on August 8, in which it took the victim about an hour to die. He strangled her twice into unconsciousness and then stabbed her in the throat, but she remained alive and aware of his intent. After she finally died, he rolled her into a ditch, covered her with twigs, and took her handbag. He removed a watch from it and used it as a gift for another woman. When he worried that the body might be associated with him, he returned the next day to bury it. (This is the one that was found near the five-year-old's remains, to which he'd drawn a map.) He experienced a sentimental feeling, so he'd caressed the corpse's hair and sprinkled the first layer of dirt lightly over her. After this, he had changed his weapon of choice to a dagger, because the scissors were less efficient than he'd anticipated. He tried the dagger on three people in one night, stabbing at random; these were the August 1929 incidents.

In the case of the two children killed together, he had told the older girl to go fetch him some cigarettes, and while she was away he killed the little one. He'd nearly finished strangling the older one when she revived and screamed. Kürten returned home that night, having a "natural" conversation with his wife and then mingling with crowds the next day near the crime scene to savor the effect of what he'd done. "It gave me pleasure that the lovely bright Sunday in Düsseldorf had been shattered as by a lightning stroke,"[4] he said. However, his obsession remained unquenched, perhaps because he was still trying out his new weapon, so he went out that evening and attacked another woman. However, he broke his dagger during the attack, so he threw it away.

Next, he tried a chisel and then decided on a hammer. After attacking several people with it, the weapon broke on a prostitute. Kürten remarked that she had disgusted him, due to her profession, and as a rule he never accosted such women. Returning to the scissors, he stabbed his final murder victim, the five-year-old child. However, he continued to strangle women, all of whom fought him off. His motive had been to avenge himself on society for the wrongs he'd suffered. He was angry, and he wanted someone to pay.

With one woman, he described stabbing the neck and breast while drinking the blood, which then made him vomit. He also drank from the mechanic's temple wound and from a child. Another time, he kept hitting a woman with the hammer as he raped her to maintain his erection: "Without violence, my member slackens quickly in the vagina."[5] In the incident in which he had broken the hammer, he'd experienced no arousal.

3

Berg considered Kürten the most interesting personality in criminal history, due to his cleverness and diversity. What stood out was Kürten's unusually accurate memory, which clearly facilitated his waking fantasies, and his sharp eye for minor details that alerted him to a vulnerable person. His first murder had been impulsive. The child was there, asleep. He'd tried to tear open her vagina, but it did not arouse him so he'd cut her throat instead. *This* had worked.

Kürten, Berg decided, was a psychopath whose sex impulse was perverted in an abnormal psychic constitution. He was born with a "predisposition for deviation," and his early experiences conditioned him toward abnormality. With fantasies, he reinforced it. In fact, after going through quite a number of evaluations, Kürten remembered an incident from his childhood. When he was nine years old, he was playing with other boys on an improvised raft. One boy fell off and Kürten pushed him under, drowning him.

On another occasion, he pushed a boy off the raft to let the current carry him away. In both incidents, Kürten knew he'd done something wrong but felt pleasure rather than remorse. Thereafter, he cultivated an inclination to lie. He learned how to pass as a normal person, but he kept the fire of his secret perversions alive. Berg estimated that Kürten's condition was 90 percent sadism and 10 percent atonement for injustice done to him.

Among the things Berg learned were that Kürten sometimes sought out pain, saying that he provoked the victims to strike him, indicating a masochistic component to his arousal. He visited his victims' graves repeatedly, digging with his fingers into the dirt to renew his excitement; he also went back to where he had violated certain victims. He once witnessed a man fall under a train, and he pretended to help just to get near the blood, which produced an orgasm. Kürten expressed indifference about his weapon choice. He merely wanted something that would produce blood (e.g., he stated, "I can hear the bleeding even when the stabbing is through the clothing"),[6] although a hammer produced postmortem twitches that he also enjoyed. He'd confided to a warden, who told Berg, that his greatest enjoyment was having bitten a woman's genitals until they'd bled. Just before he was caught, Kürten had cut the throat of a swan and drunk its blood. He enjoyed reading crime accounts in the newspapers and had read about Jack the Ripper several times. He'd considered nailing one body to a tree to produce public excitement, he claimed, and added that he preferred movies that promised the possibility of someone being strangled or stabbed.

Berg's detailed study of this killer set a standard for the future. Going beyond mere case analysis, Berg offered a means for other professionals to consider the psychological details of sadism. He decided that Kürten's father had been an "egotistical type" who'd imposed his will on others and spent most of what he'd earned on himself, despite his large family. Kürten had no moral restraints, and his family history included thieves and alcoholics but no mental illness. Two of Kürten's brothers had also ended up in prison. Kürten was the eldest, so he'd witnessed the most abuse when his father became violent. He'd developed a sense of enragement, which he'd kept to himself, but he would wander from home for weeks at a time, stealing to survive. "In short," Kürten had said, "my youth was a martyrdom."[7] He ran away for good when he was sixteen, and whenever he was caught for petty crimes like theft he suffered humiliations and extreme punishments in prison, which further enraged him. "Nothing is worse than the spiritual suffering of one who is tortured through the infliction of pain."[8]

He believed he'd come away from prison with a form of psychosis that thwarted proper decision making. Like his father before him, he claimed that he was subject to uncontrollable rages.

Although Berg dutifully took notes, he was aware that prison officials described Kürten as quick to assess any situation and use it to his advantage; he was a talented chameleon who knew how to win people over and he might well be telling lies or exaggerating for effect. Berg could see that Kürten Berg felt entitled to more than he'd received from life and thought it was possible that he suffered from low self-esteem over the small size of his penis. To one surviving victim, he had hinted that his "tail" was barely there. Prior to his arrest, he had put effort into making himself look good, and he admittedly enjoyed standing in front of mirrors to admire himself. Slim and blond with blue eyes, he realized that people considered him a good-looking man.

Kürten's wife, it turns out, was also a killer. Before meeting her husband she had shot a man for jilting her and had spent five years in prison. Kürten had seduced her (via threat) before marrying her, but apparently realized that she could support him, so he'd married her instead. She was aware of his many infidelities, yet continued to stand by him. Even so, she swore she had never suspected that he was the infamous Düsseldorf Murderer.

It's instructive for the present study that Kürten had sustained a head wound in 1922 from a falling piece of iron, which was the source of head-aches for years afterward. Little was known in 1929 about what brain damage can contribute to violent aggression, but his description of the consequences could indicate a certain type of organic damage.

For a while, Kürten denied any sexual contact with his victims, but as Berg won him over with the assurance of confidentiality and a show of concern, he began to reveal more about his secret motives and activities. Berg later stated, "He gave me a completely free hand to make use of his statements for the purpose of science."[9]

Berg sometimes confronted Kürten and once told him that the uniformity of his accounts revealed deception: it seemed that he was merely trying to create an impression. Kürten admitted that he'd read Cesare Lombroso, which had helped him to formulate a credible description. Yet he insisted he had a strong sex drive, constantly felt an urge to kill, and went out to seek a victim every time his wife went to work. He often envisioned killing a lot of people at once, mostly because of the public reaction it would engender. "Sometimes even when I seized my victim's throat, I had an orgasm."[10] If not, then it happened when he stabbed the person. Killing was how he got sexual satisfaction, especially during a struggle. He claimed that he could ejaculate without erection, which was "much nicer" because it gave him "a shudder down the whole back."[11] Although he fingered victims' genitals, it was stabbing or choking that excited him. Sometimes he returned to undiscovered bodies to relive the experience. With Scheer, a male, he had climaxed upon hearing the blood gurgle forth. He'd also ejaculated while standing near officials who were investigating his crimes. His night prowling never caused him fatigue.

Although Kürten denied that he'd been crueler than other boys toward animals, he described how stabbing sheep pleased him, and when he cut off a dog's head, he first became conscious that it felt sexual. It was the way the blood rushed out that fascinated him. He was thirteen when he first experienced an orgasm while wounding an animal, and he also found setting fires stimulating, largely because of the way they sent people into action. Although he had access to girls for sex, he found himself strangely uninterested in normal intercourse. It succeeded only when he treated his partner badly or made her fight him. He eventually envisioned murder, which gave him a great deal of sexual excitement. He noticed that in prison, while others were fantasizing about naked girls, he envisioned slitting someone's stomach. His fantasies about wounding others kept him from killing himself. He did this so often that once he was released, he was ready to act out what he'd rehearsed in his mind. (He did mention how surprised he was that after beating or throttling some women, they still went out with him again.)

Berg decided that Kürten stood as an example of a depraved sadistic psychopath with no particular victim preference who would have continued to kill had he not been stopped. While he added nothing particular to the studies of sadism to that point, the fact that he had chosen different types of victims was interesting, as was the fact that his method had sometimes deviated. Typically, sadists have a well-defined means for arousing lust, and they stick to their habits. However, Kürten admitted that in part he was attempting to deflect the investigation by making it appear that several different people were committing the murders. Thus, his sense of self-protection dominated his patterns of arousal.

He was also one of the rare killers who utilized a variety of murder weapons. His change from one to another had been experimental, he explained, or from mere practicality after something broke. He thought scissors was the least suspicious of all weapons to carry on his person, but they hadn't been effective for quick and decisive attacks.

Another unique characteristic is that after being caught, he went to great lengths to ensure that his wife would live out her days a rich widow. In other words, Kürten presented an odd collection of traits and behaviors that defy the serial killer stereotypes we have today.

Yet, we have stereotypes for a reason. Not long afterward in America, a renowned psychiatrist would evaluate a killer who did fit—almost too perfectly.

CHAPTER 4

Carl Panzram and Karl Menninger

1

Although nineteenth-century alienists had shepherded the psychotic, the demand for treatment of neuroses had drawn many new psychiatrists away from asylums. Patients could now go to clinics or spas for relief from daily anxieties. Many embraced the inner study of their defense mechanisms, so the psychiatric enterprise moved toward a private practice model. By the 1920s, depth psychology in the form of Freudian psychoanalysis framed the manner in which mental illness was understood, including extreme criminality.[1]

Psychoanalysis resisted the division of mental illness into categories. Freud had surmised that repressed childhood sexual memories and fantasies influenced adult neuroses. To cure these conditions, the patient had to dig deep into some mental disorder via a regular ritual of free association, dream analysis, and analyzing the symptoms of transference. The emotional womb into which the doctor and patient entered often filled a void in the patient's life. Freud's emphasis on intense introspection made the patient feel as if every minute detail of his or her life was magnified in significance. Add sexual material to a culturally repressed individual, and the titillation factor was hard to resist. By this time, many sexual perversions had been detailed and discussed *ad nauseam* among professionals, with clinical detachment. In addition, mentorship offered emerging professionals the aura of membership in an exclusive club.

"Gone forever is the notion that the mentally ill person is the exception," said Karl Menninger, who was often referred to as one of the most astute American interpreters of Freud. "It is now accepted that most people have some degree of mental illness at some time, and many of them have a degree of mental illness most of the time."[2] Menninger figures large in a case from 1929.

2

From his jail cell, Carl Panzram scribbled a 20,000-word criminal autobiography that bears strong kinship with the narratives that Lacassagne encouraged during the 1890s. Although he wrote it for a prison guard, it came into Menninger's hands to read and interpret. While caution is always warranted regarding self-report—especially from someone like Panzram, who had a thirst for attention and who loved to brag—there were few other sources of information about him than this self-analysis.

"I started doing time when I was eleven years old," it opens, "and have been doing practically nothing else since then."[3] Panzram was in his mid-thirties when he wrote this narrative, and he devoted a lot of time to blaming others for his anger—especially mistreatment by his family, reform school, priests, and prison guards. The result was not to "whip the demons" out of him but to *feed* them until they grew explosive. "I have no desire to reform myself. My only desire is to reform people who try to reform me. And I believe that the only way to reform people is to kill 'em."[4] He claimed to have set many fires, committed thousands of burglaries and sodomies, and murdered twenty-one people. "For all of this, I am not the least bit sorry. . . . I don't believe in man, God nor Devil. I hate the whole human race, including myself."[5] Affirming his adopted philosophy that "might makes right," he proceeded to lay out the details of his life and crimes.

Panzram was born on June 28, 1891, in rural Warren, Minnesota. His strict, religious parents had emigrated there from Germany to find work and raise a family. As a boy, Panzram acted out to get attention, which drew swift punishment from his short-tempered father. He grew to resent his parents, and his anger precipitated more bad behavior. Arrested for drunkenness when he was only eight, Panzram lived a hard life. His father abandoned the family, and he found himself forced into chores on the farm. He seemed unable to absorb life's frustrations. Instead, he saved injustices like pennies in a piggy bank, waiting for payback day. The more he collected, the worse it would be.

Resenting what others had that he did not, Panzram began to burglarize neighbors' homes, which got him a stint when he was eleven in the military-style Minnesota State Training School. While there, he would later claim, he was brutalized, whipped, and raped. Still just a boy, he grew hard inside and began setting fires. He wanted nothing but revenge against those who'd hurt him. Released from reform school, he was humiliated and bullied by other kids, so he continued to set fires. Back he went for another year in the hated reform school.

Instead of returning home, he took to hopping trains to get places, and in one box car four men restrained and sodomized him. He learned that he must act first to impose his will, because people in positions of strength create the rules. From that moment on, he'd force himself on other men, and once when a brakeman caught him raping two "hoboes," he drew a gun, raped the train official, and forced the hoboes to do the same.

At age seventeen, Panzram lied his way into the army, but he misbehaved so often, including burning down the prison laundry, that he spent three years in a military prison. He worked on toughening his body and mind, so that by the time he was released, he was a six-foot, 190-pound hard body with a spitfire attitude. Indifferent to his court-martial and dishonorable discharge, by this point he was resolved to commit mayhem wherever he went.

Panzram worked some brief stints as a strikebreaker and a soldier in the Foreign Legion, but got caught up in a vicious cycle of burglary, imprisonment, and escape, often bursting into rages while incarcerated that caused a lot of damage. He referred to himself as "the spirit of meanness personified" and attributed his foul temper to a lack of love and kindness in his life, as well as to endless abuse from family, religion, other inmates, and prison guards. He often said that he regretted not being born dead.

He successfully escaped prison and, at the age of twenty-seven, Panzram burglarized the New Haven, Connecticut, home of U.S. Secretary of War Howard Taft.[6] With a stolen handgun and money, he purchased a yacht, using it to lure sailors to their deaths off the coast of Long Island. He would pretend to hire them, two at a time; get them drunk; then rape, rob, and kill them. He claimed to have murdered ten men in this manner before the yacht hit some rocks and sank.

From there, Panzram traveled to West Africa. He killed a boy by bludgeoning him in the head and then hired six natives to help him hunt crocodiles. During the trip, Panzram shot the men and left the remains for the crocodiles. Then he traveled for a while, raping and killing, before he returned to the United States. In Massachusetts in 1922, he raped and murdered a twelve-year-old boy, and he did the same thing the following year in Connecticut.

Caught for burglary in Larchmont, New York, Panzram received a five-year prison sentence. He tried to escape, but suffered severe breaks in his legs, ankles, and spine. Medical attention was slow in coming, so he ended up with poorly healed bones and one leg shorter than the other. He served the rest of his time, but once out, he committed a dozen more burglaries, killing a man in Philadelphia. He threatened to poison the water supply of some major city, blow up a railway tunnel, or even sink a military ship to start a war, but he lasted only a month outside prison walls. He was next arrested in Baltimore for breaking into a house, so he ended up in a cell in a district jail in Washington, D.C.

His escape attempt from this jail was met with a severe beating for several days that required the observation of a doctor to ensure he did not die. His hands were tied behind his back, and he was heaved up by the wrists to place his full weight painfully on his shoulder sockets. This he endured for twelve hours straight.

Prison guard Henry Lesser was shocked by this illegal and inhumane treatment. He took pity on the angry convict and sent him a dollar. Panzram was so surprised by this act of kindness that the two men became friends. Soon, Panzram agreed to write his life story, and they made a clandestine arrangement: when Panzram had written fifteen to twenty pages, he would leave it between the bars of his cell. When Lesser made his late-night rounds, he would pick it up.

In this extraordinary confession, Panzram provided his numerous aliases and the details, places, and dates of his crimes. His international one-man, eighteen-year crime spree spanned thirty-one countries and two continents. He viewed killing as fun. Comparing himself to a caged tiger cub, he said that, when mistreated, the tiger grows savage and bloodthirsty. When turned loose, it preys on the world. After a rare period of care, he later wrote to Lesser, "If in the beginning I had been treated as I am now, then there wouldn't have been quite so many people in this world that have been robbed, raped, and killed."[7] Despite his poor formal education, Panzram had read many works about prison reform, and even enjoyed psychiatric and philosophical literature—mostly of a pessimistic bent.

One item of note was that Panzram had endured surgery at the age of nine for "mastoid trouble," and afterward he experienced discharges from his ear, as if from an internal infection. He wondered if it had any causal influence on his behavior afterward. He did ask Lesser to ask some psychiatrists about it, because if there was an answer as to why he'd become such a monster, he wanted to know. (Later, a doctor surmised that a brain infection could have caused his impulsive temper tantrums.)

The only time that Panzram seemed to experience guilt was when he betrayed a progressive prison warden, Charles Murphy, who had noted his intelligence and shown him a degree of trust. He'd allowed Panzram on unsupervised outings, believing he'd always return. Panzram got drunk one night and failed to show, and that was the end of the prison reform program. (Note, however, that clearly others had also been kind to Panzram.)

While he was in the D.C. jail, other jurisdictions issued warrants for his arrest for the murders to which he'd confessed. It soon became clear to him that even if he got out of one sentence, he faced many more, especially when witnesses were found to corroborate some of his claims.

Panzram defended himself in court on November 12, 1928, on charges of burglary and told the surprised jury that he was indeed guilty. He'd even waited in the house he'd robbed to murder the owners when they came home. Then he said, "There's something else you ought to know. While you were trying me here, I was trying all of you, too. I've found you guilty. Some of you, I've executed. If I live, I'll execute more of you. I hate the whole human race."[8] The jury took one minute to convict him, and the judge sentenced him to twenty-five years in the federal penitentiary at Leavenworth in Kansas. "Visit me," he spat at the court official. He'd been in this prison before, so he knew the ropes.

Upon his arrival, Panzram warned the deputy warden that he would kill any man who messed with him. The person who did was Robert Warnke, the civilian laundry supervisor. He sent Panzram to solitary confinement, but once free, Panzram wrote a note to Lesser to say that something was about to change. Back in the laundry, Panzram picked up a heavy iron support bar and fatally bludgeoned Warnke, hitting the man five times on the head. One story says that Panzram then went after the other prisoners, who were locked in with him, beating several and breaking one man's arm. However, another account indicates that Panzram went looking for the warden, but failed to find him before guards apprehended him. A third tale holds that he dropped the bar and waited for the inevitable reaction. Panzram was locked up once more in solitary confinement until his trial the following year. He seemed pleased with his rampage.

After his indictment in December, Panzram told the warden that he would plead not guilty to force the prosecutor to make a strong case, but he would put on no defense. He would then take the stand and admit to everything. For him, this was the end of the line. He intended to hang. He asked the judge to allow him to represent himself, but in case it was all just a pose, the judge appointed an attorney and ordered an assessment by a Sanity Commission.

For the first time, despite everything he'd done, Panzram was on trial for murder. On April 15, 1930, as he'd said he would, he pled not guilty. Several eyewitnesses testified against him, and he refused to help his attorney. "This is your show," he said. He was convicted and sentenced to be hanged. Consistently defiant, Panzram reported looking forward to this like "some folks do with their wedding night."[9]

He spent most of his remaining time reading the depressing writings of the philosophers Arthur Schopenhauer and Friedrich Nietzsche, declaring repeatedly to anyone who listened that he wished he could kill the whole human race. When advocates from the Society for the Abolishment of

Capital Punishment tried to intervene, Panzram sent them a note in which he said, "The only thanks you or your kind will ever get from me for your efforts on my behalf is that I wish you all had one neck and that I had my hands around it."[10] He also sent a letter to President Herbert Hoover to dissuade him from listening to this group. Afraid they might succeed, Panzram attempted to kill himself. He survived, but no appeal succeeded, so within months, he was on his way to the hangman's noose. The night before he died, he paced his cell, singing a self-composed pornographic song.

Panzram was hanged on September 5, 1930, the first man to be executed at this prison (Kansas was anti–death penalty, but this was a federal institution). Panzram's memorable final words were to the hangman himself; they were reported in different versions, but in essence he said, "Hurry it up, you Hoosier bastard! I could hang a dozen men while you're fooling around." He also tried to spit in the man's face, as he'd bragged for weeks that he would.[11] Panzram was buried in Leavenworth's cemetery in row 24 under marker 31614, his prison number. He left behind one of the most self-probing memoirs ever written by a killer. (Lacassagne would have been pleased.) Lesser donated it, along with their extensive correspondence, to the University of San Diego.

3

From the moment he heard about Panzram, Dr. Karl Menninger took a keen interest. He was a member of the famous Menninger family, many of them psychiatrists. He had graduated from Harvard Medical School in 1917, and two years later went into business with his father, Charles F. Menninger, to found the Menninger Clinic in Topeka, Kansas. Later, they built a sanitarium and created a foundation.

Menninger was a solid Freudian, although he had a philosophical ability for theoretical evaluation. He was most keenly interested in Freud's notion of the life and death instincts (sometimes called Eros and Thanatos), especially as it applied to suicidal impulses. "It is to psycho-analysis," he once wrote, "that we owe the credit for giving us the courage and the techniques for penetrating below the obvious explanations of human motives that pass currently among us."[12]

In his first book, *The Human Mind*, published in 1930, Menninger discussed the scientific nature of psychiatry and began to form his theory that mental health and illness were on a continuum. He also believed that psychiatric treatment could prevent crime and would one day replace the prison system, which he deplored. Offenders, he thought, should be treated for their mental illness. Thus, a hospital or clinic was a better place for them. The child, he said, is a born criminal, concerned only with the satisfaction of his own needs and desires; when thwarted, he grows angry and may hurt others. The "unyielding facts of reality" will either mature him or turn him into a perpetual criminal. Religious beliefs influenced Menninger's practice to the point where he believed in the idea of sin and the possibility of demonic possession. Much later, he came to believe that mental illness was just a "conversion" stage along life's way and that many patients could probably improve on their own.

As Panzram's trial approached, Lesser sent his manuscript to Menninger, who resided near where Panzram was imprisoned. Menninger was impressed by the degree of anger and brutality in its handwritten pages. He was surprised to learn that Panzram would be tried right there in Topeka. Just as he was growing aware of the possibility of being involved, he received a request from an attorney, Ralph O'Neil, who'd been appointed by the court to represent Panzram. He wanted to go with an insanity defense, and he hoped Menninger would agree to participate on the Sanity Commission. O'Neil barely needed to ask; Menninger was ready.

Early on a rainy morning of the first day of the trial, Menninger awaited Panzram in a special office in the courthouse. Panzram entered, wearing a suit but heavily manacled and under the guard of three strong men. He took short, hobbled steps toward a chair. Despite knowing that he probably looked like a large man to Panzram, Menninger had the feeling that Panzram could kill everyone in the room. He felt a thrill at the idea of such power coursing through this convict, and he recalled the enraged rhetoric he'd read. He was now face-to-face with the man who not only allegedly wanted to strangle the whole human race but also believed the world *could* be a better place.

Panzram had read about the Sanity Commission in the newspaper, so he scrutinized the psychiatrist and made it clear in a gruff voice that he wanted no interference to being convicted and hanged. (He'd confided quite rationally to Lesser that life without liberty is not worth living, but he knew he was "not fit" to live among civilized people. "If the law won't kill me, I shall kill myself.")[13] Panzram claimed to be proud of the murders he'd committed and only wished he'd managed a few more. With a cruel look, he told Menninger that he was no more insane than the psychiatrist was. He refused to tell Menninger anything about his life, depriving him of the possibility of finding mitigating factors from his childhood or any reason to say that he had not been responsible for what he'd done. In short order, the interview ended and Panzram stood, rattled his chains in a threatening manner, and exited, but Menninger remained fascinated.

With his background reading on Panzram, he believed he'd seen deeply into this man's soul. He'd seen bloodthirst, of course, but he'd also recognized the Thanatos instinct, in which the desire to die outpaced the desire to live. "He had been hurt so much that he no longer had any compunction about hurting anybody and everybody and virtually begged for death to put him out of the misery of his feelings of vengeance."[14]

This was the very embodiment of the type of person Menninger wished to study, one of the worst offenders he'd ever heard about, but one who was intelligent enough to be self-analytical. "The same psychological factors later discovered in the psychoanalytic investigation were recognized in himself by this extraordinary fellow and set down by him in these comments about his own psychology. . . . They are, in short, that hate breeds hate . . . that the wages of sin is death . . . that to kill is only to be killed, that there is no real atonement but only suffering."[15]

Menninger reported his impressions to the judge but did not testify. He then sent a letter to the warden at Leavenworth, requesting a second interview with Panzram. This time, he decided, he would be more prepared. He hoped to accomplish something much more ambitious than a mere competency assessment; he wanted to study Panzram for scientific purposes. Menninger was convinced that, with enough details gleaned from an in-depth interview, he could identify the forces behind Panzram's mental instability. In fact, he'd made over 1,000 pages of notes on Panzram's manuscript. However, the warden declined to honor his request, and there is no record of what Panzram might have said about his brief encounter with Menninger.[16]

In 1933, over two years after Panzram's death, Menninger published an essay for *Kansas Magazine* about the psychology of crime. In it, he used Panzram anonymously as an example. He also returned the manuscript of Panzram's confession to Lesser and stated his desire to include a full analysis of it in the psychiatric literature. Lesser did not respond, perhaps because he was attempting to get the manuscript published via literary great H. L. Mencken, but its contents were proving too strong for editors. However, Panzram emerged in 1938 in Menninger's next book, *Man against Himself.*

Disguising Panzram as "John Smith," Menninger offered his analysis. He blamed Panzram's hostility on the treatment he'd received as a child in the Minnesota reform school and noted the psychological damage done to Panzram at an early age. Menninger thought that the injustices perpetrated on Panzram had aroused a need for retaliation, which he had repressed of necessity but later expressed in his brutality and murder. Because Panzram was highly intelligent as well as enraged, he went further than most others who'd endured similar treatment. He required intelligent, compassionate handling, which one did not see in reform schools or prisons.

Menninger confirmed an idea expressed in a study from that era that criminality was one of the last remaining outlets for masculine sovereignty to express itself and resist becoming a cog in the social machine. It represented the part of American democracy that affirmed the individual, because certain criminals are self-made men, successful in their own worlds. Menninger added his own notion that common to these cases was "a great wish to remain a dependent child and great resentment against the social, economic, and other forces which thwarted their satisfactions, with the consequent combination of mixed feelings of revenge, self-assertion, and guilt."[17] Some criminality, he suggested, was the result of overwhelming hate that started in childhood, and the aggression it inspired also set up the conditions for capture and punishment that the child felt he deserved. Consciously, the offender does not believe he should be punished, but subconsciously he does, and subconscious forces are stronger.

Menninger was impressed with Panzram's frank admissions that no one liked him, that he wasn't likable, and that he was in fact destructive. However, Panzram had also seemed to realize that his life could have been productive and he might have performed many good works if only he'd been treated better. The hatred and rage he'd felt had not been natural parts of his life but had been instilled by the inhumanity of others.

"I have never seen an individual whose destructive impulses were so completely accepted and acknowledged by his conscious ego," Menninger wrote. "He outlined to me in detail a plan he had conceived for bringing about the destruction of the entire human race."[18] He compared it to looking into a human body torn open, "with all the vital organs laid bare, the person retaining consciousness with a superhuman ability to endure pain so that he could calmly discuss the accident and his approaching death."[19] Menninger concluded that Panzram's execution was nothing short of suicide, the accomplishment of what he'd sought once his life had become a living hell.

Panzram clearly had entitlement issues. When he was told upon his return from boarding school to get to work on the farm, he decided that he wanted more out of life and that it was owed to him. Thus, he tried helping himself to what neighbors had. When punished, he grew angry. He was like many offenders whose rage and self-centeredness empower their aggression. Given their infantile level of narcissism, they will not resolve their anger—and don't wish to. For some, such resolution is equivalent to being weak or less masculine. Instead, they let it build. They ruminate, get depressed, feel mistreated, dwell on past experiences, and probably minimize their role while exaggerating the role of others. Blame is a strong factor in keeping anger alive. Those "others" who caused the distressing situation will now become objects in their fantasy, upon which they will take out their rage. But by Menninger's theory, they're really indirectly attacking themselves. The victims are symbolic punching bags. They bear the brunt of the killers' need, and they are forced to feel the pain that the killers have long harbored inside themselves, but they're also the means by which to be caught and punished.

When interviewed, several killers motivated by rage say that murder is a way to express (and derive relief from) their frustration. They target victims who symbolize their anger, due to their looks, their profession, their age, or the way the person treats them. Anger provides an adrenaline rush, and when it's coupled with poor impulse control, there's little to hinder a person intent on rage-motivated murder. In the moment, it feels good. They've rehearsed this solution to frustration in their fantasies, so the pleasure from killing has become a routine response.

Over half a century later, Duncan Cartwright studied the predisposing personality of the rage murderer, based on a study of nine offenders, and found that they were able to split reality into external and internal worlds. A degree of dissociation occurs during the act of murder, which is often triggered by some innocuous external event. In other words, the explosive intensity of rage murder is well beyond what the stimulus should have provoked. Like Menninger, Cartwright describes the origination of murderous impulses from the feeling of internal threat, so the person decides to annihilate the threat. It's a defense against potential damage to an already vulnerable or deficient personality. Aggression preserves the person's inner world (like Panzram raping before he could be raped). Early problems in childhood, be they from abuse or an inability to adapt to the world, can make the person inflexible, with a tendency to control (or overcontrol) situations. But their hostility and rigidity set them up for failure, which escalates their desperation to keep their inner world intact. When the triggers are just right, they can react quickly and with extreme violence. When this possibility is removed, they may act to manipulate the system to end their lives.[20]

When Menninger wrote his article in 1933 about how the penal system makes criminals worse, he was pleased to report that Wichita, Kansas, had a police school that relied on scientific methods of catching criminals and psychological methods for dealing with them, with a view toward using insights gained to prevent future crime.

If Menninger had known about another killer from his era, not yet caught, he'd have wanted to interview this man as well, but the next tale features another psychiatrist, equally noted for his ideas and experience.

CHAPTER 5

Albert Fish and Fredric Wertham

1

Even today, Albert Fish stands as one of the most deviant sex offenders in U.S. history. It's not that he killed the most people, but that his sexual appetites, his bizarre rituals, and his need to torment himself as much as others have no equal. The psychiatrist who most fully evaluated him, Dr. Fredric Wertham, was so fascinated with this offender that he made a detailed study. He also spoke the most compassionately on his behalf, throwing blame on unfortunate life events. Since Wertham was an outspoken advocate for the criminally mentally ill, his account is particularly valuable.

Wertham, one of the foremost psychiatrists in America during the first half of the twentieth century, became renowned for his moralistic stand against comic books. He claimed that reading them was a significant factor in juvenile delinquency. Within this context, Wertham believed there was nothing mysterious or irrational driving criminals; social and environmental factors were chiefly responsible.

Educated in Germany and England, and an associate of Sigmund Freud, Wertham became head of the Mental Hygiene Clinic at Queens General Hospital in New York and president of the Association for the Advancement of Psychotherapy. He also ran the Lafarge Clinic in Harlem. In 1941, Wertham published *Dark Legend*, a detective story based on a juvenile murderer with a dark fantasy life. He also undertook a scientific study of murder, which provided the material for another book, *The Show of Violence*.

Wertham never hesitated to state his disapproval. He made clear what he thought about psychiatrists participating in the court system—they should be involved in treatment, he stated, not contention. He even predicted that in the future, thanks to better treatment and outright cures, psychiatrists wouldn't need to be part of the legal process, because they will have prevented many crimes. Wertham especially despised the vagueness of the legal definition of "insanity," because it encouraged psychiatrists to work on behalf of either side and thereby make their profession appear to be full of holes. "The whole relationship of psychiatry to the law," he said, "is highlighted by the development of the insanity plea."[1] Going back to a case in 1740, he named the "Swiss psychiatrist Plater" as the first advocate for a physician's involvement in a legal case of derangement and described the pre-Lombroso origins of the concept of the "born criminal."[2]

Wertham pinpointed a difficulty that pervades insanity cases in many states even today: the legal definition of "insanity" is too crude to include the nuances of delusion. An emotionally sick murderer may know that what he's doing is wrong, but within his private, distorted values, he may believe he's right. The true value of a psychiatrist, Wertham stated, is the manner in which he can get at the facts. He is trained to find out the circumstances of a defendant's mental and physical development, and thereby to offer an informed opinion from within the person's life story about the criminal motive. Thus, he should not be an "opinion ped-dler." With Fish, Wertham certainly had his hands full. It was a "life story" unlike any he'd ever heard.

2

On June 3, 1928, Grace Budd went missing from her Manhattan home. A middle-aged man had taken her away. He'd called himself Frank How-ard, but he'd given a false address. It had been his second visit to the residence. The first had been in response to an ad placed by the Budd's eighteen-year-old son, Edward, seeking work in the country. While in the residence, Howard had seen ten-year-old Grace and asked if he could take her to a party for his niece.

Only a year before, young Billy Gaffney had been kidnapped from Brooklyn, and something similar had happened to eight-year-old Francis McDonnell on Staten Island in July 1924. He'd been assaulted, strangled, and placed under some branches, naked from the waist down. Both incidents were associated with an older man who'd been seen in the area.

In the Budd incident, an officer asked telegraph agencies to look for forms that Howard had used to send a telegram to the Budds on June 2, which had announced his arrival. This discovery produced a sample of his handwriting.

The case had many twists and turns, with hopes for Grace's return raised and dashed, until it was clear that the girl was gone and proba-bly dead. William F. King, a detective lieutenant at the Missing Persons Bureau, took over the Budd investigation, but it would be more than three years before the case finally came to a resolution.

On November 11, 1934, Delia Budd received a letter, sent from the Grand Central post office. She did not read, so Edward looked over the contents, which were so disgusting that he was certain it was from Grace's kidnapper. He took the missive straight to Detective King.

"My dear Mrs. Budd," the writer began. He went on to state that in 1894, a friend of his had shipped as a deck hand on the steamer *Tacoma*, going to Hong Kong. They got drunk and missed getting back on the boat, so they were stranded in a country suffering from famine.

"So great was the suffering among the very poor that all children under 12 were sold for food in order to keep others from starving. A boy or girl under 14 was not safe in the street. You could go in any shop and ask for steak—chops—or stew meat. Part of the naked body of a boy or girl would be brought out and just what you wanted cut from it. A boy or girls behind which is the sweetest part of the body and sold as veal cutlet brought the highest price."

So this man reportedly had acquired a taste for human flesh, and when he finally returned to New York, he kidnapped two young boys. He bound and tortured them to make their "meat" tender. Then he killed and ate them.

"He told me so often how good Human flesh was I made up my mind to taste it. On Sunday June the 3—1928 I called on you at 406 W 15 St. Brought you pot cheese—strawberries. We had lunch. Grace sat in my lap and kissed me. I made up my mind to eat her. On the pretense of taking her to a party. You said Yes she could go. I took her to an empty house in Westchester I had already picked out. When we got there, I told her to remain outside. She picked wildflowers. I went upstairs and stripped all my clothes off. I knew if I did not I would get her blood on them. When all was ready I went to the window and called her. Then I hid in a closet until she was in the room. When she saw me all naked she began to cry and tried to run down the stairs. I grabbed her and she said she would tell her mamma. First I stripped her naked. How she did kick—bite and scratch. I choked her to death, then cut her in small pieces so I could take my meat to my rooms. Cook and eat it. How sweet and tender her little ass was roasted in the oven. It took me 9 days to eat her entire body. I did not fuck her tho I could of had I wished. She died a virgin."[3]

The letter was unsigned, but the handwriting was identical to that on the Western Union form from the 1928 telegram Frank Howard had sent the Budds.

Detective King examined the stationery and the envelope in which the letter had arrived. He noticed an emblem, partially scratched out. It was hexagonal and bore the letters "N.Y.P.C.B.A.," which stood for the New

York Private Chauffeur's Benevolent Association. He called the organization's president, Arthur Ennis, and asked for a meeting. Then he assigned other detectives to start looking at each person's handwriting. No one's handwriting matched Frank Howard's. King asked the members whether someone else had access to the organization's stationery.

Lee Sicowski, who worked there part-time as a janitor, admitted to taking a few sheets and envelopes. He gave King several addresses for boardinghouses, including one at 200 East 52nd Street. King found a promising lead there: the occupant in Room 7 after Sicowski was Albert H. Fish, and his description resembled the man who'd visited the Budds on that fateful day. His handwriting also matched that on the telegram form. King learned that Fish's son sent him regular checks and that one more would be coming. Thus, Fish would be returning to this very building. King alerted postal inspectors to be watching for it and set up round-the-clock surveillance at the boardinghouse. Then the check arrived. A week later, a short, elderly man came to the building. King arrested him and took him to police headquarters.

This "undersized wizened house painter with restless eyes and thin, nervous hands," as reporters referred to him, denied everything before finally confessing in lurid detail. At no point during the hours he talked did he display emotion. He signed six separate confessions.

Fish said that he had originally meant to kidnap Edward Budd, but the boy was too big. When he spotted Grace, he decided to kill her instead. On his way to the Budd home, he'd stashed away a package containing the "implements of hell" (a saw, butcher knife, and cleaver). As he left with Grace, he retrieved the package and took her on a train to Westchester County. He knew of an isolated, abandoned house there called Wisteria Cottage.

Once they arrived, he let her play in the yard while he undressed. He then called her to come in. She was shocked to see him naked, but he grabbed and strangled her. He told one person he had ejaculated twice during her struggle. Then he cut her head off, draining the blood into a can. He tried to drink it, but it made him ill. He sawed the body in two and left the lower torso and legs behind the door. Taking the head outside, he covered it with paper. He also removed some of the flesh, which he packaged up and took home. This is what he claimed he had mixed with carrots and potatoes to make a stew. In a state of sexual arousal that lasted over a week, he consumed it. Four days after the murder, he returned to the cottage; took the torso, legs, and head into the woods; and threw them over a stone wall.

Fish agreed to take police to Worthington Woods to show them the place where he had killed Grace and tossed her remains. Her skull was visible in the dirt behind the stone wall, where a rusty cleaver, a saw, and the rest of Grace's bones were found.[4]

3

Dr. Fredric Wertham, then the senior psychiatrist at Bellevue Hospital, evaluated Fish for the defense. Two other psychiatrists did so as well, along with four mental health professionals for the prosecution. Wertham's first impression of Fish was of a meek, gentle, and benevolent old man. "If you wanted someone to entrust your children to, he would be the one you would choose."[5]

Wertham spent over twelve hours with him, working to win his trust and then trying to understand his many deviances. He believed it was a psychiatrist's duty to get all the details of a life story to make sense of the illness. He administered several standard psychological tests, including the Rorschach, and discovered that when Fish realized Wertham had a genuinely scientific interest in him, he cooperated.

Fish claimed he had married four times (two of those women denied it), and after having six children with his first wife, she ran off with another man, taking all the furniture and leaving the children for him to raise. It was clear that he loved them, despite his crimes against other children, but none had guessed the extent of his problems. They had thought him merely eccentric. Fish claimed that his wife's departure, and her betrayal, opened up the floodgates of his sexual troubles. He allowed himself to express his desires, uninhibited.

Wertham described Fish as having an "unparalleled perversity." He counted eighteen different paraphilias, including cannibalism, coprophagia, masochism, sadism, vampirism, and necrophilia. "There was no known perversion that he did not practice, and practice frequently."[6] He also believed that Fish was psychotic, infantile, and prone to religious complexes.

Wertham decided that Fish's perverse predilections had begun early, when he was a child, arising from episodes of severe spanking by a female teacher at an orphan home. (Fish's father had died when he was five, and his mother had placed him there.) The act of spanking had piqued his interest, and while watching this teacher paddle the bare bottoms of other children, he grew aroused. Thus, his developing sexual desire centered on children, especially the buttocks. He was a fidgety child who suffered from bedwetting. Mostly, he was a masochist. "I have always had the desire to inflict pain on others and to have others inflict pain on me," Fish told the psychiatrist. But Fish went to extremes when looking for things with which to hurt himself. He would insert the stems of roses into his urethra or stick needles in his testicles, although he found the pain too intense. "If only pain were not so painful!" he stated.[7]

Fish compared himself with Harry Thaw, a millionaire who'd committed the sensational murder of architect Stanford White in 1906. Paranoid and mentally unstable, Thaw had been found not guilty by reason of insanity. Although he was incarcerated in a mental hospital, he enjoyed complete freedom and was eventually released. He continued to abuse people as much as he'd always done.

Believing himself at times to be Christ or Abraham, and obsessed with sin and atonement, Fish had made a practice of beating his naked body with spiked paddles and sticking lighted cotton balls, soaked in alcohol, inside his anus. "The trouble with pain," he said, "is you get tough and always have to invent something worse."[8] He also believed he needed to kill children ("lambs") as a human sacrifice to please God and/or save their souls. He enjoyed hearing their cries of pain. Whatever he did he justified with quotes from the Bible. (He'd once been a church caretaker and had even painted angels on its ceiling.) Among the things he did to children were binding, castration, removing parts of the penis, anal assault, and beatings. He would then leave them, sometimes bound, for someone else to find. In fact, he had intended to castrate the Budd boy, and had even tried to castrate himself.

Wertham was skeptical about one claim, but evidence proved it to be true. In his drive to feel pain, Fish actually shoved needles into the area of his groin between the anus and scrotum, and according to X-ray evidence, over two dozen were still there. It seemed astounding that a man would do this, but Fish had many different religious delusions that involved being a martyr. He claimed he'd performed a similar act on some of his victims. In fact, he estimated that he'd sexually abused over one hundred children in twenty-three states.

Fish readily described his method for seducing and bribing children, often going naked under his painter's overalls so he could quickly remove his clothing, ready for sexual abuse. He used many different aliases and chose victims from the poorest classes, especially "colored children," because he knew they were least likely to raise a fuss, tell on him, or inspire an investigation. One little girl had procured boys for him for money. Still, he'd been forced to leave town many times when adults heard rumors about him. He also enjoyed writing obscene letters to strangers, hoping someone would respond with a similar inclination. He was constantly looking for a kindred soul with whom to inflict and receive physical abuse.

Wertham noted that Fish admired the work of a notorious killer from Germany, Fritz Haarmann, the "Hanover Vampire," who'd been convicted in 1924. Since Fish had a number of clippings about the man in his possession, Wertham looked into the case. This case proved to be just as disturbing as Fish's in its depravity. Haarmann was a butcher with a record of past commitments in a mental institution. He would invite wayward young men to his home for a meal, force sex on them, and murder them. Worse, as he sodomized them, he often chewed into their necks to drink the gushing blood. Under arrest, Haarmann had confessed to fifty murders, referring to his victims as "game." He would cut the flesh from their bodies, he had admitted; eat some or store it under his bed; and sell the rest as butchered meat.

To Wertham's astonishment, when he did background research, he found that Fish had twice been committed to Bellevue, but no one there had spotted his demented fantasies as a danger to anyone. He was also picked up several times in New York City for the impairment of the morals of a minor, yet no one had connected him to the high-profile case of Grace Budd.

In their talks together, Wertham realized that Fish was no ordinary mental patient. He had devised a clever and detailed plan to kill a child and had used a trustworthy persona to snatch her from the bosom of her family. He had a cover story, a murder kit, an alias, a means to commit the crime in private, and a way to evade the law. Although his letter six years later was a clear impulse from his unconscious, Wertham concluded that Fish was a predator. He was abnormal and even suffered from psychotic delusions at times, but when it came to murder, he was not *legally* insane. Yet Wertham believed that one could be psychotic and still have intact reasoning.

Wertham did not consider the category of "psychopath" because, in 1935, it was a hodgepodge diagnostic category for a "mild kind of abnormality." Its criteria lay somewhere between normal and mentally diseased, so that those for whom a diagnosis was difficult to make were usually labeled psychopaths. Wertham knew this meant only that they had an abnormal mental makeup. But to sum up Fish's case, he wrote, "However you define the medical and legal borders of sanity, this certainly is beyond that border."[9] By his estimate, Fish had killed as many as five children and had intended, or tried, to kill a few more.

Fish entered a plea of not guilty by reason of insanity, and he was transported to Westchester for a first-degree murder trial. Just before it commenced in March 1935, Fish used a sharpened fishbone from his soup to cut his chest and abdomen. However, his injuries were not serious. Some guards believed he was merely searching for a way to inflict pain. However, Fish had also expressed a fear of the electric chair.

Fish's letter to the Budds, along with his most detailed confession, was read to the jury. His attorney, James Dempsey, hoped to use the fact that Fish had been a house painter for many years to introduce the possibility of lead poisoning. However, Detective King testified that Fish had admitted that he knew that what he had done to Grace was wrong. Still, Fish had also said that "God still has work for me to do." He'd told Dr. Wertham that if the murder was not justified, an angel would have stopped him, as one had done in the Bible before Abraham nearly slew Isaac.[10]

Wertham had labored over a forty-five-page report, from which he quoted when he testified for the defense. He said that Fish had practiced "every known sexual abnormality," although his prepared list of eighteen separate fetishes was not admitted. Giving a diagnosis of paranoid psychosis, he described Fish's extensive family history of abnormal personalities, including several with schizophrenia. Fish's mental problems had developed after he'd become obsessed with religion. He believed he could use murder to atone for his sins, and with Grace he'd had a premonition of some future outrage to her, so he had murdered her to save her. Mixed up with all this was his insistence that God had commanded him to sacrifice a virgin. He had told Wertham that right after the murder he'd felt overwhelming remorse. Fish, Wertham said, had no rational control. He was dangerous but insane and should be institutionalized in a psychiatric facility. In support, Fish's children testified about having witnessed his self-torture and exhibitionism, and Wertham added that to be aware of right and wrong, one had to *feel* it.

"I stated that the knowledge of right and wrong," he later wrote, "is quite different from the knowledge that two plus two equals four. It requires intactness of the whole personality."[11]

For the prosecution, Dr. Charles Lambert and Dr. James Vavasour, who had seen Fish for about three hours, refuted Wertham and another psychiatrist for the defense, finding that Fish was legally sane. Despite his delusions, Fish had known at the time of the crime that what he had done was wrong. There was no clearer evidence than his use of a pseudonym, his carefully planned agenda, the manner in which he'd hidden his "death tools," and the isolated location.

In closing, Dempsey insisted that Fish was a psychiatric phenomenon, stating that "no single case history report, either in legal or medical annals, contains a record of one individual who possessed all of these sexual abnormalities."[12] He reiterated Wertham's plea to send the man to a facility that could treat him.

After deliberation, the jury convicted Fish of murder. (Som.
they agreed that he was insane but still believed he should be ̔
As Fish awaited his sentencing, he confessed in writing to the n
the Gaffney boy, in which he had long been a suspect. He said he .
the boy into pieces and roasted his buttocks with onions and carrot,
suming the tender meat over the course of four days. The police immediately went to question him in the presence of District Attorney Walter
Ferris, and he confessed orally, affirming that what he had written was
true. He also admitted to the murder of the McDonnell boy on Staten
Island. If he had not been interrupted, he said, he would have dismembered the body.

On June 17, 1935, Fish, now sixty-five, went to the electric chair at
Ossining (Sing Sing) Prison, his hands clasped together as if in prayer. In
just three minutes, he was dead. He offered no last words, although supposedly he'd anticipated that the experience of electrocution would be a
supreme thrill.

4

Two years later, Wertham proposed a theory about offenders like Fish. He
accepted the notion of "catathymia" to explain the recurrence of violent
sexual compulsions. A German psychologist had coined the word in 1912
in the context of paranoia, deriving it from two Greek words, *kata* and
thymos, which refer to emotions. Accordingly, an emotionally charged
idea temporarily overwhelms a person and pushes him or her off balance.

Wertham explained catathymic behavior as occurring when a person
acquires an idea that he believes he must carry through to a violent act.
This person develops a plan and feels an urge in the form of emotional
tension to put the plan into action, imbuing the violence with symbolic
meaning. His thinking acquires a delusional quality, marked by rigidity and poor logical coherence. When the act commences, he feels calm
again.

The eight stages of catathymic crisis play out thus:

1. Following a traumatic experience, an unsolvable internal state leads
   to emotional tension.
2. The person projects blame for this tension onto an external source.
3. His thinking becomes more egocentric and self-protective.
4. Violence is perceived as the only way out, so he crystallizes a plan.
5. To safeguard the personality, the extreme emotional tension culmi-
   nates in the violent crisis—either acted out or attempted.

6. The tension is relieved.
7. Superficial normality occurs.
8. Inner equilibrium is recovered, with the development of insight.

Thus, Fish could have been in catathymic crisis just before each incident of murder.[13]

In 1954, Wertham took on the big question: why do men kill. He dismissed "irrational forces" from "unfathomable depths" that turn murder into a romantic mystery. Equally erroneous is that murderers are all abnormal. He discussed his examination of the "Lonely Hearts Killers" Raymond Fernandez and Martha Beck. He had tried hard to find symptoms of disease, but found only greed and jealousy. He went on to describe motives for murder as mixes of complex forces, not the least of which was the contagion of violence. "The more we inculcate in young people the false idea that there is something courageous about killing, the more do we foster it in susceptible individuals."[14] Murder, in fact, is full of cowardice. Society must ask itself if it wants a violent or nonviolent world and set rules on all levels accordingly. Wertham's stand against comics, in fact, was instrumental in the creation of the sanitizing Comics Code.

To this point, few female offenders were considered severe enough for this type of detailed study. In 1908, Cesare Lombroso had offered an interpretation of Norwegian American serial murderer Belle Gunness, but since she was either dead or on the run, she wasn't around to respond to probing questions. In general, females were thought to lack the propensity for truly cold and brutal offenses, despite the fact that among the first serial killers on record were Locusta, a poisoner from ancient Rome, and the seventeenth century's Countess Erzsebet Báthory, who possibly had hundreds of victims. It is even less likely that anyone would expect such behavior from a child, but the next case surprised everyone. Only an observant police psychiatrist saw through her to counter the story she told with behavioral evidence.

CHAPTER 6

Chloe Davis and J. Paul de River

1

While it was rare during the 1940s to even consider females as extreme offenders, one case grabbed a psychiatrist's attention and engrossed him so much that he lost sight of his limitations. At the time, Dr. J. Paul de River was the founder and head of the Los Angeles Police Department's (LAPD) newly formed Sex Offense Bureau, and he consulted on crime scenes with a sexual component (thousands of cases, he said). He reported the results in a unique and graphically illustrated book, *The Sexual Criminal*, in 1949, shortly after he was involved in a scandal regarding the infamous Black Dahlia murder.[1] The New Orleans–born de River liked to devise brief profiles whenever he studied a crime. He offered one for a sensational triple homicide that put him firmly on the map with the LAPD. While it is not easy to glean genuinely shrewd observations from his subjective opinions, his place in the history of criminal psychology is firmly established. After surgeon Thomas Bond offered a profile of Jack the Ripper in 1888, de River became the next professional to construct an official consultant's profile from crime scene data—and the first psychiatrist to do so. He also founded the first police-based sex offenders database and the first bureau in the United States to focus on sexual offenses. He gained support from investigators after his work on a high-profile case.

On June 26, 1937, three girls went missing in Inglewood, California. Two were sisters: Madeline Everett, age seven, and Melba Everett, nine. Accompanying them was their eight-year-old friend, Jeannette Stephens. All three were seen that Saturday talking to a man and leaving Centinela Park. Two days later, volunteer Boy Scouts found their bodies in a weed-strewn gully in the nearby Baldwin Hills. They had been strangled, sexually assaulted, and seemingly subjected to an odd ritual. Despite an intense search, there were no leads, and the LAPD hit a dead end. They consulted a psychiatrist with whom they had previously worked on probation cases, Dr. Joseph Paul de River.

He viewed the condition of the bodies in the morgue and went to the crime scene. He knew from photos that the girls had lain close together, face-down, their dresses pulled up, and their shoes removed and placed in a row, side by side. He considered all of this and described the type of person the police should be seeking: a sadistic pedophile in his twenties who was meticulous in appearance, religious, and remorseful. He might have a past arrest record for annoying children or hanging out where they played. The crime had been planned, and he'd known how to approach the girls without frightening them. They had trusted him.

Although no one could run down a suspect with such a general description, investigators began with known sex offenders, bachelors who lived in the area, and men with whom the girls might have been acquainted. De River helped to question suspects. His description fit a school crossing guard, Albert Dyer, who had been at the crime scene as a volunteer searcher and had acted strangely afterward. He'd even presented himself, unsolicited, at the police department, insisting on knowing why they wanted to question him. Although Dyer initially denied it, with de River's assistance, the man confessed that he'd killed the girls. As a member of the search team, he'd become hysterical when the bodies were found, ordering everyone there to show respect. He'd also insisted on helping to remove the bodies. However, contrary to the profile, he was thirty-two, was married, and had never been arrested for bothering children. His postcrime behavior, as he described it, reflected the private joy of a sadist rather than remorse. His wife reluctantly admitted that since the girls had gone missing, he'd been keeping a scrapbook of clippings.

Once he'd come clean, Dyer described how he'd planned the crime. He'd lured the girls into the secluded gully with a story about rabbits and then separated them. One at a time, he'd strangled them with his bare hands, tying clothesline tight around their necks to ensure they were dead. He'd then had postmortem sex with them, burning the bloody handkerchief he'd used to wipe off his penis. Dyer had then removed the girls' shoes, placed them in a row, and prayed over the bodies. Although he eventually recanted, with similar clothesline from his home and the crime details he'd provided, he was convicted and then quickly hanged.[2]

De River's description had not helped to find or identify the perpetrator, but its accuracy on certain points confirmed the psychiatrist's value as a consultant. The LAPD made him the go-to man for sexually bizarre crimes in the greater metropolitan area. He felt good about that, and whenever he believed he'd been ignored, he complained. *He* was the sex expert, after all, and he'd created the country's first Sex Offense Bureau.

He'd been its director and sole employee for two years in April 1940 when a shocking case came his way.

Nothing would have captured his interest more than the arrest of a female murderer—in the form of a pigtailed little girl with a bizarre and bloody story. She was a find, with the potential to solidify his status and legacy among his colleagues. He wrote that it is wise to remember "that we must never trust appearances,"[3] and this would certainly apply to a young girl suspected in a controlled and bloody quadruple homicide. Almost anyone with a weak character, de River would say, could develop a "misdirected sexual impulse" and thereby become a monster.

De River's method was to learn as much as possible about a suspect's family background and sexual habits. Dyer, for example, had admitted to a preference for anal sex, female buttocks, the smell of children, the idea of sexual control, and having sex during menstruation. De River also examined medical records and past criminal history, if any. He made a determination of each suspect's IQ and decided whether he or she was medically and legally sane. De River would then assign the person to a category, based on the crime details, and place the record in his files with others of this same type. He used these files to then practice a primitive form of "dangerousness" assessment of anyone brought in on a morals charge. Although he kept his public image low-key, he rapidly gained elite status among the city's most powerful officials.

The psychopathology of the sexual instinct in psychopaths, de River believed, derived largely from childhood complexes. At the time, it was believed that people became sexual predators due to character weakness and imbalanced psychology. The offenders were considered unreflective and self-centered (i.e., they had superegos that made them abnormally proud of their degeneracy), and thus they would break laws and harm others to fulfill their own needs. Treatment during these times was to persuade offenders to gain insight about their degeneracy and to understand the need to exert their will to return to a normal state. De River hoped to succeed in this way with his young female mass murderer.

2

Chloe Davis was eleven years old. On the afternoon of April 4, she called her father where he managed a grocery store and told him to come right home. Her voice sounded urgent, but she would not tell him what was wrong. When Frank Barton Davis arrived at his two-bedroom bungalow on West 58th Place, Los Angeles, he saw a crowd of neighbors, so he pushed through them. Chloe stood on the porch near the front door, her forehead bleeding. She ignored his concern and insisted that he go at once into the kitchen. Davis entered, struck by the smell of something burned. He was completely unprepared for the bloodbath that awaited him. In the kitchen he saw his three-year-old son, Marquis, and seven-year-old daughter, Deborah Ann, lying face up on the blood-stained linoleum. Both had been bludgeoned. Chloe pushed her stunned father out toward the hallway. There he found his wife, Lolita, staring up from a mattress on the floor amid a flurry of gore and feathers; she'd been bludgeoned and burned. In a bathroom he found his ten-year-old daughter, Daphne. Davis looked around at the crimson splotches and lumps of brain matter on the walls, ceiling, and furniture. He could barely register that he'd lost nearly his entire family. Then he ran. Screaming, he went into the street, insisting that he should die, too. Chloe went after him and told him to "brace up." An ambulance arrived, called by neighbors, and Chloe was taken to the police emergency hospital.

Chloe's wound was superficial, so after it was treated, police officer Rose Pickerel and Dr. Speak came to her room to question her. Since Chloe had witnessed this atrocity, they had to speak with her as quickly as possible, despite her recent trauma. Although this was not a sex crime, de River accompanied Captain Edgar Edwards to help.

Oddly, Chloe did not appear to be too disturbed. She answered their questions readily, and to their surprise, the incident had not been the work of some lunatic intruder, perpetrated while Chloe hid. In a clear voice, she claimed that her mother had done it. Then she described the morning's horrible work. Chloe woke up to a lot of racket and went out to find her mother hitting the other children. Chloe asked what was going on, and stated that "she told me demons were after all of us and she was going to kill all us kids and then kill herself."[4]

Lolita had allegedly heard demons that day and had believed they were inhabiting her children. When Chloe came running in response to the screams, Lolita hit her with a glancing blow, but the child had resisted further attacks. Lolita claimed she'd killed Chloe's cousin years earlier because she could wish people dead with her mind. She then grabbed a box of matches and tried to light Chloe's hair, but Chloe blew them out. Lolita then retreated to her bedroom and pulled a mattress off the bed. She dragged it into the hall and lay down. After setting her own hair on fire, she ordered Chloe to burn her nightgown, which the girl did, "because she was suffering." Lolita reportedly begged Chloe to hit her with the hammer. "She told me to hit her over the head and to keep on hitting until she couldn't talk."[5]

Chloe described how she'd hit her mother repeatedly, about twenty times, stopping to get a drink between blows. At this time she had seen her ten-year-old sister, curled up, naked, and unconscious in the bathtub. Lolita ordered Chloe to keep striking her. After a while, the hammer's head broke off. (Chloe showed de River the blister she'd received to the base of her right thumb while wielding the hammer.) Feeling tired, she went into the kitchen to see what time it was and to get a new hammer. There she encountered her wounded sister and brother. Lying across the threshold, Marquis was moaning in pain. Chloe stepped over him to get the hammer and returned to her mother. It didn't work, so Chloe picked up the handle of the broken hammer and hit her mother, she estimated, another thirty times.

Still, her mother remained alive, so Chloe asked if she should finish off her brother and put him out of his misery. When Lolita nodded, Chloe went in the kitchen and hit her brother on the head three times. Then she returned to her mother, who supposedly told her to keep hitting until she could no longer talk. When it was over and the house was silent, Chloe took time to wash the blood off herself and clean what she could reach of the gore-spattered walls. She removed her bloody pajamas and put on a dress and shoes. She went outside and pulled the door behind her, locking it "to keep out the demons." She went to a neighbor's house to call her father. Returning to the porch, she waited by the front door.

The two sisters, while unconscious, were not yet dead. They were transported to the hospital, and there is an indication in de River's notes that Daphne had told doctors that Chloe had attacked her. (Chloe herself mentioned this "rumor" and vehemently denied it.) Both girls died soon after arrival, their stories forever sealed.

When Chloe was asked if she was angry with her mother, she said, "Mother never mistreated me. She was all right. I stopped beating her when she stopped breathing."[6]

De River found Chloe's deliberate and precocious manner intriguing, especially her lack of mourning for her dead mother and siblings. Most interesting was the fact that she had not once sought assistance during the slaughter, as he believed a normal child would do. Instead, she'd stood unruffled in the midst of a bloody mess that must have smelled awful. Even there in the hospital, the girl was cold and unfeeling, and she even seemed to be having a bit of fun as she offered treats from a bag of candy someone had given her and flexed her bicep to show how strong she was. De River concluded that she, not Lolita, had killed them all: she was a sadist, a rare female psychopath. Edwards agreed. Together they reconstructed the incident into other possible scenarios: Chloe had killed her mother first, getting her out of the way, before turning her wrath on her siblings. Or she had killed her youngest siblings in the kitchen, drawing her mother into the hall in response to their cries of pain; there, in the hallway, Chloe killed Lolita before going into the bathroom to bludgeon her other sister. She had then fabricated a cover story about her mother's crazy idea about demons before calling her father to come home. In short, she had done the whole thing, De River believed, and had presented a detailed lie.

De River based his theory on the idea that any child, even one with a strong bond with her mother, would refuse to carry out the horrific act that her mother had supposedly demanded. Chloe was not intellectually slow; on the contrary, she appeared to be quite bright. De River tentatively diagnosed her as suffering from "hereditary mania" and possibly the Electra complex—an obsessive jealousy over her father's affections and the desire to displace the mother.

After completing her narrative, Chloe added a detail she'd forgotten: oh yes, her mother had asked her to retrieve a razor for slashing her wrists, and she had watched as Lolita cut into herself. Oddly, Chloe had added this last piece of information as an afterthought, just before the questioning ended. That day, Chloe became the youngest person to have been arrested in Los Angeles for murder; because of her behavior with her brother, she was detained in a juvenile facility. She'd confessed to that one, as well as to the fatal beating of her mother. The police viewed her as coldhearted and without remorse. That she was a girl raised the stakes and turned the story into a media sensation. De River assured reporters that no third-degree interrogation tactics had been used. Chloe had been cooperative from the start.

The next day, the coroner's office had a startling announcement. Although Lolita had been bludgeoned in the head many times, she had not died from blows to the skull; her skull was not fractured. However, she'd succumbed to loss of blood due to her wrists being slashed. In the home, police found a bloody razor blade near where Lolita's corpse had lain.

The girl was brought in for another round of questions, as well as taken through the crime scene so she could point out where and how the events had occurred. She denied having ever been scared—"I didn't cry, if that's what you mean." She remained calm and repeated her story without alteration, over and over, for hours. She reenacted parts and added that her mother had said she could kill with her mind. Lolita had been seeing several doctors, who'd given her injections, but her condition had worsened. She'd complained of being unable to sleep and had made several remarks that demons had given her certain powers.

Chloe's father hired an attorney, Mitchel Moidel, who stopped the questioning on April 6. He stated that this many hours of interrogation constituted third-degree treatment and insisted that a child her age could not form criminal intent. It was a confusing issue at this time, because there had been very few cases in America of psychopathic children—in particular girls—who knew what they were doing and that it was wrong. Moidel hired his own psychiatrist, Dr. Samuel Marcus. Following the psychiatric evaluation, Moidel told the press that Chloe had been suffering from shock directly after the incident, and that the team who had interrogated her had failed to take this into consideration. De River was now on the hot seat, and his defense was to repeat that he had treated Chloe respectfully, without leading questions.

Then, more information came out. Davis admitted that his wife had not been as normal as he'd initially insisted: she'd seen two doctors and a psychiatrist for her illness, and had been getting shots for anemia. But she had asked him to purchase chloroform that she could pour on her children when the demons came to torture them, she had asked him to help her commit suicide, and in front of the children one day recently she had asked what the best way to kill a person was. "I'm convinced that Chloe is telling the truth," he stated. "When I talked to her yesterday, she said, 'Daddy, they are trying to make me say something I didn't do and I won't say I did it.'"[7]

A doctor confirmed that Davis had feared his wife was going insane, but there was no reported word from the psychiatrist she had seen. Neighbors, too, affirmed Lolita's odd comments and said that she was obsessed with tales about violent deaths. One person said that she had asked him about where in the head was the best place to hit someone for fatal results. However, there was also commentary on Chloe. A friend indicated that she had seen Chloe grab her mother by the hair over a petty squabble and knock her head hard against a concrete wall. Chloe was just a head shorter than her mother, and muscular, and could easily have committed this attack.

Even before all of the reports were in, a coroner's jury was formed. They considered the physical evidence in the context of Chloe's story and ruled that Lolita Davis had killed three of her children before killing herself. They also decided that Chloe had not really understood what she was telling the police. When a judge stated that she had been under her mother's domination and was therefore not responsible for her acts, he undermined de River's credibility. In fact, he nearly ruined the psychiatrist's career when he instructed that de River was never again to question a child under the age of eighteen. Effectively, he removed de River's ability to assess juvenile sex offenders. Although de River retained his position with the police, he lost both access and support for doing the work he wanted to do. He devoted much of his time offering armchair criminal analyses to a tabloid reporter—including cases on which he was still consulting for the LAPD.[8]

Despite the case resolution, de River continued to view Chloe Davis as uniquely coldblooded and labeled her a "female juvenile sadist" with a "cold, autistic personality."[9]

3

De River reiterated that "S" (the way he referred to Chloe in his case book, *The Sexual Criminal*) was suffering from the Electra complex (probably based on her admission that she disliked how her father gave all his attention to her youngest sister), but he added the Cain complex (rivalry between siblings) and the Destruction complex (a deadly component of Electra and Cain). In addition, he found a "marked element of spectacularism."[10] He noted that Chloe enjoyed good health, was athletic, and was fond of reading and of drawing pictures of wild animals and dinosaurs. Although de River was trying to learn if Chloe had liked crime stories, she shrugged it off, saying she preferred fiction, especially "Indian stories." However, her father claimed that she and her mother had shared an interest in crime novels.

"The eyes," de River said about the strange girl, "have an excited look with a bright, faraway stare, as if in person she were with you but in mind, miles away."[11] He noted that she had not yet entered puberty. When answering questions, she'd been calm and articulate, with a solid vocabulary and acute memory for details. Her stamina amazed her interrogators. De River saw no evidence of brain trauma, impairment, or shock. Chloe admitted to having a quick temper at times, and he thought her poise was more like that of a girl some years older. He determined that she possessed insight and was aware of the difference between right and wrong. He classified her as being emotionally frigid, characteristic of the "despotic type." The only time she cried during her questioning was when she sensed her questioners doubted her. She did not cry in the presence of her weeping father, and any emotion she did express was short-lived. She bounced back easily into her normal state of calm, readily posed for pictures, and was easily distracted by things in the room. De River had the impression he was watching an actress.

In his book, he provided a partial transcript of the girl's sessions with him, making comments throughout about how abnormal Chloe was. Each time she stated something that confirmed his ideas, he asks readers to note this. Clearly, he made a startling diagnosis and looked for confirming evidence rather than validating what she had told him with forensic evidence; he should also have learned more about her from a wide variety of sources, including teachers, friends, and surviving family members. Thus, de River could be guilty of cherry picking, looking for something specific and ignoring anything that failed to confirm what he believed. He did learn from Frank Davis that Lolita had been anemic, and he suspected that she'd been mentally disturbed. De River made a tentative diagnosis of the deceased Lolita of schizophrenia or paranoid praecox. Thus, it seemed likely to him that Chloe might have inherited a "schizoid temperament." She had then been exposed to an unsettling environment, which could have exacerbated her own unbalanced character. He believed that, at the very least, Chloe had been an easy and willing accomplice to the crimes.

In 1940, there was as yet no crystallized diagnosis of a psychopath, but by the time de River had collected and published his cases, a prison psychiatrist had published a groundbreaking book. Hervey Cleckley wrote *The Mask of Sanity* to make better sense of the condition often called "constitutional psychopathic inferiority." In the prisons, he'd met some rather distinct and charming manipulators who were in a category all their own. He called them "psychopaths." He discussed how typical psychopaths would seem agreeable, alert, friendly, and well adjusted. Devising sixteen distinct clinical criteria for assessment, Cleckley described these people as charming, manipulative, irresponsible, self-centered, shallow, lacking in empathy or anxiety, and likely to commit more types of crimes than other offenders. They were also more impulsively violent, more likely to recidivate, and less likely to respond to treatment. They displayed no sense of conscience.

De River believed that Chloe possessed the hallmarks of an insensitive sadistic child who, even in the most benign scenario, had no feelings for her dying mother and no problem with deciding to kill her brother. She showed no signs of shock, horror, or grief afterward. Her intent had been to punish her father while becoming the sole object of his affection and the central actress in an unfolding drama. Her postcrime behavior with him was revelatory—especially when they kissed each other on the lips when Chloe was released to his care.

If de River's transcript is accurately rendered, this is indeed a rather shocking way for a child to think, let alone act. Even so, there are no reports of Chloe acting out again, so it's possible that she was not as heartless and crafty as de River portrayed her.

About Chloe's tale, people tend to go one of two ways: (1) the fantastical demon story is absurd and Frank Davis fabricated these notions to save his child, so Chloe is therefore a mass murderer; or (2) testimony from Davis and others that Lolita was losing her bearings makes the tale Chloe told plausible. Mothers do sometimes kill their children over delusions about demons. (Even so, Chloe's manner, lack of fear, and lack of grief belie the notion of an innocent child simply obeying her mother.)

What adds more flavor to this story is de River's behavior on a case nine years later, when he falsely accused a young man of murdering and bisecting Elizabeth Short, the so-called Black Dahlia. A reporter researched de River's stated credentials and discovered that he had fabricated at least three of his previous medical posts. All of this found its way into the news, further disgracing the once-esteemed psychiatrist. It appeared that the LAPD's qualifications check for his current position had been "loose." Eventually, he even lost his support system among the police. Finally, his career ended badly.

While de River did help to create the nation's first sex offender registry in 1947, he derived many of his psychiatric insights from pseudoscience. Nevertheless, in a book that resembles von Krafft-Ebing's tome, de River's assemblage of criminal case histories has no equal from that era. His means of privileged access to the criminal mind was to wedge his way in and make sure that he was the only person to *have* access, effectively undercutting the ability of anyone else to contradict his expert opinions. After de River was briefly suspended and finally fired in 1950, the LAPD decided there was no further need for an official police psychiatrist.

Another young girl figures into the next case, and her part in it would inspire violent team killers for years to come. But it was the young man who led their spree of carnage across the Midwest who drew a psychiatrist's interest.

CHAPTER 7

Charles Starkweather and James Melvin Reinhardt

1

In 1948, a committee for the American Psychiatric Association concentrated on the task of devising a national classification system for mental illness. The membership discussed several drafts, and in 1952, this became the first version of the *Diagnostic and Statistical Manual of Mental Disorders*. This early incarnation was heavily psychoanalytic, with largely Freudian interpretations for psychoneurotic disorders. So during the 1950s, psychiatry became almost synonymous with psychoanalysis, which framed how our next case, the eight-day rampage of Charles Starkweather, was handled.[1]

From the beginning, experts in abnormal psychology from the fields of criminology and psychiatry were involved. Files were developed to give context, a report was written that synthesized the information for the court, and recommendations were made regarding the defendant's state of mental health. In addition, Dr. James M. Reinhardt, professor of sociology and criminology at the University of Nebraska, decided to interview Starkweather. With no monetary interest, he was in a position to be more objective than the mental health experts hired by the attorneys. Reinhardt had just published a scientific study, *Sex Perversions and Sex Crimes*, so he was granted access. Although this murder spree was not a sexual crime, he'd written about the "remorseless ego," and within this frame he had offered a theory for thinking about the type of offenders who kill without shame or conscience. His study would later assist the first FBI profilers, and in fact Reinhardt had been lecturing at the FBI since 1945. He was perfectly positioned to look closely at Starkweather and Caril Ann Fugate, the killing couple.

2

In Lincoln, Nebraska, Charles Starkweather was nineteen and angry. Born in 1938, Starkweather had grown up in abject poverty with his six siblings. Since he was five, he'd felt shame about himself, his circumstances, and certain aspects of his appearance. His father was a handyman and his mother had a job, too, during a time when few housewives worked outside the home. This had become one source of Starkweather's shame.

Even worse than the poverty of Starkweather's childhood were his physical shortcomings: he was myopic, bowlegged, short, and red-headed, and he suffered from a minor speech impediment. From his first day at school, he'd been teased about one thing or another—mostly his red hair and bowed legs; classmates called him "Red-headed Peckerwood," which had resulted in what he would describe to Reinhardt as "black moods," helping him to develop "a hate as hard as iron"[2] against those who humiliated or ostracized him. At times he would manage to do something that pleased his teachers, but other children would trash it.

Thus, in comparison with his comfortable home life, he grew to perceive the outside world as a hostile, unsafe place. "They hated me because of the way I looked and because I was poor," he would later complain.[3] This feeling that he was unacceptable never left him, no matter how hard his siblings and teachers tried to persuade him otherwise.

By the time he was an adolescent, Starkweather had decided that all he needed was a girlfriend and a gun. "I had hated and been hated," Starkweather once said; "I had my little world to keep alive as long as possible and my gun. That was my answer."[4]

Fourteen-year-old Caril Ann Fugate became his love interest, in part because he believed that she would "go all the way" with him (i.e., that she would embrace death, if need be). This notion seemed to comfort him, because Starkweather had a fantasy relationship with death. He confided to at least one person that the figure of Death often visited him. They had a "deal," and he believed that making plans that promised him a future would undermine it. Death would not allow him to get away with that.

Starkweather might have devised this fantasy because he believed the world had designated him for society's bottom rung, symbolized to him each day when his older brother called him to the garbage detail. He'd had a better job, but he'd lost it and now he was picking up garbage—the worst existence he could imagine. Starkweather wondered if he would ever manage to better himself and acquire the things to which he felt entitled. He wanted to visit New York City, see baseball games, and do other things that he imagined rich people doing. The apparent impossibility of attaining status fueled his anger. He couldn't even pay the meager rent for his single room, let alone buy his girlfriend a gift. He believed if he couldn't make her happy, he would lose her. They had good times together, he and Caril Ann, making love and laughing. Pressure mounted, giving him headaches, as he tried hard to think of a way to make some extra money.

As Christmas 1957 approached, Starkweather came up with a plan. He started to hang out at a local gas station in Lincoln, Nebraska, showing interest in the change of shifts at 11:00 P.M., when they counted the money. No one thought much of it, because there wasn't much crime in that area. Then, on December 1, Starkweather decided to make his move.

He placed a bandanna over his face and told the attendant, twenty-one-year-old Robert Colvert, to hand over all the money. The scared young man said he did not know how to access the safe. Starkweather grew angry. He wasn't about to just leave. He grabbed over $100 in loose change from the till and then made Colvert drive him to a stretch of country road. It was a cold winter night, but he made Colvert get out of the car. As the young man stood shivering, scared of what might happen, Starkweather shot him in the head. He would later say that it had felt good. Afterward, his incessant headaches diminished and finally stopped. He waited for a few days for someone to arrest him, but despite the fact that people were aware of his habit of hanging aimlessly around the station, he was never a suspect. No one even questioned him. He used the money openly to pay his rent that he owed from months earlier, buy some clothes, and purchase a gift for Caril.

However, Starkweather believed that people were trying to separate him from his girl, so he wanted to take her away, deep into the mountains, where no one would find them. Thus, the stage was set for a brutal murder spree that involved them both. Caril Ann's family disliked Starkweather, especially when he showed up with his rifle, so one day her mother, Velda Bartlett, forbade her to see him. Caril Ann grew upset. Starkweather later said that she told him to keep coming over.

On January 21, 1958, Starkweather was evicted for nonpayment of rent. The money he'd stolen was all gone. He went to Caril Ann's house, and Velda ordered him to stay away. Starkweather grew angry, cocked his rifle, and shot her. Then he shot her husband. When their three-year-old daughter began to scream, Starkweather used the butt of his rifle to break her skull, killing her. It's not clear whether Caril Ann was present, but even if she wasn't, once she arrived home, she realized what Starkweather had done. She did not try to run away or call the police.

They remained in the house for about a week, making plans to leave only after suspicious relatives began to come over and knock on the door, including Starkweather's older brother. When the coast was clear, they took off. Finally, relatives who did not believe the notes that Caril Ann had left on the door broke in and discovered the three bodies in the outhouse. This occurred on January 28. An investigation ensued, but the lovers were already in Bennett, sixteen miles away. They intended to seek the help of a Starkweather family friend, seventy-year-old August Meyer, but something apparently went wrong because Starkweather fatally shot this man from behind and then killed his dog. Rather than hide out on the farm, they decided to leave, but their car got stuck in mud. Not far away, they discovered a storm cellar on the grounds of an abandoned school and sought shelter inside. However, January in Nebraska can be bitter. When this plan failed, they returned to Meyer's house to work on getting their car out of the rut. Finally, they picked up their weapons and started to walk. Starkweather knew they could find another car. He had a gun.

It was now dark. Seventeen-year-old Robert Jensen, who was out for a short drive with his girlfriend, Carol King, saw them walking. He pulled over and offered them a ride into Bennett. Starkweather instead took their money and forced them to drive to the storm cellar he'd recently found. As Jensen went down the steps, Starkweather shot him in the head three times. He then forced Carol King into the enclosed area. He shot her, removed her jeans, and forced a knife into her vagina. He left her lying on top of Jensen's body.

Next, Starkweather and Fugate returned to Lincoln and entered the Lauer Ward home, located in an upscale neighborhood where Starkweather had his garbage route. The Ward's deaf maid answered the door, and Starkweather took this frightened woman, along with Mrs. Ward, hostage. He forced Mrs. Ward to make him pancakes and waffles, relishing his new position of power. However, she got her hands on a shotgun, aimed it at him, and fired. When she missed, he threw a knife at her and forced her into the bedroom, where he tied her to the bed and stabbed her repeatedly. Starkweather then killed the maid and waited for Mr. Ward to come home. It wasn't long before there were three dead people in the house, and the fugitives were fleeing in the Ward's car. They hid Jensen's stolen car inside the garage.

By now, authorities knew exactly who they were looking for and the manhunt expanded exponentially. The governor had deployed the National Guard to protect the streets of Lincoln, and the police had even distributed guns to civilians. The other bodies were discovered, one by one. Starkweather was considered armed and dangerous, and no one knew whether Caril Ann was an accomplice or a hostage. Around the time police entered the Ward home, Starkweather had killed a salesman napping in his car on a deserted Wyoming highway, shooting the vulnerable man eight times. However, when he tried and failed to start the car, a truck driver came along to assist. He saw the body on the passenger side and struggled with Starkweather over the gun. Just then, a highway patrol officer crested the hill. Caril Ann ran toward it, shouting that Starkweather had killed everyone. Apparently, she'd had enough.

In custody, Caril Ann claimed that Starkweather had taken her against her will, although the evidence clearly said otherwise. In short order, Starkweather confessed, initially taking the blame but eventually sharing equal responsibility with Fugate. He even stated that she'd killed Carol King out of jealousy. At no time did Starkweather show remorse. Instead, he claimed to have acted in self-defense. As he listened to news reports, he was pleased to learn that his killing spree was rare, because he believed he would now be famous. This gave his relationship with "Death" a new meaning.[5]

3

At this point, no criminologist had made a theoretical distinction between a mass murderer and a spree killer. There were too few cases of either to pinpoint the differences, so it would be over two decades before this distinction was articulated. Instead, all cases of multiple murder were referred to as "multicides."

Starkweather and Fugate were held for separate trials. Fugate took every opportunity to try to convince people she'd been a victim and that she had not known that her parents were dead until the police told her upon her arrest. However, it soon became clear that she'd had ample opportunities to get away from Starkweather had she really wanted to, and her youth hardly seemed a factor in her supposed inability to act. Starkweather covered for her at first, but when she turned on him he stated that she'd participated in some of the murders. This was believable when Caril came off as tough as nails in press interviews. (Her degree of participation, if any, was never resolved.)

Starkweather's defense attorney believed his only recourse was to plead insanity and blame a hostile, deprived environment. Who in his right mind would randomly kill all these people? However, the prosecutor, Elmer Scheele, was intent on convicting Starkweather, and possibly Caril Ann, of capital murder. He wanted someone to pay with his (and/or her) life. Both sides lined up their mental health experts.

Due to the shockingly explosive nature of their crimes, and with the death penalty pending, Reinhardt made the necessary preparations to interview Starkweather. Although this young killer was not a sex offender, Reinhardt viewed him as suffering from the "brutal hopelessness of [his] fears and failures" and with a "capacity for remorselessness." In the book he later wrote about his encounters with Starkweather, *The Murderous Trail of Charles Starkweather*, he used the term "chain killer."[6]

Starkweather proved to be a willing subject, in part because he expected to become quite famous for this brutal episode. Reinhardt spent about thirty hours interviewing him and reading his numerous writings (including a scribbled autobiography for *Parade* magazine) before making his report. Reinhardt also attended all hearings and the trial, getting assigned a seat in the reporters' area. To make a full assessment, he spoke with people who had known Starkweather throughout his life: teachers, family members, schoolmates, coworkers, and former employers. He described the killer as having a suspicious, unrealistic assessment of the world around him, and noted a delusional quality in many of his responses. Starkweather, he thought, bordered on a dysfunctional, albeit nonpsychotic, paranoia. The young prisoner made odd claims about how he could make things around him do his will, but he had firmly resisted an insanity defense. More important to Reinhardt was the condition of Starkweather's ego, which he found "empty and defeated."[7]

The overriding theme of their sessions was Starkweather's enraged exaggeration of what people had done to him, so as to justify his hatred. He viewed himself as a nobody who *should* be a somebody. Thus, to him the world was unfair and someone had to pay a price. In his fantasies, he imagined how he could get renown; as well, he endlessly pondered acts of revenge. However, said Reinhardt, "The time came when the ego demands could no longer be contained in the inner-world of his fantasy."[8]

Starkweather complained constantly about how "society" had treated him. While this was consistent with the way sociology and psychiatry viewed offenders at this time, with the optimistic idea that a better society would reduce or eliminate criminality, Reinhardt opted to locate the causal mechanisms for the murders in Starkweather's personal pathology.[9] He believed that the same nervous system that makes a baby laugh was also the "nursery house for grudges, anxieties, and fears."[10] A decade earlier, Reinhardt had written that children, lacking the means to gain prestige and respectability, would use their imagination to manipulate their sense of reality. That is, they would get it one way or another. It was a vital life force. Still, he saw no red flags in Starkweather's genetic legacy or in his earlier behavior that would have marked him as a destined killer.

Merely carrying grudges and spouting threats were no guarantees of fatal action. In fact, each time he had drawn a gun at his own reflection, it was at himself that he'd aimed. In short, said Reinhardt, his hatred against society was a form of projected self-hatred: he had to do something that was essentially suicidal in order to free himself of the shame and disgust he felt about himself.

With an IQ in the average range, added to a below-average education, he was aware that his options were limited. He could foresee no escape from his sorry state. In 1956, he had watched James Dean play a disillusioned adolescent, Jim Stark, in *Rebel without a Cause*. Instantly, he had a hero. Stark expressed the same alienation and emptiness that *he* felt. Not only that, but also they very nearly shared the same last name. From that day, Starkweather viewed himself as a misunderstood drifter with a sexy appeal.

It was around this time that Starkweather became obsessed with his delusion that Death visited him and wanted something from him. Referring to his amorous image as "she" and "her," he described to Reinhardt how she had first appeared in a dream, assuring him that he was marked and she would not forget. Once, Death came in a coffin, and he saw himself sailing away in it as it burned. He knew his "earth-time" was coming to a close. He confided that after each dream, he had an accident, as if he needed a conscious reminder of what lay ahead. Sometimes he also said this image looked at him through his window. That's why he'd needed a girlfriend like Caril Ann, because when the time came, she would join him in death. Reinhardt believed that Starkweather developed an unconscious search for some way to die. After the Colvert murder on that cold December night, Starkweather told Reinhardt that he'd looked at the stars and wondered how it felt to be dead.

Reinhardt found little abuse in Starkweather's background. On the contrary, aside from being bullied at school, there wasn't much cruelty in his life. While he learned about a couple of instances of head injury, Reinhardt placed no significance on them. Instead, he emphasized factors that had made Starkweather normal. He was from a two-parent family, and before he'd gone to school he'd had a happy childhood. His murderous rage seemed to be rooted in the cruelties that peers had inflicted, as well as in his inability to forgive. Dropping out of school during the ninth grade, he found a job in a warehouse. One day, a machine lever had hit him just above his left eye. Afterward, he'd experienced frequent headaches as well as periods of confusion. It's possible that the head injury caused or contributed to the lack of inhibition he would soon experience, but no one at this time knew much about the neurological components of violence.

He lost this job, and having few options, Starkweather joined his brother hauling garbage. As they worked their way through wealthy neighborhoods, Starkweather saw what he could never have and grew to resent the residents. He hated them for his sorry lot in life. The one person who comforted him was Caril Ann. In his sparsely furnished rented room, they danced, made love, laughed together, and practiced knife throwing. However, just before Starkweather had started to kill, people who knew him later told Reinhardt that they'd seen a marked change: he'd withdrawn and become uncommunicative. He seemed to speak only to his girlfriend.

Reinhardt later wrote an article for the Associated Press, "Why Did He Kill?" denying that Starkweather's environment had been to blame. He cited a law-abiding family, public schools, an average childhood, a dog, and a good relationship with his father and siblings as the basis for his conclusion that Starkweather was a child set apart. The pathology was inside him, not caused by these other things that thousands of children across America shared. Starkweather had acquired a shallow set of values from television shows and comic books. Even though he supposedly had a religious conversion in prison, he never showed an ounce of remorse. Starkweather, he said, had come to believe that fame would happen only if he excelled at something, and his best skills had been shooting and knife throwing.

His "grotesque," power-hungry fantasies had removed him from a normal ability to adapt. He had created a world in his imagination in which he felt cornered and without options, save violence. Once he was convinced that other children were nasty and mean, he could never dig himself out. A perceptual feedback loop gave him a negative perspective that inhibited trust, intimacy, and affection. What most children would get over, Reinhardt said, Starkweather hung on to and magnified.

"I often experimented with the effort only to witness the consolidation of his defenses," Reinhardt wrote, "and to watch his temper rise."[11] In this regard, Starkweather never disappointed. Reinhardt described one episode in which he had watched rage fill the prisoner, twisting his body, curling his lips, and distorting his face. "Every sharp word, every angry look invaded the marrow of his being. It never escaped. It stayed inside him. These words, looks, and gestures formed an impenetrable encrustation of hate. Hate imprisoned him; it shut him up inside himself."[12]

It was the filter through which Starkweather had viewed the rest of humanity that made him resistant to happiness. Despite his own pain, he could not identify with the pain that he caused to others. Thus, he made his deal with Death. In this way, stated Reinhardt, the "hidden world of Charles Starkweather was generating its own psychic energies. . . . It was profoundly affected by each surging response to some threatening attack or blow from the outer world."[13]

Even so, despite all his existential musing, Starkweather also took pride in what he'd done. He wanted to stay alive long enough to write a novel and witness his resulting fame. Sometimes he said he'd like to prevent other boys from following in his footsteps, but to Reinhardt it was clear that Starkweather sought to be renowned for his own self-centered purposes.

4

When Starkweather went on trial for the cold-blooded murder of Robert Jensen, each side had hired experts to assess and testify about his mental competence, in part because his string of murders revealed no ordinary motive. The murder of Robert Colvert had been to eliminate a witness to robbery, but the rest seemed like the work of a lunatic.

In an age of dueling experts with little basis in science, they predictably contradicted one another. The prosecutor's experts said there was no evidence of brain damage or psychosis. Starkweather possessed an antisocial personality disorder and a degree of immaturity that had contributed to his hostile attitude but had not prevented him from knowing the difference between right and wrong. He'd also shown evidence of careful planning in terms of thwarting discovery.

Starkweather's attorney attempted to prove that the defendant could not have premeditated the killings because he either was insane or had an organic brain disorder. The psychiatrists who had assessed him stated that Starkweather had a paranoid view of the world, a consuming hatred, and an inability to cope effectively with stress. Since he'd given several different versions of what he and Fugate had done, they interpreted this as a "processing disorder." One professional stated that Starkweather had been afraid of Jensen's large size. In short, they concluded that he was not entirely responsible for his actions.

Starkweather was angry about this attempt to portray him as insane. One reason he gave was to spare his family the inevitable "taunt" (taint), and the other was that he feared that he would be dismissed as a lunatic. Thus, he would be forgotten. It was important to him to be remembered for ages to come as a rare type of killer. He wanted to ensure that the people who had once mocked him realized what he'd harbored in his heart. He even considered selling his story in segments, so as to receive more money via the enticement factor.

The jury rejected the expert opinion about his diminished capacity, and Starkweather was found guilty and sentenced to die. But what he and

Fugate had done in attacking strangers had alerted people to a pervasive sense of vulnerability. If a mass killer starts traveling, and even enters homes as these two had done, anyone could become a target.

On the day of his execution in 1959, Starkweather walked quickly to the execution chamber. He had already expressed his opinion that the state's form of murder was more brutal than anything he had done to his victims. In fact, as he entered the chamber, there was a thunder clap outside, which he interpreted as a warning to those who were about to kill him. He listened to the chaplain read Psalm 23, his favorite, and climbed onto the chair without assistance. His final words were to request that the straps be tightened. He was correct that he had left a legacy, but mostly because he'd taken Caril Ann Fugate with him.

Reinhardt provided the bottom line: Starkweather's warm childhood memories had created a fictional idealized world that had failed to measure up against the real world; this division had worsened over time until he decided that someone had to pay for violating the womb. "He had no moral armor from a real world, and no moral defenses."[14] Starkweather had cast all blame for his actions on others, and ultimately on the figure of Death itself. Life was unfair, and he could not have what he wanted, so there was no reason to stick around. His final revenge was to testify against Fugate at her trial, still insisting that she'd helped to kill people, so that she'd end up in prison. She did not, however, suffer quite as much as he'd hoped. Although she got a life sentence, she had served only eighteen years when she was released in 1976.

As the 1950s melted into the 1960s, this shocking crime seemed to have been the initiator of the age of serial murder. Ed Gein and Harvey Glatman had made their own headlines in the 1950s, and soon killers began picking off multiple victims with more frequency. The case of one who was killing women in Boston apartments remains controversial today, despite what a renowned psychiatrist had to say about him. Around this time, a strictly Freudian interpretation of a criminal case was beginning to lose its gloss.

CHAPTER 8

Albert DeSalvo and James Brussel

1

In 1955, Bernard Brodie and his research team discovered that if you gave reserpine to animals, serotonin vanished from their tissues.[1] This proved to be one of the earliest links between behavior and the body's biochemistry, restoring interest in the connection between biology and psychology. There was also an upsurge in illegal drug use, especially amphetamines and hallucinogens, and drugs like these contributed to violence.[2] Over the next few years, psychiatric drugs were manufactured that changed brain chemistry and alleviated the symptoms of mental illness. Soon, researchers realized just how these drugs worked, although it would be two decades before brain imaging confirmed it. Until then, the oedipal logic of psychoanalysis dominated the field, although Hervey Cleckley's new editions of *The Mask of Sanity* became more influential. The analytic notions filtered into interpretations of crime, since criminal consultants were often psychiatrists. One who came to prominence toward the end of the 1950s was James A. Brussel in Manhattan. "A psychiatrist's dominant characteristic," he once wrote, "is his curiosity. He wonders about people."[3]

Gerold Frank, who wrote *The Boston Strangler*, described Brussel in a foreword to Brussel's 1967 memoir as a "wiry, sharp-witted, no nonsense super sleuth" and compared him to Sherlock Holmes.[4] He noted Brussel's distinctive voice and opinions. Brussel had published half a dozen books, including a novel and a basic guide to psychiatry.

Just as Brussel entered the case of the Boston Strangler in 1964, discussions were under way for the second edition of the *Diagnostic and Statistical Manual of Mental Disorders* (DSM-II), which was scheduled for publication in 1968. Its psychoanalytic stance remained intact, although some concepts and terminology had evolved to better correspond to Europe's diagnostic tool, the *International Classification of Diseases*.[5] The move was toward making multiple diagnoses of comorbid conditions.[6]

Brussel showed a definite inclination to associate crime by males to issues with mothers, and he offered a simple explanation: "The two most influential people in an average child's life are his mother and his father. They usually, more than anyone else, shape his character as their genes have shaped his physical appearance."[7] He mentioned the widespread professional belief in the Oedipus complex, noting the strong feelings that boys develop toward their mothers. Most get over it with maturation, but for some it remains a driving force. No one had yet solved the mystery of why some boys become productive adults in good relationships and others had trouble. "All that is known is that it happens."[8]

Brussel was well placed for forensic work, due to his close association with the chief of the Bureau of Missing Persons; he'd also been a speaker at several conventions for police chiefs. A graduate of the University of Pennsylvania and its medical school, Brussel had served a psychiatric residency on Long Island before he became chief of the Army's neuro-psychiatric service at Fort Dix, New Jersey. He then went to New York to take charge of the Army's mentally ill criminals. During the Korean War, he served another military stint, then returned to Manhattan, where he would eventually become assistant commissioner for the Department of Mental Hygiene. Along the way, he consulted on counterespionage tactics for the FBI and CIA.

Brussel claims in his *Casebook of a Crime Psychiatrist* that he was invited into the Boston Strangler case in February 1964, via a telegram from Assistant Attorney General of Massachusetts John Bottomly, who was gathering a committee to brainstorm about the unknown repeat offender. He'd just worked a case that had estranged him from New York law enforcement, and he saw the Strangler case as a way back into the game.

In fact, his version fails to mention that he'd already indirectly inserted himself. He'd seen the headlines about the series of murders in Boston and had written an article for the October 1963 issue of *Pageant* magazine. It seems clear that he hoped to attract the attention of the task force, just in case they did not realize how central he'd been in an infamous New York–based case.

2

Over three dozen minor bombs had exploded in Manhattan between 1940 and 1956, most of them in public places such as Grand Central Station. The apparent bomber had claimed credit in numerous angry letters sent to the area newspapers, various politicians, and a utility company,

Consolidated Edison. While no bomb had been lethal, the attacks had grown more dangerous, so in 1956, police asked Brussel for an analysis. The idea of using a psychiatric consultant in forensic analysis was rare, but the detectives on the "Mad Bomber" case had unsuccessfully tried other venues. Thus, three investigators arrived at Brussel's office one day to show him the collection of letters and photos from the sixteen-year spree.

Expecting to find a method to the bomber's madness, Brussel, who was also a skilled graphologist, studied the material and provided details: since the first letter had been sent to Consolidated Edison, he surmised that the offender was probably a former employee with a grudge. Because bombs were the weapons of choice, he thought the perpetrator was a male European immigrant, which also revealed his likely religion: Roman Catholic. His progressively more paranoid messages placed his age between forty and fifty and suggested he was a fastidious loner. Thus, he probably lived with an older female—a mother figure—who took care of his basic needs. Since the letters were often mailed in Westchester County, New York, if one considered this to be halfway between his home and his target, he probably resided in an ethnic community not far from the city. The bomber probably attended church and was quiet, polite, and helpful, although he would have difficulty managing his anger. He would also be miserly, and he'd wear an old-fashioned double-breasted suit. As per his rigid personality, he'd keep it buttoned. In addition, although the Mad Bomber had been meticulous in his missives about forming each letter of the alphabet with straight lines, the "w" was always rounded. This signaled to the psychiatrist sexual issues and a deep love for his mother.

Years later, Brussel explained that his deductions were based on simple probability, flavored by his clinical experience. He did offer erroneous notions about the offender, such as having a facial scar, being of Germanic extraction, and living in White Plains, New York, but having no precedent for such an analysis, Brussel was cutting his own pattern. When reporters asked him what proportion of his assessments were based in science, he would tell them he always began with science—by which he meant psychoanalysis—but then intuition and imagination took over. Even so, he'd check his hunches against research data and he trusted in the law of averages. Mostly, he utilized mental immersion: "When you think about an unknown criminal long enough, when you've assembled all the known facts about him and poked at them and stirred them about in your mind, you begin to see the man."[9]

He also suggested a strategy for how to use his analysis. Upon completing the profile, Brussel urged the police to publish it in the newspapers, because he was certain from the emotional tone in the letters it would provoke a reaction. The Bomber wanted people to see how important he was, which he seemed to measure by newspaper coverage.

Brussel's suggestion worked. Although the profile sparked several false leads and drew an abundance of tips that wasted police resources, the perpetrator himself also responded, pointing out errors and revealing the date of the incident that had so angered him. With that, it was possible for Consolidated Edison to check through its abundant employee records. Early in 1957, it was a Con Ed clerk, Alice Kelly, who broke the case when she matched unique phrases the Bomber had used to phrases in written complaints to the company. The complainant had signed them.

When the police finally arrested George Metesky, age fifty-four, in Waterbury, Connecticut, he was in his robe and pajamas. He did live with two unmarried older sisters, and he was of the correct ethnicity and religion. He owned a typewriter, which was matched to the letters, and had a workshop stocked with tools and materials for making the bombs. The police told him to get dressed, and he returned (according to Brussel's memoir) buttoning up a double-breasted suit. Nevertheless, it was not the profile's details that had assisted the police but the way it had provoked Metesky to reveal himself. Thus, Brussel received credit for assisting.[10]

He was soon in demand for similar consultations until one of them annoyed the police sufficiently to stop calling him. Around this time, he wrote his armchair analysis for *Pageant* of the unknown perpetrator who was terrorizing Boston. Bottomly obviously took note, and he invited Brussel onto the Medical-Psychiatric Committee.

3

Other participants included a gynecologist, an internist, medical examiners who had performed autopsies on the victims, a chemist, a graphologist, and several psychiatrists. The committee's task was to examine the information already gathered to produce a psychiatric profile, akin to what Brussel had done in New York. At the time they met, there had not been a strangling in three months. The committee members looked over crime scene reports and photos before they separated for three weeks to think about the offender (or offenders). They all had the following information.

The first victim, killed on June 14, 1962, was fifty-five-year-old Anna Slesars. She'd been murdered in her home by bludgeoning and strangulation with the cord from her bathrobe. It had even been tied into a bow. She had been posed as well as sexually assaulted. Nothing of value was missing, although the place was ransacked. Two weeks later, Nina

Nichols, age sixty-eight, was strangled. The murder weapon—two nylon stockings—was also tied into a bow, which linked these two crimes, although semen had been deposited on Nichols's thigh. Helen Blake, also in her sixties, was murdered on the same day, followed by similar fatal attacks on two more elderly women. A pillowcase had been used on one, stockings on the other. All of these victims had been left in sexually exposed positions, as if purposely insulted and posed for effect. Because there was no evidence of someone breaking in, the police believed these women had let their killer in voluntarily. This was especially disturbing in light of the growing publicity about the danger to elderly women living alone. It seemed likely that this killer was posing as a handyman or some other official.

Then the assault pattern changed. Twenty-year-old Sophie Clark, an African American student at the Carnegie Institute of Medical Technology, was found strangled in her home, as was Patricia Bissette, twenty-three. A blouse was tied around her neck, left in a bow. Then four months later, sixty-eight-year-old Mary Brown was found beaten, strangled, and raped, followed by a graduate student, Beverly Samans, although the latter victim had been stabbed, not strangled. Still, scarves were arranged around her neck. A new development was semen found inside her vagina. Detectives knew there was every possibility that, with all the publicity about these cases, they could easily be dealing with copycats.

Boston and surrounding areas were in turmoil, so Attorney General Edward Brooke formed the "Strangler Bureau," assigning a team to collect and assimilate the growing amount of information. Hundreds of potential suspects were fingerprinted, and many took lie detector tests. Police tracked down known sex offenders and checked patient leaves from mental institutions. Governor Endicott Peabody offered a $10,000 reward.

The murders continued. On September 8, fifty-six-year-old Evelyn Corbin was discovered strangled in her home. Two months later, Joann Graff, twenty-three, was raped and murdered in her apartment. Police found two brown nylon stockings and a black leotard tied around her neck in a flamboyant bow. She also bore many bite marks like Evelyn Corbin, and semen was smeared on her. Mary Sullivan, just nineteen, turned out to be the final victim. The killer had forced a broomstick handle into her vagina after strangling her and then propped a card against her foot on which was written, "Happy New Year." Two scarves were tied into a bow around her neck, and semen dripped from her mouth onto her breast.[11]

It's not clear at what point during the investigations Brussel took up his analytical pen, since the lead time between submission and publication in *Pageant* magazine is unknown, but it was certainly at a time when the majority of victims were elderly women. Brussel described the offender as athletic, muscular, energetic, and paranoid, and predicted that he was between thirty and forty, unmarried, sexually abnormal, and difficult to employ. Brussel believed the killings were about some issue between the offender and his mother and that there would be a "hospital angle," because many of the victims were associated with hospitals. This man would live alone near the city center.

Boston investigators took note of this profile and compared their suspects against it, but no one stood out who could also be linked to all of the murders. Thus, Assistant Attorney General John Bottomly, when assigned to coordinate the investigation, stated his intention to try "unusual methods," such as creating the Medical-Psychiatric Committee.

When these professionals reconvened at Boston University's School of Legal Medicine, they offered one another their thoughts. Given the diverse victimology, most members of the team believed there were two or more killers involved, but Brussel insisted that only one man was responsible for all eleven murders. He admitted that he was puzzled by the dissimilarities among the crimes and had not known whether to emphasize the similarities or the differences. He'd finally decided on the former, and to explain the shifting patterns between the five elderly women and six younger "career girls," he suggested a series of life upheavals during the process of maturation.

"What has happened to him, in two words," Brussel said, "is instant maturity. In this two-year period, he has suddenly grown, psychosexually, from infancy to puberty to manhood."[12] In other words, he thought the Strangler had originally struck out at his mother, symbolized by the older women. Brussel suspected they'd probably turned their backs to him at some point during his "visit," setting him off. Then, once he'd resolved his Oedipus complex (desire for mother), he was able to sexually respond to younger women. That's why, Brussel explained, there was semen at these murder scenes. However, the offender remained angry at his mother, so he'd continued to kill. "He had to commit these murders to achieve his growth. It was the only way to solve his problems, finding himself sexually, and to become a grown man among men."[13]

Although there was logic for his explanations, Brussel failed to address why the offender had killed two older women after he'd turned on the younger women. It seemed inconsistent with Brussel's theory. He did believe that, with the excessive and defiant treatment of the last victim, Mary Sullivan, the killer was ultimately finished. He'd been cured. He no longer needed to prove anything with murder, because he'd realized his potency as a man.

Brussel's colleagues were unimpressed, but he stood by his interpretation. Still, they all agreed that the Strangler would be nondescript, not too tall and not too short. Probably muscular. He knew how to get past locks, or he used a persuasive pretext to get inside homes and apartments without having to break in. He left his victims in degrading positions to make it appear that they had enticed him and therefore should be punished.

Brussel reiterated his opinion that the Strangler was in his thirties or forties (although he also said late twenties) and of southern European stock (Spanish or Italian). He'd be average in every way in his dress and appearance, and he could mingle easily with ordinary people. He would come forward on his own to confess.

4

On November 5, 1964, Albert DeSalvo was arrested for a series of rapes attributed to the "Green Man," so-named because of his green work clothing. He'd already served time for sexual assault as the "Measuring Man." He confessed to being the Boston Strangler, and his attorney, F. Lee Bailey, worked out a deal that would send him to trial for only his sexual offenses. Bailey decided that he would propose an insanity defense for the rapes that would also include details from the murders. (It should be noted that DeSalvo was never actually tried for the murders, and many people today dispute that he was even the Strangler; he himself reportedly told psychiatrist Ames Robey that he was not, but DeSalvo was murdered in prison in 1973 before he could reveal more. His confession did contain numerous erroneous details, his DNA did not match that lifted from the exhumed body of Mary Sullivan, and several exposés of the Boston Strangler investigation have turned up better suspects for many of the murders.)[14]

Once DeSalvo confessed, offering some fifty hours of taped material, Brussel was proud to have been the one to state that a single perpetrator had been responsible. To his delight, F. Lee Bailey contacted him and invited him onto the defense team. This gave Brussel an exciting opportunity to get close to DeSalvo and make a more personal study. Brussel had decided that if DeSalvo turned out to be a psychopath, he would not testify for the defense. He would participate only if DeSalvo had schizophrenia.

Brussel went to meet DeSalvo for the first time on August 16, 1966. A colleague of his did the objective diagnostic examination via standard assessments like the Rorschach Inkblot Test. Remaining intentionally ignorant of the results, Brussel went on his own to meet DeSalvo.

"It is one thing to speculate about a criminal before he is caught," Brussel wrote. "It is quite another to sit across a table from him and talk to him. . . . I did not expect that I was going to enjoy my talks with him. I wasn't looking forward to them. I was curious, yes—but also acutely uneasy."[15]

In a bare interview room, Brussel conducted two long sessions. DeSalvo had been eager to talk with him, because he wanted a scientific man to understand and possibly help him. At the very least, DeSalvo hoped that Brussel could explain *why* he had committed these crimes. DeSalvo was especially interested in Brussel's prediction that the offender would have a "problem," possibly because he hoped for some mitigating factor to help him avoid prison. In other words, his interest in Brussel was a mix of supposed altruism and personal gain.

Brussel learned several things from the prisoner that contradicted his theory. DeSalvo was married rather than a loner bachelor, and he'd never been impotent as Brussel had believed. Instead, he reported being insatiable and even bragged that he'd committed over 1,000 rapes. Despite being grandiose, he was quite chatty and personable. Even with an IQ in the average range (some sources dispute this and place it above average), DeSalvo had been able to pump the police for information to insert into his lengthy confession. Brussel was often surprised by the sophistication evident in the way DeSalvo spoke.

He found DeSalvo, of Italian descent, to be polite, alert, cooperative, and gracious, although he possessed the slick charm of a salesman. The five-foot-nine DeSalvo was thirty-three at the time, and he had broad shoulders, a remarkably large nose, and a muscular build. He willingly answered all questions, so Brussel had an easy time writing a report.

DeSalvo had been born on September 3, 1931, and raised in Massachusetts. He had five siblings, who attested to the fact that their father had been abusive and sexually inappropriate in many ways. This had affected Albert, who became delinquent, cruel to animals, and sexually inappropriate with his brothers. To Brussel's surprise, DeSalvo reported that his relationship with his mother, who'd tried to keep him out of trouble, was reasonably good. Still, Brussel believed that DeSalvo's problems with crime stemmed from maternal neglect. "This neglect, which spawned the emotional trauma of maternal rejection, eventually became part of the launching mechanism for Albert's strangling."[16]

DeSalvo had once served a military stint, meeting his future wife, Irmgard, while stationed in Germany. They married and had their first child. However, their daughter had congenital pelvic disease, forcing her to wear a cast to keep her legs stationary in a frog-like position. Brussel thought it mirrored the posed position of DeSalvo's victims. He wondered if the way DeSalvo had tied bows on the child's cast indicated that he'd had sexual feelings for his daughter. Irmgard began to avoid sex, afraid she would bear another handicapped child, but DeSalvo's sexual appetite was demanding. Irmgard began to reject him, just like Brussel believed his mother had. By not having sex, she was "turning her back," so he had looked elsewhere for it.

Between 1956 and 1960, DeSalvo began to break into apartments. He was arrested several times, but he always managed to get a suspended sentence. In 1960, he and Irmgard had a second child, a son, who seemed fine. DeSalvo worked several different blue-collar jobs, and one boss described him as a decent family man and reliable employee. DeSalvo told Brussel that he'd entered at least four hundred apartments and had assaulted hundreds of women in a four-state area. Many of them had been willing, he insisted. He also described each murder incident, giving Brussel plenty of material to fill out his theory.

"Twined and twisted throughout his personality," Brussel wrote, "were the two dangerous factors that had been part of his life since childhood: the overwhelming obsession with sex and the need for a mother's love."[7] He uncritically accepted DeSalvo's claim that whenever a woman had turned her back on him, he'd felt an irresistible impulse to act out violently against her. Although this notion was easily testable in a controlled condition, Brussel never bothered to see if DeSalvo really did have a physical reaction when a woman turned her back. Brussel concluded that DeSalvo's home life was largely to blame for what he'd become. "In a good home, he might have grown to become an ordinary respected citizen."[18]

Brussel believed he could demonstrate that DeSalvo had a mental illness that had rendered him incapable of controlling his urges during the commission of each murder. He decided that a "constitutional weakness" had prevented DeSalvo from responding appropriately to his troubles, and that the violent part of him was hidden from the normal part—what Brussel viewed as the "classic split mind" of schizophrenia (although this is not actually what "schizophrenia" means). DeSalvo's brother, Richard, corroborated some of the tales, but it was clear that DeSalvo exaggerated how bad things had been. No one seemed to notice that Richard DeSalvo, who endured the same parental neglect and abuse, had become not a rapist or killer but a responsible family man. Still, Brussel maintained his position that a cold, indifferent mother who had failed to provide a decent home life had been instrumental in DeSalvo's criminality. Under cross-examination in court, he admitted that DeSalvo did not specifically fit the criteria for his diagnosis. He also made an unsupported and seemingly inconsistent claim that while DeSalvo was driven by an irresist-ible impulse—a "brain sensation"—he was nevertheless able to take pre-cautions to avoid being caught or identified.[19]

It seems that Brussel's pride in predicting from the crimes who the offender would be influenced how he perceived the makeup of DeSalvo's character. It was also clear that he wanted to be part of the defense team. Thus, his objectivity in this case is questionable. In fact, as soon as he'd satisfied himself that DeSalvo was schizophrenic, he'd agreed to be an expert witness in DeSalvo's trial, so as to help get him into a psychiat-ric institution rather than a prison. He did not check the records from Bridgewater State Hospital in Bridgewater, Massachusetts, where DeSalvo had been held for several months, or question any of his guards to see if he might have shown psychotic behavior. So, Brussel had not done his homework. He should have. This case was no slam-dunk for the defense.

When Brussel saw the members of the jury, he perceived them as straitlaced, disapproving people who seemed uninterested in any expla-nation or mitigating factors—not even when DeSalvo cried. On the stand, Brussel insisted that DeSalvo could not control himself when a woman turned her back, because subconsciously this represented his cold wife and mother. Again, no one seized the opportunity to test it. Even DeSalvo knew that an irresistible impulse meant that he would commit the act even if a police officer were standing at his elbow, so they could have had a woman walk up to him and turn her back, just to see.

In any event, the jury did not accept the diagnosis of either defense psychiatrist. Its members quickly convicted DeSalvo of the rape charges and gave him a life sentence. It remains unknown to this day whether physical evidence would have corroborated DeSalvo's confession to mur-der. He did believe he'd be able to collect the reward money, so he had an incentive to lie. In fact, he eventually recanted his confession. To this day, it remains controversial whether there was a single Boston Strangler, and if so, whether it was DeSalvo or someone else.

With more sophisticated data about predatory serial killers, it seems naïve for Brussel to have theorized that killing older women could "resolve" a man's "mother issues," so that he could move on to raping and killing younger women. In addition, Brussel predicted that with the mur-der of Mary Sullivan, the Strangler was done. Crime does not cure killers, and serial killers rarely just stop because they've "matured"—especially if their behavior has become more brazen and brutal. Even if Brussel was correct about DeSalvo being the Strangler, DeSalvo's sexual history under-mines the possibility that he could control his behavior to this extent. In short, Brussel's reliance on psychoanalytic theory, coupled with his desire to be viewed as one of the country's top experts, may have warped his ability to observe and let the data speak for themselves.

Just after this terror episode in Boston, Charles Schmid committed three murders in Tucson, Arizona, that made it into *Life* magazine, as did a shocking mass murder in Chicago that seemed to precipitate the age of violence. The 1960s in America were a time of social upheaval, widespread violence, political assassinations, and pervasive fear. Another psychiatrist decided to venture close to an extreme offender to study the forces that had made a man as violent as the notorious Richard Speck.

CHAPTER 9

Richard Speck and Marvin Ziporyn

1

Twelve days before he encountered one of the country's most infamous mass murderers, Chicago psychiatrist Marvin Ziporyn was quoted in a *Time* magazine article about physicians who administer the hallucinogen LSD. Ziporyn had given it to fifty patients, as well as taken it himself. Along with many colleagues, he viewed the "hippie" drug, discovered in 1947, as a way to get intimate information about a patient. "LSD is, if you like, a psychiatric X ray," he told the reporter. "With LSD you have no greater vision of the universe than you did before. It no more expands your consciousness than an X ray expands your lungs when you see them on the screen. All you do is get a better look."[1]

At this time, he was serving part time as the prison psychiatrist for Cook County (Illinois) Jail. His predecessor had abruptly resigned, and Ziporyn accepted the job on the spot. A graduate of the Chicago Medical School, he had been a professor of psychiatry, as well as an accomplished violinist.

Ziporyn had read in the papers on July 14 about a horrendous event in the area on the night before—the slaughter of eight nurses. He knew the police had picked up a suspect, Richard Speck, and he saw Speck being placed in a bed in Ward I. He noted that the young man appeared haggard, apprehensive, and pale. Ziporyn was asked to assess Speck, who had slit his wrists just hours before, for his current suicide risk.

The psychiatrist's first impression of Speck, twenty-four, was of a gentle, confused man who had no recollection of the incident of which he was accused: he claimed he'd been drinking and taking drugs for hours the day before, but he accepted that if people said he did it, then he did. Ziporyn spent about an hour with Speck that day and reported to the warden that his suicide risk was high: the man was depressed, unstable, and disoriented, and he probably suffered from brain damage. Speck had readily described the many times he'd hit his head, or been hit, and the headaches that had plagued him all his life.

Ziporyn was assigned to monitor Speck, so he set up a schedule to meet with him twice a week and immediately began to work at getting the prisoner to trust him. He stated in the book he later wrote, *Born to Raise Hell*, that this would be a measure of his success as a psychiatrist. He found Speck to be a man of shifting moods who responded well to kindness. Ziporyn performed small favors, such as getting him his favorite brand of cigarettes or purchasing a paint set, which broke the ice. At times, Speck even expressed curiosity about why he might have killed the nurses—each time denying any memory of the incident. Between July 29, 1966, and February 13, 1967, Ziporyn visited Speck in his cell, staying for one to three hours. About two months into this project, he decided to record each session verbatim for a book. He believed he had a rare opportunity—the enigma of a surviving mass murderer—and that learning about Speck's complex makeup would be of vital importance to society. He obtained Speck's handwritten consent for him to go ahead. The note stated, "I understand that Dr. Ziporyn is writing a book about me. I am glad he is doing this, because he is the only person who knows anything about me. I want the world to know what I am really like, and I fell [*sic*] he is the one who can tell about me."[2]

Although Ziporyn accused all other psychiatrists who examined Speck of "interpreter's bias," and believed that he alone knew the prisoner, he seemed blind to his own interpreter's bias that Speck was sincerely amnestic, not responsible for his crime, and just as sympathetic as the victims. This seems to have helped Ziporyn accept as a friend a man who was capable of such unthinkable acts against defenseless young women. In addition, since Speck never talked about the crime, Ziporyn did not really deliver as his book title promises. Nevertheless, his reports do provide an intimate portrait of the way a killer played games with officials. Speck confessed to a reporter in 1978, so in retrospect, we know that he never had amnesia and never felt remorse. He fooled Ziporyn and used him for his own ends.

2

Speck had always believed he was destined to shock the world. He didn't plan how he would do it, but when the opportunity arrived, he grabbed it. Eight nurses and nursing students lived in a townhouse at 2319 East 100 Street in a suburb of Chicago in July 1966 when Richard F. Speck arrived in town. His sister there gave him a hand, but he spent her money on drugs and booze. He found a job, only to learn that he'd lost it before it had even begun. Frustrated, he drank throughout most of the day. Then he took a walk. He was near the Maritime Union Hall, where he went each day to look at job postings for seamen, when he went over to the nurses' house nearby and knocked on the door. It was around 11:00 P.M. Corazon Amurao, awakened from sleep, answered the door, expecting that one of her housemates had locked herself out.

To her shock, Speck pushed his way in, holding a gun trained directly at her. He took her and another girl to the south bedroom and ordered them to stay there. Soon he found four other young women, one of whom was just visiting, and brought those four to join Amurao and her roommate. He told them that he was there for money so he could fund a trip to New Orleans, and each gave him all she had. Still, he cut sheets into strips to bind their wrists. Then they all heard someone enter the house downstairs.

Gloria Davy, an attractive woman, was home from her date. Speck met her and forced her to join the others, although she showed a spirited resistance. Amurao later said that Speck's demeanor completely changed. Davy made him angry.

Then the doorbell rang, and Speck forced two women to accompany him to let whoever was there inside. But no one was at the door. (Later, it turned out that another student had come by to borrow something, but to her good fortune she had left when no one answered.)

Speck went upstairs to finish binding his captives. He sat on the floor, asking odd questions and growing more agitated. He kept looking at Davy. Then he stood up. He untied Pamela Wilkening's ankles and led her out alone. She spit on him. Outside their range of vision, the others heard her make a sound like a sigh. That was all.

A noise indicated that the last two residents were home. Speck met them and ushered the startled women to the south bedroom, but then he forced them out again. The bound women still in the room heard muffled screams and a struggle. After a brief period of silence, they heard water running in the bathroom. Speck appeared once more at the door. He looked around and selected Nina Schmale.

Some of them tried to hide under the beds, but when Speck returned for them, one at a time, he pulled them out and took them away. By this time, they knew that he was going to kill them all. Helpless, they mourned their friends and awaited their fate.

When only Davy and Amurao were left, Speck came in and turned his attention on Davy. Amurao, under a bed against a far wall, listened as Speck raped Davy there in the room for about twenty minutes. He even stopped and asked her to wrap her legs around his back. Then he took her out.

Amurao awaited his final visit, trying not to let her pounding heart betray her. He came in, stood still as if listening, and then left. She kept her head down. Sometime later, she heard an alarm clock ring, which had been set for a morning shift. The house was otherwise silent. Still, she waited.

Finally it became clear to her that the intruder had overlooked her. He might have left or fallen asleep somewhere in the house, but she knew she had to get help. Cautiously listening and peering about, she saw in the other bedrooms what she had feared: the eight nurses had all been stabbed or strangled to death, some bearing more wounds than others.

Not daring to go downstairs, Amurao stepped over three bodies—one of which lay on top of another—to push out a window from the front bedroom, climb onto a ledge, and scream, "Help me! They are all dead! My friends are all dead!"

A neighbor who saw her fetched the police, while others tried to calm her. The first responding officer entered the house and saw a nude female body on the living room couch. The victim had been raped and strangled with a strip of material. It was Gloria Davy.

Upstairs, officers found the other seven victims. One girl lay in a bathroom, choked to death. Another lay across a threshold, stabbed numerous times. A third girl, stabbed and strangled, lay on her back in torn underwear. Near her was a victim stabbed several times in the neck. Police found one stabbed in the left breast and asphyxiated with a strip from a sheet, and another had been dumped over the top of a girl killed before her. Both had been stabbed and strangled, as had the final victim, who lay on a bed.

Gasping, Amurao offered a description of the man who had done this, and they sent it out to all police units in the vicinity. She could not tell them how long ago he had left, and she was taken straight to a hospital for treatment.

A drawing of the intruder was published in newspapers, under blaring headlines about the massacre. He had blue eyes, a pockmarked face, and light-colored hair. At the Maritime Union Hall, the police learned about a man by that description inquiring about jobs. They soon discovered his name, Richard Speck, and learned that he had an identifying tattoo: "Born to Raise Hell." They tried luring him via his sister with the promise of a job, and he seemed to bite but then failed to show up for his appointment. Acquiring a photo of Speck from Coast Guard files, they showed it to Amurao, along with dozens more photos, and she made a positive identification. Three fingerprints from the house matched Speck's as well.

In the meantime, Speck had hired a prostitute and the police actually encountered him when a motel manager called them about a complaint involving a man with a gun—Speck. However, they did not yet know that Speck was the man they were seeking. They let him go. Speck, too, did not yet realize he was being sought.

On July 15, he heard a radio announcement about the murders and commented offhandedly that he hoped they caught the son of a bitch. The next day, his name was in the press. Speck heard this and bought a bottle of wine. Checking into a flophouse, he lay on the grubby mattress and got drunk. Then he slashed his right wrist in a suicide attempt, but as he bled he sought assistance. The police arrived to take him away, a routine case to their minds, and under his bed they found a Chicago newspaper that bore the headline, "Police Say Nurse Survivor Can Identify Slayer of 8." Still, they did not know this was the man being sought all over the city.

They took Speck to a hospital, and it was the attending doctor who thought their flophouse suicide case resembled the sketch in the papers. He washed enough blood off Speck's arm to uncover the tattoo and turned him in. Amurao confirmed her identification. Speck was taken to the Cook County Jail to await trial.

3

To Ziporyn, Speck denied culpability. He said he did not remember anything after an evening of drinking and claimed that a stranger had given him an injection of speed. Ziporyn bought it. He did not know that in a past case, Speck had successfully claimed amnesia to sidestep an arrest for assault. He'd figured out before this time how to play the system to his advantage.

Ziporyn began the process of finding out who Speck was, paying special attention to incidents that had resulted in a head injury or substance abuse. Born on December 6, 1941, into a family of eight children in Kirkwood, Illinois, Speck had been a sickly child. At age five, he suffered a severe head injury from a hammer, and the following year he fell out of a tree, getting knocked unconscious. Later he ran into an awning, which resulted in severe repetitive headaches, then had an accident that resulted in yet another head injury.

His father died when he was five, so his mother moved with Speck and his sister to Dallas, Texas. Eventually, his mother married an ex-con. Speck grew to resent her and her new husband, perhaps because he felt neglected. The sulky boy began drinking around age twelve, and from that time on he was frequently in trouble with the law for various infractions. When he flunked the ninth grade, he dropped out. He suffered from fierce headaches that he claimed made him drink even more, and he often added drugs into the mix.

When he was eighteen, he beat up his mother. He was developing the attitude that women did not deserve to be treated well, because they always disappointed. Nevertheless, when Speck was twenty, he married Shirley Annette Malone, a fifteen-year-old. After they had a daughter, Speck tattooed the child's name on his arm. Yet he could not hold down a job or a relationship, and his marriage quickly failed.

Speck spent several years in prison, one term of which was for assault on a woman with a knife. During that time, Shirley filed for divorce. Speck vowed revenge. To his mind, she was no better than a cheating spouse. She remarried quickly, confirming his suspicion that she had betrayed him. He was fiercely angry at his ex-wife to the point of blind hate.

Speck returned to Illinois, where he still had family, although he vowed to return to Texas one day to kill his wife. Around that time, another woman whom he had encountered disappeared and was found murdered, and he became a suspect. Landing a job on a barge, his drinking got him into trouble and he found himself unemployed.

Speck doled out his life history to Ziporyn in bits and pieces, sometimes expressing outrage over crimes other people had committed. When he read about an eighteen-year-old man killing five women in Arizona, he stated that since the young man had been inspired by *him*, he now had thirteen deaths on his conscience. Ziporyn believed everything Speck told him. While he relied on a text that described antisocial personality consistent with Speck's traits and behaviors, he failed to see or accept that Speck was callous, believed his criminal acts were reasonable, had no critical awareness of his behavior, suffered no guilt, was devoid of shame, and was able to give a false impression of reliability and affection.

Ziporyn believed that all humans have murderous impulses, and as a "strict determinist," or someone who believed that all events result from antecedent conditions, he viewed Speck as the "mechanical expression" of his heredity and environment. Thus, Ziporyn asked Speck's sisters and mother about what Speck had been like as a child; he learned that Speck had been especially close to his youngest sister, his father, and his daughter (although he had decided the child was not really his). One sister mentioned that Gloria Davy was so similar in appearance to Speck's estranged wife, Shirley, that she could have been her twin.

This information gave Ziporyn an idea. He got a *Time* magazine article about the murders and cut out the photos of each victim. He then placed these clips, one at a time, into Speck's hand and asked him to say whatever came into his mind. Mostly, he commented on how pretty each one was, but when Ziporyn placed the photo of Gloria Davy into Speck's hand, Speck froze. He drew his hand back, and his lips quivered. When he finally touched it, he himself said the victim was a dead ringer for Shirley. Ziporyn had already decided it was this resemblance that had set Speck off. He offered Speck an out: you were only intending to steal money, but she came in and sent you into a blind fury. Speck shrugged and would not agree. All he would say is "She sure is pretty."

Ziporyn was not deterred and remained vigilant for ways to persuade Speck of his interpretation of Speck's acts. Convinced that Speck was no psychopath, he worked hard to try to get Speck to behave in ways he thought were appropriate for a man who genuinely felt remorse. When Speck laughed during hearings or claimed he suffered from no nightmares about the murders (as Ziporyn thought he should), Ziporyn explained this behavior as repression. He looked for signs that Speck was becoming "healthier," and it bothered him that among the psychiatrists hired to interview Speck before his trial was Dr. Hervey Cleckley, renowned for his seminal book, *The Mask of Sanity*, on the diagnosis of psychopathy. Ziporyn was angry that Speck had not told Cleckley about his head injuries.

Oddly enough, Ziporyn grew exasperated from constantly reminding Speck that he was not a sociopath and that he was capable of friendship, caring, and remorse: "I've told you over and over," Ziporyn said. "I believe you weren't responsible."[3] He likened Speck to a jar that leaks: you can't blame the jar, but have to blame the manufacturing process. "We react the way we were made."[4] His frustration indicated that Speck was not falling into line. Ziporyn naïvely believed that Speck could be persuaded to do something one day that would neutralize the harm he'd done, and that he could give back to the world.

Ziporyn, who thought he might be a witness for the defense, prepared a summary of his ideas about Speck's mental state that included depression, anxiety, and remorse. He was angry that a team of esteemed professionals had diagnosed Speck as a sociopath, because he believed that Speck had solid relationships with his family and that he'd never tried to manipulate the facts to his advantage. Ziporyn thought Speck had an obsessive-compulsive personality, possible ambivalence about his sexuality, and a "Madonna–whore" attitude toward women. The latter is a psychoanalytic notion that women are divided into perfect types; for Speck, some were untainted (e.g., his mother, he said, although he'd once assaulted her), but all others were worthless (e.g., his ex-wife). Ziporyn also diagnosed organic brain syndrome, which he believed was the result of Speck's multiple head injuries, and he believed that while Speck might be competent to stand trial, due to the mix of brain damage, alcohol, and drugs in his history, he could not have been responsible for his violent acts. He had therefore been legally insane during the slaughter. His amnesia from that night, Ziporyn said, was proof that he could not have appreciated right from wrong, because he had "blacked out" while committing the atrocities.

Although Speck's attorney listened to all of this, he did not invite Ziporyn to testify. Both sides had learned that he was writing a book with Speck's cooperation and believed that he could not possibly be unbiased.

Speck showed only boredom throughout the proceedings and would not even look at Corazon Amurao when she stood before him to identify him. Based mostly on three fingerprints from the bedroom door at the crime scene and the strength of Amurao's defiant testimony, Speck was quickly convicted. In the same breath, the jury recommended death.

Ziporyn's relationship with Speck came to an end, as did his stint at the prison. The warden fired him for writing the book, which was considered a violation of confidentiality. However, Ziporyn would one day have reason to revisit the case, because contrary to expectations Speck survived another twenty-five years.

In 1972, after intense deliberation, the U.S. Supreme Court issued a moratorium on the death penalty; all capital sentences around the country were commuted. In place of his death sentence, Speck received eight life sentences, to be served at the Statesville Correctional Center at Joliet, Illinois. In 1978, he admitted to a *Chicago Tribune* reporter, "Yeah, I killed them. I stabbed them and choked them."[5] He also told this to Special Agent John Douglas during the FBI's effort to collect data from convicted murderers. He said that he'd raped Gloria Davy, but none of the others. Douglas describes his impression of Speck and relates a story he heard while at the prison: Speck had made a pet out of a sparrow, but when he learned he could not keep it, he tossed it into a fan to prevent anyone else from having it. Clearly, he had little concern for the pain he had caused this defenseless creature.[6]

Former Special Agent Robert Ressler believed that Speck had no insight into his behavior. "Speck displayed a callousness for human life," Ressler wrote in *Whoever Fights Monsters*, "admitting that he had killed his victims so they couldn't testify against him."[7]

4

Just short of his fiftieth birthday in 1991, Richard Speck suffered a heart attack and died. His remains were cremated, but his brain was saved for analysis. He'd been repeatedly rejected for parole, but he had not seemed to mind. The reason surfaced in 1996. A reporter discovered a clandestine two-hour tape of his prison activities, which indicated that he seemed right at home. He was getting drunk and taking drugs—snorting cocaine on camera with a $100 bill—and, grotesquely, he had turned himself into a woman. The film shows him with large breasts and a flabby body, dressed in silky bikini briefs and acting as a sex object for another man. Through this gimmick, he received favors and gifts from other prisoners. On this film, the interviewer pointedly asked Speck how he'd felt about the murders back in 1966. He shrugged. "Like I always felt," he said. "Had no feelings. If you are asking if I felt sorry, no." When asked for a motive, he said, "It just wasn't their night."[8] He then described what it was like to strangle another person: "It ain't like you see on TV. You have to go at it for about three and a half minutes. It takes a lot of strength."

Upon viewing the video, Ziporyn held firm to his own theory. He said that Speck had punished himself by forfeiting his manhood and offering himself to be used by other men in the same way he had degraded the nurses. Ziporyn still believed that Speck felt remorse.

In fact, it does appear he was correct about the brain abnormality. After Speck's death, Dr. Jan E. Leestma, who was a neuropathologist at the Chicago Institute of Neurosurgery, performed an autopsy and discovered a striking abnormality in Speck's brain. In the limbic system, the hippocampus, an area that involves memory, encroached upon the amygdala, which deals with rage, fear, and other strong emotions. Because he found this so unusual, Leestma made slides of the brain tissue and showed them to other professionals in his field. Many agreed that his findings were unique. However, when Leestma sent his samples to a Boston neurologist, they were lost.[9]

Two weeks after Speck's massacre, Charles Whitman killed his wife and mother and climbed the tower on the University of Texas at Austin campus. From there, he shot more than forty people, killing fourteen. By the decade's end, the so-called Zodiac was killing couples in California, and Charles Manson had led a hippie raid on two homes, resulting in seven murders in two days. Then another town in California endured three multiple murderers in the span of two years, and because one psychologist observed all three defendants, he made some significant contributions to the psychology of violence.

CHAPTER 10

The Santa Cruz Triple and Donald Lunde

1

The beach town of Santa Cruz lies south of San Francisco on the Pacific Coast. Although it is a tourist town, during the fall of 1970 an influx of "hippies" arrived, thanks in part to the presence of the University of California's latest campus there. In addition, townspeople were disturbed about a series of incidents the year before in Los Angeles: Charles Manson and his "family" had invaded two homes and massacred seven people.

It turns out that Santa Cruz residents had reason to worry. On October 19, 1970, John Linley Frazier hiked up the hill from his shack and murdered four members of the Ohta family, as well as Dr. Ohta's secretary. He'd bound them with silk scarves, shot them execution style by the pool, and pushed them in. He'd also left a note that said, "Today World War 3 will begin as brought to you by the people of the Free Universe."

Frazier reportedly believed he had to prevent the Ohtas from "raping" natural resources. An environmental activist with a hippie bent, he was diagnosed with paranoid schizophrenia, and there was evidence that he'd recently suffered from a severe head injury. Nevertheless, he was considered competent to stand trial. Although he was certainly delusional, hallucinogenic drugs that he'd taken had exacerbated his symptoms, so the jury was unsympathetic. They convicted him on five counts of murder. During the punishment phase, Frazier's sanity became a key issue, as did his courtroom behavior.

Frazier offered his evaluators several versions, but, essentially, on the fatal afternoon Frazier had gone to the Ohta residence and found Virginia Ohta home alone. Threatening her with a .38 revolver, he managed to bind her hands. He then waited in the house until the rest of the family arrived. Each one was tied up before all were forced outside to the pool, where they were killed.

Donald T. Lunde was among the psychiatrists who evaluated Frazier. As a member of the Medical School faculty at Stanford University, he taught human sexuality and had coauthored a textbook on the subject. He also taught a seminar on criminal law in the law school. While in the U.S. Navy, he'd served as trial counsel for special court-martials and had consulted for area psychiatric hospitals. He considered courtroom attitudes about mental illness and insanity archaic and the legal terminology meaningless in the twentieth century. Some attorneys, he noticed, still referred to psychiatrists as "alienists," a term from the nineteenth century. In fact, the first time he'd agreed to evaluate a murderer, he'd found that the information about motivations and personality types was based largely in superficial stereotypes. Thus, he decided to fully research the history of criminal psychiatry, to keep detailed records of murderers he examined, and to do much more than was typical of a psychiatric expert. Lunde also recorded and transcribed his interviews with defendants, and during a five-year period he acquired information about forty murderers, including three who had committed multiple murders. In fact, Lunde was one of the first to make a psychiatric distinction among multiple-murder offenders, because within a two-year span he had privileged access in the Santa Cruz area to a mass murderer, a spree killer, and a serial killer.[1]

2

After Frazier's massacre, Lunde examined him in the standard fashion, but then interviewed his wife and acquaintances. Lunde believed that Frazier suffered from paranoid schizophrenia and that at the time of the murders he'd been incapable of knowing that what he was doing was wrong. Lunde accepted the likelihood that Frazier actually believed what he claimed: that he was a special agent sent from God to save the earth. His wife said that she'd heard these delusions on several occasions, including earlier in the day before Frazier committed the Ohta murders. Apparently, Frazier had grown increasingly more paranoid until he'd finally just abandoned her to go live in a rundown shack in the woods. He seemed to get along better on his own, although he was an angry man. When he killed the family, he believed he was doing the right thing for the environment. "He's crazy," Lunde had stated in court, amending it to "He is unable to appreciate society's standards."[2]

However, District Attorney Peter Chang had experts, too, who contradicted this idea. Dr. John Peschau stated that Frazier was a sociopath. Thus, he appreciated what he had done and knew it was wrong, but just didn't care. Not only that, but also Frazier would not learn from punishment and was dangerous. He was sane and should not be released into the community.

Lunde stood by his own diagnosis. In *Murder and Madness*, he provided a comprehensive account of Frazier's developing psychosis, indicating that it revealed a number of issues that were key to his growing alienation and estrangement from society.[3]

When he was just two, Frazier's parents had separated, and because his mother could not afford to care for him on her own, when he was five she placed him in foster care. He did not do well there: he ran away, was arrested for theft, and ended up in several different juvenile detention facilities. Lunde noted that he also had a history of bedwetting, sleepwalking, and terrible nightmares, which could indicate impulse disorders. Eventually Frazier was reunited with his mother. He managed to get a steady job and to get married. His life seemed to have improved, but in the spring of 1970 an automobile accident resulted in a serious head injury. Frazier told people he was receiving messages from God to stop driving. If he didn't, he'd die. Then he decided he had a mission to save the earth from materialism. He believed the end of the world was at hand and there would be a revolution. As he sat looking at the Ohta home high on the hill above his shack, it came to represent the utter evil of the material life. It was then that his nebulous "mission" crystallized into a plan: he would murder the homeowners and burn down the place. Then nature could restore itself.

Although Lunde found no mention in Frazier's juvenile records about possible treatment for mental illness, he was aware that the symptoms of schizophrenia often set in during the late teens or early adulthood. Perhaps Frazier had been stable up until then, so no one had noticed. But Frazier's recent obsessions, along with his efforts to convert people into disciples, were signs of psychosis. Lunde watched his behavior during the trial with concern. Frazier showed awareness of the attempts to prove his mental illness, and like many such individuals, he had just enough ability to try to thwart it.

On December 3, Frazier surprised everyone. He'd shaved half of his head and face, including an eyebrow. Dr. David Marlowe explained that Frazier wanted the jury to believe he was faking insanity. This was because he did not want to be sent to a mental institution—a "fascist head factory." However, Marlowe told the court, this behavior was merely an indication of just how distorted his thoughts were. It was a futile attempt to appear to be in charge.

The trial continued for two more weeks, and on December 16, Frazier pulled another stunt: he showed up with no hair at all. During the judge's instructions, he sat reading George Orwell's novel *1984*. The jury accommodated him by convicting him and sentencing him to death. However, he escaped this punishment in 1976 when the Supreme Court placed a temporary moratorium on capital punishment. At this time, officials commuted Frazier's sentence to life in prison, as was the case with other death row prisoners across the country. He served it at San Quentin. Periodically, he requested to be released, but was always denied. In 2009, at the age of sixty-two, he hanged himself in his prison cell.

Despite the legal verdict, Lunde stated that Frazier was a clear example of a psychotic killer who was detached from social reality. Had people not been so frightened about the Manson cult murders during this time, he believed the jury might have appreciated the influence of Frazier's untreated mental illness.

Erroneously, Lunde made a sweeping statement about mass murder: "Mass murderers are almost always insane, and they differ in many other respects from those who kill only one person."[4] He grouped them as paranoid schizophrenics or sexual sadists. However, since the two he evaluated did have delusions, and Howard Unruh from 1949, as well as Richard Speck and Charles Whitman from 1966, also had serious mental health issues, his statement is understandable. Over the decades since the 1970s, however, it's become clear that few mass murderers possess the delusional quality of psychosis. Instead, they're largely angry, rigid, and unable to cope with life's hard knocks. They're often suicidal.

Lunde also dismissed the notion of a female mass murderer, but there have been a few since his day. However, he did note an important factor: mass murderers tend not to know their victims. While they may harbor grudges against a specific person or people, strangers at a mall, workplace, or government facility represent to them the thing they're attacking—usually society. In some instances, it's personal and their victims are people they know. The mass murderer, Lunde said, "often perceives his victims as having certain attributes which torment him."[5] Sometimes, he said, they believe that their victims are actually aware of their place in the murderer's delusions. He based this on another Santa Cruz case.

3

In contrast to Frazier, Lunde found another Santa Cruz offender to be a sadistic predator, and he showed how their respective lives displayed quite diverse causal factors. In addition, Lunde was evaluating a delusional spree killer who was operating at the same time. By this time, the *Diagnostic and Statistical Manual of Mental Disorders*, 2nd edition (DSM-II, published in 1968), had become more influential, and among its diagnostic categories were the character disorders. In a psychoanalytic frame, there were organized reactions to a fixation at one of the key developmental stages: oral, anal, or genital. Psychologists, however, were describing "personality disorders," which revealed a mix of inborn temperament, moral development, and environmental influences.[6]

Starting late in 1972, across four months, another stunning series of murders occurred in the Santa Cruz area. The police finally arrested the killer, Herbert Mullin. Although he'd been institutionalized periodically and some psychologists had even evaluated him as a danger to others, he'd managed to get outpatient status. While he'd roamed around, he stopped taking his antipsychotic medication. Soon he "heard" a voice that ordered him to kill. Around this time, Mullin linked his birthday, April 18, to the date of the 1906 San Francisco earthquake and the 1955 death of Albert Einstein. He'd studied earthquakes versus births and deaths from around the world and believed that human beings had protected themselves from these cataclysms throughout history by means of murder: "a minor natural disaster avoids a major natural disaster. . . . Therefore we will always murder."[7]

In 1972, someone predicted a massive earthquake for January 4, 1973, and Mullin absorbed this imminent forecast into his worsening delusions. He believed that an earthquake would soon occur that would cause the state of California to dissolve into the ocean. It was his job, he believed, to save its residents. In his mind, this meant he had to "sing the die song," which he believed would persuade thirteen people to kill themselves or to allow themselves to be human sacrifices. He'd known who they were via telepathy. Whenever he heard the voice, he picked up a weapon, whether a knife, gun, or baseball bat, to go out and slay someone. After the police arrested Mullin, Lunde did a considerable amount of work to get his records from different psychiatric hospitals.

About Mullin, Lunde wrote that he had been a fairly normal child, raised Catholic. The family lived in San Francisco, and there was no lack of love in the two-parent home. They had little money, but they lived in a good neighborhood. Mullin did well in school and had friends. By his junior year in high school, the family had moved to Santa Cruz, where Mullin found a girlfriend and developed a strong friendship with a boy named Dean. He played sports and excelled in school. During the summer of 1965, just after the boys graduated from high school, Dean was killed in a car accident. This destroyed Mullin and he withdrew into social isolation. At some point he developed delusions that his parents were retarding his development and were telepathically communicating to others to stay away from their son; in other words, his isolation was their fault.

He also started dabbling with drugs, starting with marijuana. He went to college, changing his interests and career plans every few months. He became engaged, but his moodiness and strange statements gave his fiancée doubts. She broke up with him, and his ideas became more unrealistic. In 1969, he was admitted to a mental hospital but stayed for only six weeks. Mullin then began to wander, hearing command hallucinations, and was soon institutionalized again. Calling himself a "human sacrifice," he began an excessive letter-writing campaign, endured several more hospitalizations, and became increasingly more aggressive. He was consistently diagnosed with paranoid schizophrenia and given medication, but he took it sporadically. He needed long-term hospitalization, but the political climate in 1972, which favored deinstitutionalization, thwarted this.

Mullin heard a command hallucination in his father's voice, "Herb, I want you to kill me somebody," and became obsessed with charts about birth and death rates. On October 13, 1972, Mullin began his murder spree by clubbing a man with a baseball bat. He stabbed the next person, a female hitchhiker, and then entered a confessional on All Soul's Day and stabbed a priest. Each person who died, he believed, protected millions of others. He purchased a handgun and tried to enlist in the military. Failing this, he went in search of the man who'd first given him marijuana so that he could kill him. On that day, he murdered five people, including a mother and her two children, and not long after he massacred four teenagers who were camping illegally in a state park. He shot one more man, who was out working in his yard, before the police caught up with him on February 13, 1973. Strangely enough, he'd managed to kill exactly thirteen people, his goal. He explained his actions thus: "A rock doesn't make a decision while falling, it just falls."[8]

All mental health personnel involved in Mullin's trial agreed that he was seriously mentally ill. Yet, because he seemed to be aware that murder was against the law, he was considered sane and was therefore convicted. Lunde considered the deplorable conditions of the mental health system to be responsible for these deaths, as the lack of funding for psychiatric hospitals had resulted in Mullin's haphazard handling. He'd been considered a danger to others and yet had been released.

"In the case of Herb Mullin," Lunde wrote, "the problem and the solution seemed self-evident. He was obviously mentally ill and dangerous. Had he been institutionalized and received continuous treatment, thirteen killings might have been prevented."[9]

While Mullin was barely aware of reality and it was fairly easy to trace the development of his mental illness to the point where he acted under a command hallucination, the same cannot be said about the third multiple killer whom Lunde evaluated. This one was truly a challenge.

4

Besides Frazier's massacre and Mullin's string of murders, starting in May 1972 female hitchhikers had been disappearing. The local authorities later tried to blame them on the imprisoned Mullin to assure local residents that there would be no more murders, but the actual offender in these cases was a serial killer, Edmund Kemper III.[10]

While Mullin had shared similarities with Frazier in terms of psychotic delusions, Kemper was another type of case altogether. When he was just fifteen (but already six feet four inches tall), he'd murdered his grandparents in a double homicide. Shy and awkward, he'd had a difficult time with his parents' divorce, especially since it felt to him as if neither wanted him. In fact, Kemper sensed that his mother, Clarnell, was afraid of him, and that his grandmother was just as bad. He developed brutal fantasies that involved killing them and cutting up their bodies. In fact, anyone who made him angry got the same treatment in his mental life. Kemper sometimes wished that everyone would die. But until the double homicide, he took out his frustrations on animals, tormenting and killing cats.

Since Kemper was still a juvenile when he shot his grandparents, he was sent for psychiatric testing. One psychiatrist decided that he had a developing form of paranoid schizophrenia, so he ended up at Atascadero State Hospital for the Criminally Insane. As he went through more assessments, his evaluators realized that his IQ was well above average. They even allowed him to handle the assessment devices. Not just smart but also cunning, Kemper exploited the opportunity, memorizing the right answers to twenty-eight different instruments and thereby gaining the tools he needed to convince doctors that he would be safe to release when he turned twenty-one. He didn't exactly have a plan, but he knew he wanted out.

As his release date approached, psychiatrists advised that Kemper should not be returned to Clarnell's care, because they did not get along. Living with her could trigger violence. Yet Kemper had no other means of support, so in the end he moved back in with his mother, who now worked at the University of Santa Cruz. She did not realize that her son had developed a prodigious sexual appetite, influenced by the stories that incarcerated offenders had told him. He was a budding sex offender who would soon feed his appetite for violence and mutilation.

Kemper attended the local community college with the aim to eventually become a police officer. However, officials at the police academy told him that, at his full adult height of six feet nine inches, he was too tall. Disappointed, he befriended many officers, hanging out with them in a local bar, the Jury Room. They would realize the irony only later. Most of them liked "Big Ed." He was a good listener, polite and courteous. No one realized that he had his own agenda for asking questions about their investigations—especially when women turned up missing and murdered.

As Kemper drove around, he saw many young female hitchhikers. It was an easy way to travel for a college student, but what Kemper noticed was their vulnerability. His mother had ridiculed him and told him he could never get a date with girls like these. But he knew a way he could have them. Kemper fantasized about things he could do to them and, one day, he moved into action. He prepared for what he had in mind, placing plastic bags, knives, a blanket, and handcuffs in the trunk of his car—his murder kit. Then he tested himself. He'd pick up a hitchhiker and let her go. This amused him. He thought it was almost too easy. He would later estimate (or brag) that he'd picked up around 150 hitchhikers. The next step for him was to look for places he could take them where he could do whatever he wanted without being disturbed. He also looked for places to dump their remains when he was done. Finally, he decided to go a little further. He felt what he called his "little zapples." He was excited at the prospect of getting one of these girls under his control.

On May 7, 1972, Kemper saw Mary Ann Pesce and Anita Luchessa hitchhiking. They had left Fresno State College to meet friends at Stanford. He saw to it that they never arrived. He picked them up, raped and killed them, and removed their heads. On August 15, Pesce's head was discovered in a remote area in the mountains.

A month later, on September 14, Kemper picked up dance student Aiko Koo. In October, Mullin's murder series began, and early in 1973 Kemper struck again: he picked up eighteen-year-old Cindy Schall as she hitched a ride to class. Her arms and legs were found on a cliff overlooking the Pacific Ocean, while her torso washed to shore in two pieces. A surfer found her left hand. Kemper enjoyed seeing himself called the "Chopper" and the "Butcher" in the local papers.

At this point, the murder pace picked up. Mullin shot ten people, while two female hitchhikers disappeared on February 5 and February 13, 1973. Police arrested Mullin on February 13, but he would not admit to killing the coeds. Although officials wanted to believe the murders would now end, investigators knew there were differences between those Mullin had committed and the coed killings.

On March 4, a couple of hikers came across a human skull and jawbone—the remains of two missing coeds, Rosalind Thorpe and Alice

Liu. The authorities were stymied. It seemed impossible that they had two repeat killers operating at the same time in the same place. They tried everything they could think of to identify evidence that would help them link the murdered coeds to their killer.

On April 23, 1973, they received a stunning surprise. Big Ed was calling them from a phone booth in Colorado. He insisted *he* was the Coed Killer. He said he'd just murdered his own mother and her best friend, and the bodies could be found at his mother's house. He seemed to realize that he could not control himself, and he wanted someone to pick him up so he could turn himself in. Once the officers found the dismembered remains of Clarnell and her friend, Sara Hallett, they sent someone to go get Kemper. What had seemed to them a joke had turned deadly serious.

Once in custody, the six-foot-nine, 280-pound killer started to talk and went on for hours. He described in detail what he had done to each of the six coeds, as well as his attack on his mother and Hallett. Eventually, he showed detectives where he'd buried or tossed parts of victims who had not yet been found. To their horror, Kemper described cutting off the heads and having sex with them. He said he'd enjoyed totally possessing them.

As the case against Kemper progressed, he began making noises about pleading insanity, although he also said he wished to be executed. Detectives compiled his background. Born on December 18, 1948, in California, Edmund E. Kemper III had an older and younger sister. He'd been close to his father before his parents' divorce in 1957, when he was nine. At this time, his mother took him and his sisters to live far away in Montana. Here, his mother apparently relegated him to a room in the basement. Kemper grew to hate his mother, although during his lengthy confession he often found ways to make sense of her apparent cruelty.

His sisters told his defense attorneys about him as a way to shore up an insanity defense. One had goaded him to kiss a teacher, for example, and she remembered that his response was that if he kissed her he'd have to kill her. Kemper's younger sister said that he'd once removed the heads from her dolls.

"I lived as an ordinary person most of my life," Kemper said, "even though I was living a parallel and increasingly violent other life."[11] Clarnell, he said, had verbally attacked him, aiming scorn at his sense of worth. "She's holding up these girls who she said were too good for me to get to know," he recalled. "She would say, 'You're just like your father. You don't deserve to get to know them.'"[12] This enraged him, and after such arguments he'd often cruise around looking at the very girls his mother thought he couldn't have.

"I'm picking up young women," he said in an interview for *Court TV*, "and I'm going a little bit farther each time. It's a daring kind of thing. First, there wasn't a gun. I'm driving along. We go to a vulnerable place, where there aren't people watching, where I could act out and I say, 'No, I can't.' And then a gun is in the car, hidden. And this craving, this awful raging eating feeling inside, this fantastic passion. It was overwhelming me. It was like drugs. It was like alcohol. A little isn't enough."[13]

When Kemper picked up Mary Anne Pesce and Anita Luchessa, he had initially decided only to rape them but then he figured he should leave no witnesses. "It was the first time I went looking for someone to kill. And it's two people, not one. And they're dead. Very naïve, too. Painfully naïve in that they thought they were streetwise."[14]

Once the girls were in his car, grateful for the ride, he drove to a dirt road he'd already scouted. He told them that he was going to rape them. He enjoyed how scared they looked, which made him feel powerful. They belonged totally to him. Handcuffing Pesce to the back seat to prevent her from making trouble or trying to escape, he forced Luchessa into his car trunk. Closing it, he returned to Pesce. This was his first actual attempt to kill a human being. He tried to smother her by placing a bag over her head but failed to kill her this way, so he stabbed her. When the blade hit her backbone, it stopped and would not penetrate. She struggled so much he had a hard time making it work. Then she bit through the bag and was starting to scream, so he slit her throat. As blood gushed out, she relaxed, went unconscious, and died. Kemper held her for a few moments, absorbing the experience. Then he remembered the other girl. He had to kill them both. He returned to Luchessa and killed her as well, more quickly. The experience had been more of an ordeal than he'd anticipated. He knew he needed to get better at this if he intended to continue, but now he had two corpses to enjoy. He could do whatever he wanted with them, without interruption.

Wrapping them in blankets, he placed both in the trunk and drove to his apartment. He felt great satisfaction that he'd actually accomplished not just a murder, but two at the same time. At home, Kemper made sure his mother was asleep before bringing the bodies inside. He took them into his bedroom, where he posed and photographed them. Then he found a sharp knife in the kitchen. As he cut through and removed the arms and heads, he took pictures. He told the detectives that he'd also engaged in a variety of sexual acts with the severed parts. He'd found the entire experience incredibly erotic.

Placing Pesce's parts in a trash bag, he left them in a shallow grave in the mountains. He marked the place so he could return if he wanted. He kept her head, using it for sexual purposes before he finally tossed it into a ravine. Luchessa's remains suffered the same insult. Kemper had felt good afterward, relieved and powerful, but it wasn't long before the "little zapples" impelled him to act out again, despite the fact that Pesce's head had been found.

Kemper felt invincible. He was convinced that no one could tie him to the missing coeds. In fact, on the day after he killed Aiko Koo and placed her head in the trunk of his car, Kemper appeared before a panel of psychiatrists at his parole hearing. He knew what these doctors wanted to hear, so he put on his best manipulative façade. One doctor saw no reason to consider Kemper a danger to anyone, while another used the words "normal" and "safe." Both recommended that his juvenile records be sealed. Kemper was amused. They had just made it so much easier for him to continue.

He viewed himself as smarter than all these sophisticated psychiatrists, no matter what his mother said about him. They thought they could see who he was through these interviews and test scores, but he knew they saw nothing of his secrets. He buried Koo's head and hands above Boulder Creek, then purchased a .22 caliber pistol. This time, he'd be ready if his other methods failed to work. A gun was quick and unquestionably effective. After an argument with his mother, two more girls died. In a show of defiance, he took these bodies to Clarnell's home, where he dismembered and beheaded them.

After killing six young women, Kemper made his fatal error. He killed someone that the police could definitely link to him: Clarnell. In his confession, Kemper said that he was afraid she'd found the items he'd removed from victims and kept, so he decided that he'd have to kill her to prevent her from speaking to the police. One evening, Clarnell went out with friends. She was slightly drunk when she came in, so she went to bed. Kemper went into her bedroom, and with some irritation she said, "I suppose you want to talk now." He told her no. He knew that soon enough he'd never have to listen to her again. Kemper waited until he thought his mother was asleep and then entered her room with a claw hammer in his hand. In that moment, he would later say, he both loved and hated her. He was going to bash her head in.

Kemper hit his mother several times to ensure that she was dead. There was blood all over the room, all over her, and all over him. He then removed her head and carried it into the living room, where he placed it on the mantel. He looked at it for a moment as it stared vacantly. Then he got some darts and threw them at Clarnell's head. But this was not enough. He remembered how she'd always degraded him, verbally lashing

him over his inadequacies, so he took the head down and removed the lar-
ynx. This he stuffed down the garbage disposal, but when he turned it on
to get rid of it, it came back up. Afterward, he penned a brief note: "Appx.
5:15 A.M. Saturday. No need for her to suffer anymore at the hands of this
horrible 'murderous butcher.' It was quick, sleep, the way I wanted it."[15]

Not satisfied with this grisly deed, however, Kemper decided to commit one last murder. He called Clarnell's close friend, Sara Hallett, to
invite her over. When she came, he killed her, too. Then he packed up his
car and drove until he reached Colorado. Within hours, he felt scared and
desperate, so he turned himself in.

During the investigation, Kemper showed officers the location of
Cynthia Schall's head, which he'd buried in his mother's backyard. He'd
put it there, he said, so he could secretly revel in knowing she was close
by. The head was a reminder of his "achievement."

Kemper was indicted on May 7, 1973, on eight separate counts of first-
degree murder, among other charges. Jim Jackson, Santa Cruz County's
chief public defender, accepted his case. Jackson had defended Frazier
and Mullin as well. He offered an insanity plea, although he knew he'd be
fighting a steep uphill battle. Kemper had clearly planned and prepared
for murder, he'd hidden evidence, and certainly he knew that what he'd
done was illegal and wrong. Still, Kemper had once been diagnosed with
a serious mental illness. Despite later psychiatric findings that he was
normal, clearly he hadn't been.

The trial started on October 23, 1973, and three prosecution psychiatrists testified that they had found Kemper to have been aware
of his actions and that they were wrong. Dr. Joel Fort had looked at
Kemper's juvenile records, and from what he could tell, there had been
little grounds at Atascadero to declare Kemper schizophrenic. He thought
the staff had erroneously relied on Kemper's lively fantasy life as the basis.
Armed with this information, Fort had interviewed Kemper at length.
Kemper even had a session under truth serum. During the trial, Fort testified that Kemper had probably cooked and eaten pieces of his victims
after dismembering them. Nevertheless, he had not been insane. Instead,
he had seemed thrilled about the notoriety he'd received, both before and
after he was caught. Kemper had also shown evidence of premeditation
and had stated that he knew he should eliminate witnesses.

When it was time for the defense, one defense psychiatrist testified
to Kemper's insanity based on the "product standard," which allows for
a finding of insanity if the crime is found to have been the product of a
diseased mind. However, California did not allow this type of testimony.
Kemper also took the stand. He described his mental state while killing

and tried to convince the jury that his compulsion to possess a woman, along with his acts of necrophilia, should be considered signals of his mental instability. He told the jury that he'd begun to drink excessively when remorse for his crimes overcame him. However, he undermined his own effort by describing the sexual thrill he'd received when removing a girl's head. He stated that two beings inhabited his body, and when "the killer" took over it was "kind of like blacking out." Kemper compared the experience to the time he'd shot his grandparents; he claimed he'd blacked out during this incident as well.

On November 8, the jury went into deliberations. After just five hours, they found Kemper to have been sane when he'd killed his victims. Thus, he was guilty of eight counts of first-degree murder. Although Kemper had requested the death penalty, the Supreme Court had already placed a moratorium on capital punishment. He was out of luck.

5

Although not hired in this case as a defense psychiatrist, Lunde read the trial transcripts for his study of murderers and looked at the results of Kemper's early psychological testing. Unlike Mullin or Frasier, Kemper seemed to him to have had unquestioned awareness of his acts; he'd even relished its perversion. Lunde looked at Kemper's background and confession details and decided that long-term anger and violent fantasies, nurtured from childhood, had exerted considerable influence on his sexual aggression. An ambivalent relationship with his mother was common among sexual sadists, and many had committed or fantasized about matricide.

"In rare individuals," Lunde wrote, "for reasons that are not well understood, sexual and violent aggressive impulses merge early in the child's development, ultimately finding expression in violent sexual assaults, and in the most extreme cases, sadistic murders or sex murders."[16] He had found that such murderers were inevitably white males under the age of thirty-five, with little if any normal sexual experience but with active fantasy lives. They derive pleasure from tormenting others, and their fantasies are filled with sadistic scenes. They then add masturbation, which conditions them toward violence as the ultimate thrill. However, they make an effort to appear normal. Usually their relationship with their mother is intense but ambivalent. A Freudian interpretation involved the young man being unable to get release from his sexual tension until he killed his mother.

Because psychological testing had been done on Kemper prior to the coed killings, it provided a unique way to look at both Kemper and the validity of the tests. At age nineteen, the test results were consistent with a sadistic personality but had failed to offer predictive power. The psychiatrists had administered the Rorschach Inkblot Test and the Thematic Apperception Test. Both are series of ambiguous forms or drawings, and to one Kemper had described a boy who was having problems with his father and who decided to be his own man. To Rorschach images, he had offered interpretations involving destructive animals like bear and alligators. He was found to be volatile and immature, with depression and latent hostility. Although dependent, explosive aggression was a possibility. He was lonely, lacking in confidence, and unable to deal adequately with conflict. Thus, it made sense that placing him back into his mother's care, the greatest source of his tension and low self-esteem, was a bad idea. Yet no one could say for sure that he would kill again . . . and again.[17]

Kemper's anger began early, Lunde wrote, perhaps from being separated from his father. Lunde blamed Clarnell, although she'd often been concerned about his lack of a father figure. Lunde also recorded incidents from Kemper's younger sister: "He would stage his own execution in the form of a childhood game, in which he had her lead him to a chair, blindfold him, and pull an imaginary lever, after which he would writhe about as if dying in a gas chamber."[18]

In an interview, Kemper had told Lunde about his fascination with weapons and his intense urge to kill women. "Ed also imagined such things as killing everyone in town and having sexual relations with corpses."[19] While he apparently did hope for a real relationship with a female, he felt inadequate, Lunde says, and believed he could get close to them only by killing them and having sex with their corpses.

Lunde observed that Kemper's juvenile experience in a psychiatric institution had done him little good. "There may be a point in the sexual sadist's development," he says, "beyond which sexual and violent aggressive impulses are inextricably interwoven."[20] To be effective, he believed, treatment should occur much earlier. Yet he knew it wasn't easy to identify such children in order to intervene with better guidance, because they generally kept their developing fantasies secret. Petty offenses like lies and property damage could be true of anyone during childhood, not just budding murderers.

In 1973, the American Psychiatric Association (APA) formed a task force to revise the DSM-II, and its members decided they needed something entirely different. They moved away from the psychoanalytic focus and decided to incorporate research in neurology. The diagnoses would derive not from clinical judgment and experience but from a fixed set of criteria. A standard classification system took shape that would allow easier dialogue from one clinician to another, with objective agreement about symptoms and illness.[21] The task force hoped to attain a document that would be based in science, not subjectivity. The National Institute of Mental Health sponsored trials in which hundreds of psychiatrists used drafts of the proposed DSM-III (more than three times as long as its predecessor) to diagnose 12,000 patients. Their evaluations were compared for consistency, and when the DSM-III was published in 1980, the medical model for diagnosis became the norm.

However, even as these trials were being run, the most notorious serial killer of the decade—perhaps the century—was being evaluated.

CHAPTER 11

Ted Bundy, Al Carlisle, and James Dobson

1

Although the precise start of Theodore Robert Bundy's criminal career is unclear, he came to the attention of law enforcement as "Ted" in 1974. Several young women had been assaulted or had disappeared in Oregon and Washington State, and when two suddenly vanished on the same day from Lake Sammamish State Park near Seattle, witnesses described seeing both at separate times with a slender man named "Ted." He'd been driving a tan or gold Volkswagen Beetle. Unfortunately, with such a vague description and such a popular car, the potential suspects formed a long list. Then when the remains of the two young women were found amid skeletal parts a few miles from the lake, the authorities knew they had a predator in the area. He was looking for pretty young girls and he'd killed before. What they did not realize is that he'd already moved on.

Bundy had graduated from the University of Washington with a degree in psychology and had been accepted into law school at the University of Utah. But his killing did not stop. As he roamed around Idaho, Utah, and Colorado, several more corpses of missing young women turned up. There were no central databases at the time for communicating across jurisdictions, so no one yet realized the enormity of the case. But then there was an unexpected break in Utah. A man posing as an undercover cop, "Officer Roseland," picked up nineteen-year-old Carol DaRonch on November 8, 1974. Suspecting him, she remained guarded, which helped her to fight him off when he tried handcuffing her. She escaped and called the police.[1]

When Bundy was arrested on suspicion of burglary the following August, DaRonch identified him as her would-be assailant. As Utah authorities processed Bundy for trial, psychologist Gary Jorgensen evaluated him with standard diagnostic tests such as the Minnesota Multiphasic Personality Inventory (MMPI) and found him to be free of psychiatric disorders. Before and after his conviction for aggravated kidnapping in the DaRonch incident, Bundy endured more extensive testing, including brain scans, which detected no organic disorder. His lack of remorse got him a diagnosis of personality disorder, antisocial type, from several examiners.[2]

In addition, a picture of his early life emerged. Born in a home for unwed mothers on November 24, 1946, as Theodore Robert Cowell, he was taken to Philadelphia to live with his mother's parents and be raised as her brother. For many years, he believed his grandparents were his parents. When Ted was almost five, his mother took him to Tacoma, Washington, where she married Johnnie Bundy, who adopted Ted. Four more children entered the family, and Bundy would later claim that he had grown up in a stable home with caring, churchgoing parents. He insisted that nothing they did was to blame for his actions. Still, he had shown signs of antisocial behavior even before he had a stepfather. His aunt woke up one day to find herself surrounded by knives and three-year-old Ted grinning at her. He also engaged in lies and petty theft, as well as voyeurism.

Bundy was a shy kid, subjected to some bullying before he became popular in high school. He was a good student, going on to college for Asian studies but changing to psychology. He graduated with an A– average, wrote a pamphlet about rape, designed a program for habitual criminals, and got involved in politics. He enrolled in law school but dropped out, then moved to Utah for another go at law school. There, he became a Mormon.

While at the University of Washington, Bundy had met and fallen in love with a young woman, but she found him to be deceitful and lacking in direction, so she'd ended the relationship. Many criminologists believe his anger at women began with her rejection, because many of Bundy's subsequent victims resembled her. However, they actually reunited in 1973, becoming engaged before he inexplicably dumped her (perhaps for revenge). Only a few weeks later, on January 4, 1974, Bundy killed his first documented victim in her Seattle home. (He changed his story often, sometimes claiming that his first murder was in 1969, or perhaps in 1972 or 1973, but these are not definitively documented.) During the first half of 1974, Bundy killed at least six more young women. At some point, either when he was a teenager, in college, or after his graduation, he had learned that his "older sister" was actually his mother, his "parents" were his grandparents, and his real father was unknown. (Some accounts hold that his grandfather had fathered him through incest, but this was not confirmed.) Bundy was reportedly stunned by this revelation. His parents and grandparents had deceived him for years, which may have affected his sense of stability. Since the circumstances of this discovery remain vague, it's not possible to describe a resulting change in character or demeanor.

Among those who evaluated him after his first arrest was Dr. Al C. Carlisle, a psychologist at the Utah State Prison. Although he did not realize at this time that he had a serial killer on his hands, he wasn't new to the experience. Carlisle had already evaluated Arthur Bishop, an excommunicated Mormon and former Eagle Scout who'd raped and murdered five boys, and his observations of Bundy and other serial killers led to groundbreaking ideas about how they develop into compulsively repetitive offenders.

2

After administering a test, Carlisle found Bundy's IQ to be above average, between 120 and 125. "I spent about twenty hours with Bundy on the psychological assessment," he said.[3] "I used a number of psychological tests such as the Sentence Completion Test, the Rorschach, the Thematic Apperception Test, and the Bipolar Psychological Inventory." He also engaged in a clinical interview and acquired names of people who had known Bundy before he'd gone to Utah. By talking with them, Carlisle hoped to gain more information.

"He cried in front of me twice," he recalled. "One time was when we were doing the Thematic Apperception Test [a projective assessment instrument that relies on a series of cards that depict ambiguous situations, allowing for personal interpretation]. The last card is blank and I asked him to make up a picture as well as a story. He talked about a picture in his mind of a guy coming into a room and seeing his wife or companion on the floor cleaning an oven. Tears rolled down his cheeks when he reported this story. I showed this to other psychologists and the first thing they said was, 'Did his girlfriend have an abortion?' She did, and Ted reported strong mixed feelings about it."

Carlisle noted that in prison Bundy had a regimen. He'd get up, exercise, work on legal briefs, and then read. "He liked to read about people who had committed crimes and survived. It helped him to remain strong. He wanted to keep his mind active in a forward-moving manner. He told me once that fear didn't bother him. He didn't have regrets."

After talking with some of Bundy's acquaintances, Carlisle saw a picture forming of a man with two distinct sides to his character. "The question was, how he could seem so normal and friendly at times and yet be evil at other times? Can good and evil occupy the same mind? This is the chameleon in him." Along these lines, he noted that Bundy saw women as more powerful than men, and had described his mother as the most powerful person in their family. "Some who knew him talked of his sense of feeling inferior," Carlisle observed. "One young lady said, 'He put me on a pedestal and then knocked me off.' Another said that it seemed like there was always a power struggle between them."

Carlisle decided that Bundy had a dependent personality disorder. Among the reasons for this was the obsession Bundy had described with his former fiancée. She'd moved on, but he hadn't let go. When she went out with another man, Bundy had stalked her. "He went down to the restaurant where they were at," Carlisle said, "walking back and forth, and she had to tell him to leave. When she got back to her place, he was there, crying, and they cried together. During the evaluation, Ted told me she had slept with another guy, and [as he said this] he changed, literally. There was a very angry, cold look in his eye and he said, 'That was the last straw.' This was about the time he killed his victim in '73. He couldn't live with Liz, he couldn't marry her, but he couldn't give her up."

When asked if Bundy had felt betrayed by the fact that his mother had kept the truth from him about his real father, Carlisle recalled that he had, although perhaps not as much as losing his mother's attention. "I believe that possibly a greater issue was that he was the oldest of the children and when the others came along, he felt abandoned. Also, he'd been close to his grandfather and when they moved, there was that loss. That may be when he got into the heavy fantasizing."

In Carlisle's presence, Bundy twice lost his composure to feelings of rage. "One event was when he talked about his girlfriend having sex with another man. The other one was when he learned that I had called some of his other girlfriends. He wanted to know what they were saying. I told him some were saying very good things and some were saying negative things. He changed at that point. He said, 'If you ever use that stuff, I'm going to call them into court and make them explain that, and I'll interrogate them.' He couldn't handle criticism."

One thing that Bundy was very good at, however, was supporting people in power. "When he was working on political campaigns, such as for [Daniel J. Evans, governor of Washington State] and Arthur Fletcher, he was able to achieve a level of success. He would do anything to make them successful, which would possibly allow him to ride into success on their coattails."

Carlisle noticed that Bundy could be charming and friendly while steaming inside. Throughout the psychological evaluation, he complained to his friend, Ann Rule. Having majored in psychology, he knew what the questions meant and he apparently disliked being on the receiving end. He told Rule that Carlisle had diagnosed him as being passive-aggressive and seemed to expect him to blurt out a full confession. He also told her he'd read about the Sam Sheppard case, wherein after years in prison Sheppard had been found innocent. Bundy appreciated the triumph of an innocent person falsely accused. He allowed Rule to send copies of his letters to Carlisle, but he ranted that the psychologists were trying to prove that he had a split personality. He admitted that Carlisle was probably correct that he was insecure but expressed annoyance about other findings, especially his alleged dependence on women.

But Carlisle had done his homework, collecting impressions from a wide variety of people who knew Bundy. "He was described as intelligent," he said, "high achievement-oriented, having the acumen necessary for a political career, and loyal to a cause." These items went into Carlisle's report, as did negative conclusions, which Bundy dissected point by point to Rule. Accordingly, Carlisle offered his list of observations for this chapter. About Bundy, he had written the following points, quoted below:

1. He is a private person who won't open up and reveal himself to others. He doesn't want to be known by others.
2. He became defensive and evasive when any of his girlfriends tried to get information from him.
3. Outwardly he looks very adequate. This masks strong feelings of inadequacy underneath.
4. He can't handle ambiguity.
5. Loss of a father is very significant.
6. He views women as more competent than men.
7. He demonstrates a strong dependency on women for emotional support and yet he can't settle down with one. He said he resents dependency, and yet he seems to most resent his own dependency.
8. He gets very upset when people say negative things about him.
9. There are a number of people coming in and out of his life. Most relationships were brief, suggesting instability. He would hurt deeply when he would lose someone. There is a strong sense of futility about him.
10. He is reluctant to accept help or support from anyone (except for financial support). He wants relationships with people on his terms, and he wants to be in control of the relationship at all times. He is egocentric. It is extremely important for him to be in control of emotions, interpersonal relationships, and interviews. He has a very strong fear of being hurt and he puts up strong defenses against getting close, including being touched. He has an obsession regarding controlling and structuring, and he runs from the situation or relationship when it doesn't work.

11. He shows strong suspiciousness regarding people playing games or trying to trick him, and he is always on guard. He is a very perceptive person.
12. There is a strong theme of having been put down, humiliated, and made fun of.
13. Strong sense of loneliness.
14. He has shown a rapid change in moods from pleasant to angry to depressed.
15. He lacks outward indications of guilt and tries to conceal his anxiety. However, he shows it through deep sighs and heavy perspiring.
16. His behavior is not modifiable by fear. [He states,] "I don't have fears. Fear, pain and punishment don't stick with me." [Bundy apparently exhibited fear, as evident in his stated anxieties, but denied feeling or allowing it to control him. This could also indicate how difficult he might be to rehabilitate.]

Bundy saw Carlisle's list and Rule recalled his hostile reaction: "For every conclusion that Dr. Carlisle asserted, Ted had a comeback. He denied that he 'ran from his problems,' or that he was unstable, pointing out his amazing strength under the rigors of the DaRonch trial."[4]

When Carlisle offered the report in court, Bundy picked it up and shook it. With tears running down his cheeks, he objected that it had been written to fit the crime. Nevertheless, thanks largely to DaRonch's testimony, he got a prison sentence. He could hardly believe it. But once ensconced in a cell, Bundy became quite friendly toward Carlisle. "He just seemed to want to get together and talk. All the bitterness that was in the courtroom wasn't there anymore. He was a fascinating guy. I enjoyed talking with him. He helped the other inmates work on their legal briefs, so he was popular among them."

But Carlisle wasn't fooled. He knew that when the opportunity for violence is restricted, inmates can seem more socially effective. With Bundy's lack of impulse control, if he got free, he'd return to his prior habits.

Sentenced on June 30, 1976, Bundy was transferred early the following year to Colorado to face charges in the murder of Caryn Campbell. Credit card receipts for gas put him in all the right places, and the crowbar from his car matched the wound on her skull. In addition, strands of hair consistent with hers (and another suspected victim's) were found in his car, and a witness had described someone who looked like him at the inn from which Campbell had vanished.

While researching his case in the prison's law library, Bundy jumped out a second-story window and escaped. But it was very cold that night in Aspen and he was without resources, so he was quickly caught. Carlisle was surprised to receive a phone call from him. "We talked for about fifteen minutes," he recalled. "It was much like a son calling his dad to say, 'Dad, let me tell you about the game I had, my home run.' He just seemed to want to talk."

This was the last time they spoke, but after Carlisle learned the enormity of Bundy's offenses, he studied other serial killers and devised a theory from the things they had told him.

3

Based on his research and experience, Carlisle proposes that the ability to repeatedly kill and also function as a seemingly normal person develops through the gradual evolution of three primary processes:

1. *Fantasy*: the person imagines scenarios for entertainment or self-comfort.
2. *Dissociation*: the person avoids uncomfortable feelings and memories.
3. *Compartmentalization*: the person relegates different ideas and images to specific mental frames and keeps boundaries between them.

Carlisle states that serial killers have a "compartmentalized" self, that is, they offer a public persona that appears to be "good" and nurture a dark side that allows murderous fantasies free rein. Because they have painful memories from childhood abuse, disappointment, frustration, being bullied, or whatever, they have learned to use fantasies to escape, comfort themselves, and even develop an alternate identity that feels more powerful or provides greater status. As Carlisle explained, "A child who experiences excessive emptiness and engages in extensive daydreaming may reach the point where the identity of [the] entity generated through fantasy becomes a compartmentalized and controlling factor in the person's life."[5]

In fantasies, he wrote, the expression of unacceptable impulses, desires, and aspirations gradually grows to be equally as influential as the "good" persona, but as normal life grows boring, frustrating, or disappointing, the fantasy life becomes more attractive. Eventually, the brutal dimension gains more substance through mental rehearsal, as well as opportunity, and the unrestricted fantasy develops into an unquenchable habit. Killers then learn to deflect others from discovering their secrets: they devise different sets of values for different life frames, and they can also carry on a high level of functioning even while they seek another victim.

An individual can also achieve emotional and sexual gratification with imagery, Carlisle believes, and those feelings and acts that others might disapprove get shoved into a secret compartment, to be savored and augmented when alone. Any remorse, self-hate, or guilt he may feel gets sealed away in its own mental compartment. He won't allow emotional taboos to interfere with the drive to once again achieve the high this fantasy affords. However, it fails to fully satisfy, and the dark side is full of energy that seeks expression, so it requires considerable effort to keep Jekyll and Hyde in separate rooms. The weaker the person's ego, Carlisle theorizes, the harder it is to sustain this effort, and it can psychologically overwhelm and undermine the killer, leading to decompensation, carelessness, and mistakes.[6]

When Carlisle considered Bundy in the context of this theory for the present study, he offered a more extensive analysis, comparing the dynamics of a serial killer against those of an actor as a metaphor:

> Compartmentalization is a process that all of us can engage in to one degree or another. It's a complex state of mind on a continuum that can vary from a healthy level, such as with an actor who rehearses a script so intently that when portraying that role on stage or in a film he has a deep sense of being that person. At the other end of the continuum, compartmentalization, as used by Ted Bundy and many others, is a very destructive process that can result in violence. At this level, it's a combination of addiction, intent, imagery, strong unmet needs, and some level of dissociation.
>
> The actor is satisfying his needs through compartmentalization because he creates within his mind the world of his character and he can move around within the sphere of the character he is playing without losing the essence of the part. His role is open for everyone to see. He has an audience who affirms his success in this role, and once he has completed the film or stage production, he can move on to another role. He limits his acting to the medium of the production—the movie set or on stage. Once he leaves that medium within which his craft is performed, he exits the compartment he has created in his mind for that role. If he is playing Hamlet in the theater, for example, he doesn't continue to remain in the role when he goes to the beach for the weekend with his friends. His intent is to be able to access the voice, the mannerisms, the behavior, and the emotions of his role upon cue as needed, and then to step out of the role when it's not needed. He creates the compartmentalized role, and he controls it. Although it may be somewhat difficult to give up a role once it has become such a powerful part in his life, he has control over both the creation and the completion. He uses it rather than it using him.

In the case of a Ted Bundy, most aspects of the compartmentalization are different than with the actor. Through fantasy, he creates a world in which he is able to gratify his sexual needs. The part he plays in the fantasy is kept a secret from others. There is no audience to affirm his success and, except for brief sexual satisfaction, there is no success. There is no applause, no congratulations on a job well done. There is no critique of his style and performance. He is the creator of his work, and he has no one to tell him it's wrong.

The medium of the production is both in his mind as well as in the world around him. He never completely steps out of his role whether he is living the production in his mind or is reliving it when he is on the beach. The stage, the props, the background scenery are only in his mind. The actor steps onto the stage to play out his role. The killer steps from one compartment in his mind into the other. The actor leaves the theater for a day on the beach. The killer shifts from the pathological compartment in his mind back into the socially acceptable compartment, but he never completely leaves the theater in his mind, and, in fact, it is even more active when he goes to the beach. It is with him wherever he goes, twenty-four hours a day, day in and day out.

The intent of the actor is to please his audience, his director, and those who are in the production with him. The intent of the killer is to please himself through his interaction with, generally, one person. When the actor finishes his part, he receives his accolades and moves on to the next production. The killer never receives the accolades in reality, so he has to pretend that he does, which generally consists of him congratulating himself. He may also attempt to get the victim to express admiration of him. When he finishes a fantasy episode, he feels gratified but not satisfied. There has been a temporary reduction of a powerful drive but an increase in a psychic need. The intensity of the sexual release is so powerful that the person craves for more. However, as his mind adapts to the experience, the satisfaction diminishes so he has to find ways to keep the experience exciting. In the process of doing this, he progresses from hero fantasies through control fantasies and possibly to revenge fantasies.

He knows that this style of fantasy life is unacceptable to his friends and family, so he continues to keep it secret, and since nobody can criticize him for it, he can do anything during a fantasy episode to satisfy his lusts. Since he can't experience in reality what he enjoys in fantasy, he enhances his fantasy in an attempt to approximate reality as closely as possible; and to help him experience it more fully, he blocks out everything going on around him, a process called "dissociation." The more he is lonely and uninvolved with satisfying life activities such as relationships, sports, academics, and so on, the more he has to turn to fantasy as a vicarious substitution, which he often attempts to do through pornography. The better he becomes at dissociating the world around him during a fantasy, the more real the fantasy feels to him. Instead of fulfilling his need, however, his need for similar gratification in the real world increases, which, again, leads to frustration. He increases the frequency of his sexual fantasy in an attempt to increase the intensity of the experiences, but it still doesn't give him what he is after.

He is soon spending lengthy spans of time in his make-believe world. Since he isn't satisfied with who he is in reality, he creates a more dynamic character in his mind to give the imagery more power. His growth in his day-to-day life becomes somewhat stilted, emptier, and more unfulfilling. He attempts to compensate for this by enhancing his fantasy world and stretching it into his real world. He may molest a woman in fantasy, and when he sees a desirable woman later that day he may relive the same fantasy by imagining he is doing it to her. It increases the reality of the fantasy. Gradually, the fantasy world and the real world begin to meld together. The boundary between the two worlds becomes thinner and more difficult to control.

This becomes a problem because he has to hide his fantasy world from others so they won't become aware of his pathology. He attempts to tighten his real-world compartment and may become obsessive and compulsive in some of his mannerisms, such as was seen with Ted Bundy. He has to be very careful to keep the two worlds, or two compartments in his mind, very separate.

Since it's very difficult—some would say, almost impossible—to have good and evil coexist within the same mind, he has to find a way to minimize the polarity between the two parts. His criteria for determining right from wrong gradually change over time. What was wrong for him as a child may become acceptable when he is an early teen and then desirable when he is in his late teens. He does this by finding justifications for his fantasy life. He may, for example, attempt to convince himself that there is nothing wrong with his daydreams since he isn't actually harming another person. He may tell himself that women are conniving, manipulative, and deceitful and need to be punished. He may convince himself that romance is a game, that there is no right or wrong, that it's only a matter of winning or losing, and that power, intelligence, and superiority are demonstrated by winning.

All of this activity increases in intensity and frequency, and the person may become a highly energized assailant in search of a trigger to release the explosion that has been growing within him. Then comes the first victim, and once the offender has stepped over that final boundary, which has been protecting his shaky identity, his belief about who he is permanently changes, at which time both compartments in his mind will go through an alteration. At first he may feel guilty and depressed over what he has done, but he is now more incapable of fighting his pathology. He may swear to himself that he will never do it again, but he soon finds that he is incapable of fighting off the urges to repeat his crime.

Now, he *is* the pathology. The day-by-day compartment becomes sub-servient to the greatly strengthened pathological compartment. Some offenders speak of something within them which takes over and they find themselves observers of the crime. Some say that when the killing cycle is triggered into action, they are unable to stop it without something stronger occurring, such as a police officer walking by.

Compartmentalization for the Bundy type of serial killer is the cre-ation of multiple realities in the mind which are kept separate (in com-partments) to help protect the ability of the person to live multiple, and often opposing, lifestyles which are relatively immune from detection. As to how the brain is able to do this is still open to question. However, with what we know of plasticity of the brain, is it not possible that each of these highly developed lifestyles (compartments) has a semi-independent neural circuitry system?

4

On December 30, 1977, Bundy escaped again, this time from Garfield County Jail. He left Colorado and crossed the country, considering sev-eral different Midwestern cities as his new home before he ended up in Tallahassee, Florida. He apparently believed he could live there unde-tected, but by January 15, 1978, just two weeks into his freedom, Bundy was having trouble. In short order, he deviated dramatically from his typi-cal modus operandi (MO) and made several high-risk moves.

First, he entered the Chi Omega sorority house at Florida State Univer-sity, raping, strangling, or clubbing four girls in their beds. Lisa Levy and Martha Bowman died, but the other two survived. As Bundy fled with a three-foot club, a resident saw him. In addition, he'd also bitten one of his victims, leaving a distinct, identifiable impression. Although he got away that night, and even managed to abduct twelve-year-old Kimberly Leach a month later in broad daylight in front of a school crossing guard, he finally drew police attention with a traffic violation. He was driving a sto-len Volkswagen. After being stopped, he kicked the officer and ran. The officer subdued him and placed him under arrest.

Once in custody, Bundy could barely believe they did not realize who he was, so after a few lies he finally told them. They received confirmation from states where he was wanted and learned that he was on the FBI's Ten Most Wanted list.

Bundy was once again subjected to psychological evaluations. Florida appointed Dr. Hervey Cleckley, renowned for writing *The Mask of San-ity*, to assess Bundy's competency to stand trial. He found Bundy to be a sociopath (a term that had replaced "psychopathy") who was competent.

Dr. Emanuel Tanay, an expert on criminality, interviewed Bundy and for the court Tanay stated that Bundy had an antisocial personality disorder over which he had no control and which prevented him from fully appreciating how his self-defeating behaviors could undermine his best interests. Thus, he was a danger to himself and should not be considered competent to participate in his defense. Tanay stated that while Bundy had a factual understanding of the proceedings, he did not have a rational understanding of what he actually faced. He seemed to lack an appreciation of the consequences of being found guilty. Whatever he needed in the moment deflected his appreciation of a potential death penalty. Thus, he could not accept competent advice or act in his own best interest. His masochism, need for immediate gratification, embrace of manipulation, and "malignant narcissism" ensured that he would always sabotage his attorney's efforts on his behalf.

Dorothy Ottnow Lewis, a psychiatrist out of New York, also examined him and began a correspondence with him. From her initial interview with him, she believed that Bundy suffered from a bipolar disorder, which gave him alternating states of deep depression and high energy. She also surmised that he might have multiple personality disorder.

One other professional stated that Bundy killed because he liked it.[7] Florida did not recognize the concept of an irresistible impulse as a mitigating factor, or the concept of diminished capacity. Bundy's only real hope was an insanity defense.

However, Bundy wanted nothing to do with it. His attorney, Mike Minerva, tried to get him to enter a guilty plea in exchange for life sentences, but Bundy asked the court to be relieved of counsel so he could represent himself. He was granted this right. In court, he preened, flirted with girls who flocked to see him, and winked at people he knew. However, he took such delight in questioning investigators on the stand about the details of his crimes that he angered the jury. As the psychologists had surmised, he was his own worst enemy. While questioning a witness, he also mistakenly identified himself as the offender. In addition, there was a solid case against him.

Two Florida juries convicted Bundy for three murders (including that of Leach, whose body was found raped, strangled, and dumped in an old pig shed). Still, he figured that he could at least get himself life in prison, and again he was wrong. Bundy was sentenced to death three times. Yet he had cards to play, starting with legal maneuvers.

Not only did he appeal his cases on various grounds all the way to the U.S. Supreme Court, but also he tried to persuade "scientists" that he was unique and should be kept alive and studied. To add to his notoriety, he revealed more of his crimes, eventually confessing to thirty murders in seven states: Oregon, Washington, Idaho, Utah, Colorado, California, and Florida. (Not all were corroborated with evidence.)

In 1980, Ann Rule published *The Stranger beside Me*, about her experience with Bundy in a Seattle Crisis Clinic. He'd made good grades as a psychology major, she wrote, and went to law school. He was also a compassionate hotline counselor. "I can picture him today . . . see him hunched over the phone, talking steadily, reassuringly—see him look up at me, shrug, and grin. I can hear . . . the infinite patience and caring in his voice. . . . He was never brusque, never hurried."[8] She was not surprised that he had charmed so many young women. She'd even believed in his innocence herself for quite a while, despite the mounting evidence against him.

To investigators who came to interview him, Bundy discussed his compulsions as a predator. Among the most revealing was with Supervisory Special Agent William Hagmaier from the FBI's budding Behavioral Science Unit. Bundy agreed to work closely with Hagmaier, which fed his need for attention and gave him an opportunity to prove his worth as a "scientific specimen." Hagmaier maintained correspondence with Bundy over a period of four years, until his execution, and provided the FBI with an extensive report.

Bundy's MO was to first select an appropriate disposal site—something that provided privacy or cover. Then he went looking for a victim who matched his sexual preferences. Once he spotted someone, he would fake an injury or a need for assistance (something he devised from a psychology course in which he'd participated in an experiment about the effect of a handicap on helping behavior). "He would feign an injury and indicate he needed assistance," he told Hagmaier, speaking of himself in the third person, "or he would portray an authority figure such as a police officer. He thus persuaded a victim to voluntarily accompany him to his Volkswagen where he had secreted a crowbar near the rear of the vehicle. Upon reaching the vehicle, he would retrieve the crowbar and strike the victim over the head, rendering her unconscious. He would then handcuff her and place her in the passenger side of the vehicle, which he had modified by removing the seat."[9]

Bundy usually emboldened himself with alcohol before an assault (DaRonch had smelled it on his breath), and while he most often killed by ligature strangulation from behind during a sexual act, sometimes he bludgeoned them. It depended on his mood or the demands of the situation. In many cases, he beheaded the corpse with a hacksaw, or removed the hands. Sometimes he carried the heads around with him or returned to a disposal site to have another sexual encounter. He considered the victims, once dead, as belonging to him. He was a collector. (He also had a foot fetish and collected socks.) "They are part of you," he stated, "and you are forever one. Even after twenty or thirty, it's the same thing, because you are the last one there. You feel the last bit of breath leaving their body, you're looking into their eyes. A person in that situation is God! You then possess them and they shall forever be a part of you. And the grounds where you kill them or leave them become sacred to you."[10] At one time, he had four heads in his home.

He would often drive for hours trolling for the right person, he said. He'd even made dry runs, letting some women go, and he believed that serial killers go through a developmental process, reaching their peak after considerable experience has given them a shell that buffers them from feeling anything for the victim. The early days are experimental, and thus mistakes can be made, but as the offender perfects his technique, he grows smoother. The predatory urge is like the addiction of an alcoholic, Bundy explained. It can be demanding. When he was very agitated, he would bite. He did say that once he had reached his peak and felt confident, he looked for victims he considered equal to his skill—more challenging.

Bundy often assaulted his victims in bright moonlight or under his car headlights, and he returned to nearly every crime scene. He had buried about one third of his victims or dumped them in water. On several, Bundy admitted, he'd performed acts of necrophilia. He would lie down with them, apply makeup to their decomposing faces, and then have sex. He enjoyed the fantasy of a dominant male and a submissive female—preferably a terrified one. He generally scripted his victims to perform certain acts from his fantasies—even dressing them in clothing he provided—before raping and killing them. He told Hagmaier that slasher movies or the covers of true crime detective magazines had influenced the content of his fantasies. (He told Dorothy Lewis that he'd found his grandfather's secret stash of pornography.) At times, he took pictures of victims so he could relish them later. There is some suggestion, although it might not be true, that on the day that Bundy had abducted the two young women from Lake Sammamish, he had forced one to watch him kill the other.

Bundy usually blamed his youthful interest in pornography for his developing blood lust. "The initial sexual encounter," he said, "would be more or less a voluntary one that did not wholly gratify the full spectrum of desires that he had intended. And so, his sexual desire builds back up and joins . . . this other need to totally possess her. As she lay there, somewhere between coma and sleep, he strangled her to death."[11] He said that during these encounters, some malignant part of his personality took over—he called it "the entity"—looking for satisfaction. Some people think he meant an alter personality while others say it was just a metaphor to avoid first-person narratives. Bundy enjoyed the feeling that he was smarter than the investigators (his perception), and he liked playing mind games.

Bundy's post-crime behavior was also revealing. He'd read newspaper reports about what the police knew and adjust his MO to avoid detection. He steam-cleaned his car, changed the upholstery, tossed victim clothing out of the car window as he drove, and scattered victim remains, but he was unfamiliar with forensic odontology and the ability to match his teeth to his bite mark. Hagmaier marveled at Bundy's ability to dissociate himself so fully from what he did to his victims—confirming Carlisle's theory.

In addition to information about himself, Bundy offered his expertise. As a task force investigated the forty-plus murders attributed to the Green River Killer in Washington State during the 1980s, Bundy wrote a letter to the former lead detective from his own case, Robert Keppel. He insisted that he could help investigators to "understand" the "Riverman's" mind. He knew the area intimately, so he could "figure out" how this new predator operated. Keppel came with Green River Task Force Detective Dave Reichert to question him, but as they listened they realized that Bundy was describing his own MO. They accepted his "help," allowing Bundy to believe in his superiority as America's premier serial killer. Playing off his arrogance, they closed several unsolved Seattle cases.

5

When, in January 1989, it was clear that there would be no more delays for Bundy's execution, he scrambled for new ways to make himself valuable. He agreed to tell detectives about more victims, but also said there was still a fruitful area to explore: the influence on his behavior of pornography. Although he had already talked about this at length with investigators, he asked to meet with the founder and president of Focus on the Family, the evangelical psychologist Dr. James Dobson. Here was a man with clout, he believed, who would take him seriously.

The son of a traveling preacher, with a long family legacy in the Holiness Movement, Dobson had studied psychology in order to become a Christian counselor. Earning a doctorate in child development, he became an associate clinical professor of pediatrics during the 1970s. Honored by many organizations, Dobson was invited to be a member of President

Ronald Reagan's commission on pornography. He founded the Family Research Council in 1981, and his radio show *Focus on the Family* was broadcast in a dozen languages in 164 different countries. Some publications referred to him as the nation's "most influential evangelical leader," and he emphasized tough love, the need for discipline, and the preservation of the Christian home.

By some reports, Dobson and Bundy had been corresponding intermittently, but this was going to be Bundy's "ultimate" statement about what had turned him into a monster. The interview was to be videotaped, but Bundy imposed one condition: it was not to be released until after he was dead. Bundy's time was running out and he seemed, finally, to realize it.

When Dobson arrived at the prison on January 24, he noticed the circus-like atmosphere outside, as people who were celebrating the impending execution mingled with hundreds of reporters. Dobson was aware that Bundy had decided that he could not trust the media to get his message right, so he'd chosen Dobson as his rightful messenger. In his book *Life on the Edge*, Dobson describes how he went through seven steel doors and metal detectors to reach the high-security room where the interview would take place. He watched as Bundy was brought in and strip-searched. Half a dozen guards remained close by. While Dobson and Bundy talked, the lights dimmed several times, as the guards tested the electric chair that would take Bundy's life in less than twenty-four hours.

Dobson asked Bundy, for the record, whether he had murdered all those girls, and he admitted that, yes, he had. When reminded that he'd never been physically or emotionally abused, Bundy agreed, saying, "That's part of the tragedy of this whole situation. I grew up in a wonderful home with two dedicated and loving parents, as one of five brothers and sisters. We regularly attended church. My parents did not drink or smoke or gamble. There was no physical abuse or fighting in the home."[12]

Dobson believed that alcohol and addiction to pornographic material were the primary causal factors in serial murder, and with this interview he had the most influential and credible offender confirming it. On the video, Bundy appeared humble and sincere, although he quickly and squarely placed the blame for what had happened to him on society's shoulders. *We* had relaxed the smut laws and allowed trashy material to be sold. It was our fault. "This is the message I want to get across," he said, becoming somewhat teary-eyed; "that as a young boy . . . I encountered . . . the soft-core pornography . . . as young boys do, we explored the bad roads and sideways and byways of our neighborhood, and people would often dump the garbage. . . . And from time to time we would come across books of a hard nature."[13]

Bundy described how he became increasingly more curious, and then addicted to looking at pornography. Then he'd thought obsessively about the images. "I'm not blaming pornography," he insisted. "I'm not saying it caused me to go out and do certain things. I take full responsibility for all the things that I've done. That's not the question here. The issue is how this kind of literature contributed and helped mold and shape the kinds of violent behavior."[14]

For him, pornography had fueled a thought process, crystallizing it and transforming his imagination into a separate, secret entity. Dobson led him by describing the stages, from first viewing pornography to getting obsessed to acting out. Bundy agreed. "You look for more potent, more explicit, more graphic kinds of material. Like an addiction, you keep craving something which is harder and gives you a greater sense of excitement, until you reach the point where the pornography only goes so far."[15]

Dobson asked him what had pushed him into action. When Bundy had difficulty articulating it, Dobson asked him if he would call it a sexual frenzy.

"That's one way to describe it," said Bundy, "a compulsion, a building up of this destructive energy."[16] He then said that alcohol abuse was also part of the picture. When Dobson asked Bundy to describe his first murder, he compared it to "being possessed by something so awful and alien, and the next morning waking up and remembering what happened and realizing that in the eyes of the law, and certainly in the eyes of God, you're responsible."[17] He claimed to have been horrified—an attitude that contradicted the strutting he'd often done in court and for reporters' cameras. But the drive to kill had receded, he said, and he'd felt normal again. "Those of us who have been so influenced by violence in the media, particularly pornographic violence, are not some kind of inherent monsters. We are your sons and husbands. We grew up in regular families. Pornography can reach in and snatch a kid out of any house today."[18]

Apparently Bundy hadn't quite gone far enough, so Dobson gave him a hint. "Outside these walls, there are several hundred reporters that wanted to talk to you, and you asked me to come because you had something you wanted to say. You feel that hardcore pornography, and the door to it, soft-core pornography, is doing untold damage to other people and causing other women to be abused and killed the way you did."[19]

Bundy said that in prison, he'd met a lot of men who'd committed violence. Without exception, pornography had been instrumental. "The F.B.I.'s own study on serial homicide," he added, "shows that the most common interest among serial killers is pornography. It's true."[20]

He claimed that he could now feel the pain he'd caused to the victims' families. He then warned that there were many more predators just like him, still on the loose. In a moralistic tone, he decried the sexualized slasher films of the current era that would never have been shown when he was a boy. "There is no way in the world that killing me is going to restore those beautiful children to their parents and correct and soothe the pain. But there are lots of other kids playing in streets around the country today who are going to be dead tomorrow, and the next day, because other young people are reading and seeing the kinds of things that are available in the media today."[21]

During one part of the interview, Dobson asked Bundy if he had accepted the forgiveness of Jesus Christ as his savior. Bundy affirmed it and said he drew comfort from it as he approached his own "Valley of the Shadow of Death." Whenever he felt lonely, he said, he reassured himself that everyone faces death eventually.

Dobson also asked him what was going through his mind on this, his last day on Earth. Bundy seemed near tears as he admitted that he had not yet come to terms with it. He did not want to die, but in nearly the same breath he admitted that society needed protection from people like himself.

Bundy was executed the next day, February 24, 1989, and Dobson showed the tape on television. When Ann Rule viewed it, she commented that she wished she could believe in Bundy's apparent sincerity, "but all I can see in that Dobson tape is another Ted Bundy manipulation of our minds. . . . The blunt fact is that Ted Bundy was a liar. He lied most of his life and I think he lied at the end."[22] He'd told her that he had never purchased a detective magazine—the very medium he was describing to Dobson as the cause of his fatal addiction. She was concerned about the many young women who had watched the interview and had concluded that Bundy, this conniving, deceptive torturer and murderer of many young women, was actually a good man, now repentant and humble. They wrote to her in tears, wishing he wasn't dead.

Strangely, after he was cremated, Bundy's family acceded to his request to spread his ashes on the mountains in Washington State where he had dumped several victims.

But Bundy's execution was only one of the many headlines devoted to serial killers since his capture. Even before his trial for the Chi Omega murders, John Wayne Gacy had been unmasked and his activities seemed even more disturbing. Like Bundy, Gacy blamed it all on an inner entity.

CHAPTER 12

John Wayne Gacy and Helen Morrison

1

During the 1970s, thanks in part to the emergence of killers like Bundy, the FBI had developed the Behavioral Science Unit with a handful of elite investigators who focused on serial crime. As part of this program, Special Agent Robert Ressler started to do interviews with convicted offenders to lay the foundation for a computerized database. "By 1978, I had come up with the idea of improving our instructional capabilities by conducting in-depth research into violent criminal personalities," he stated. "I suggested we go into the prisons and interview violent offenders to get a better handle on them and formulate a foundation for criminal profiling."[1]

He was aware of Ziporyn's work with Speck and Reinhardt's *Sex Perversions and Sex Crimes*, as well as the latter psychiatrist's book about Starkweather. Although Starkweather was dead, Speck went onto Ressler's list. In order to acquire consistent information across cases, he devised a standard questionnaire and interview protocol and partnered with Special Agent John Douglas. The plan involved interviewing one hundred incarcerated individuals, although they ultimately managed to interview only thirty-six. Among them were Speck, Charles Manson, Frazier, Mullin, Kemper, and Sirhan Sirhan, the convicted assassin of Robert F. Kennedy. When some of these offenders seemed unable to articulate what they had done, the project skewed toward those who were bright and willing to offer details. Data were also collected about 118 victims, from both those who'd been killed as well as several people who'd survived an attempted murder. The goal of this study was to collect information about how the offenders had planned and committed murder, what they did during the incident, what kinds of fantasies they had, their immediate postincident behavior, and what they did to prepare for the next incident, if there was one (some interviewees were not serial offenders). The agents believed it was important to learn the offenders' state of mind during each stage of their crimes, and whether the criminal acts affected their routines in ways that people who knew them might notice. Ressler named this effort the Crime Personality Research Project.

The agents did extensive research before each interview on the target offender, often from prison records, trial transcripts, or newspaper reports. After they had collected enough data from the all-male sample for a study, they found that about a third of the offenders were white, just about half had been raised in a single-parent home, three-fourths complained about an indifferent or negligent parent, many had a psychiatric history and poor employment records, their mean IQ was just above average, three fourths had described some type of paraphilia, and the same percentage reported an experience of abuse (usually physical). While the research group was small and not a scientifically designed random sample, the information was helpful. They learned about offenders' values, homicidal ideation, thinking processes, levels of post-crime recall, sense of responsibility for a crime, and crime scene rituals, as well as factors that influenced their modus operandi (MO). Several agents used these data to write a comprehensive overview for law enforcement, the *Crime Classification Manual*, to provide for the investigative world an equivalent of the *Diagnostic and Statistical Manual of Mental Disorders*. One of the offenders they interviewed had killed at least thirty-three young men. He was John Wayne Gacy.

2

In December 1978, a team of police officers dug up the dirt floor of the crawl space of Gacy's home at 8213 Summerdale Avenue in Des Plaines, Illinois. He was a suspect in the recent disappearance of an adolescent named Rob Piest, and when an officer entered his home and noted the odor of death coming through a heat duct, he requested a search warrant. At the time, no one suspected what was about to occur. Gacy was a successful and well-connected contractor in the area who frequently hired young men to work for him; he entertained sick children and was popular with his neighbors. But he was also the last person known to have spoken to Piest, so the officers took the case seriously. Supposedly, Piest had gone to ask Gacy about a job and had not returned. There was nothing to indicate that he'd run away, and there were plenty of reasons for him to stay right where he was. There were no problems within his family and no issues at school. The police agreed that his disappearance was alarming.

Once Gacy realized he was a suspect, his behavior became erratic. At times, he would invite the officers tailing him to have dinner or a drink, and other times he would threaten them with his lawyer. Sometimes he acted as if he didn't have anything to hide, while other times he sped up in his car to try to lose his tail. Rather brazenly one day, he invited several officers into his home. That's when one of them recognized the smell of death. Gacy explained it away as dog urine, but his quick lie did not work. Soon, a team descended on the house, and almost at once, down in the muck-filled crawl space, they discovered decomposing human remains. The missing persons case exploded into one of the most notorious tales of a serial killer—one who liked to keep the bodies close by.

Over the course of several days, investigators excavated the entire crawl space and dug out the remains of twenty-nine young men, all in different states of decomposition. Some were just bones, but Piest was not among them. However, Gacy remained a suspect in his disappearance. Clearly, he had a preference for young men. As he was taken to jail, Gacy's house was dismantled and his entire yard dug up with a backhoe. Then several bodies were pulled from the Des Plaines River, including that of Rob Piest. Gacy had apparently run out of space under his house and had been using the river as his personal trash can. A team of investigators and forensic specialists started the difficult task of identifying the bodies. Since Gacy had piled several victims close together, the first task was to separate the comingled remains. To assist with identification, families of missing young men offered photos, X-rays, and dental records of their sons and brothers. Many were certain they had finally come to the end of their desperate search.

Gacy's typical victim, it turned out, was a Caucasian male in his teens or early twenties. Some had been runaways, and a few had sold themselves on the streets, but one had been a Marine and another had been married. Gacy claimed that each one had come to his home to enjoy drugs and alcohol. He'd killed them in self-defense or because they deserved it. How much of his account was true remains uncertain to this day, as he changed his story many times, including recanting his various confessions.

At times, Gacy killed two victims in a single night, and after each incident he was faced with what to do with the bodies. This was especially true when he still had a wife living there. There were times when he told members of his construction crew to dig grave-like holes, so he was planning ahead. The final total of found bodies was thirty-three, although many people believe that not all of Gacy's victims had been found. Gacy was charged with multiple counts of murder.

Upon his arrest, he pretended to have an alter personality whom he called "John Hanley." It was John, he said, who was responsible for whatever had happened. His attorneys offered a defense of insanity, so both sides hired mental health experts who put Gacy through a battery of assessments. Gacy's attorney then presented testimony that Gacy had experienced an "irresistible impulse" each time he had killed. Whenever he drank, he blacked out, so he had poor recollection of what had actually happened in these incidents. He simply had no way to stop himself from raping and killing his house guests. Each of his experts, whether psychiatrist or psychologist, affirmed some version of this finding.

However, the prosecutor effectively demonstrated that Gacy had planned several of the murders. In addition, he'd had clear recall about where he'd placed each body. He'd even drawn a map. This team's psychologist insisted that a person could not plan for an irresistible impulse, and it was ludicrous to believe that Gacy had done this on thirty-three separate occasions. The jury rejected the insanity defense, and Gacy was convicted. He then received the death penalty.[2]

Thanks to his enormous notoriety as the "killer clown," Gacy received many letters from correspondents, some of them looking for their own form of fame and some of them interested in studying him in a serious context. One person who kept in continuous touch with him for a period of fourteen years, starting before his trial, was psychiatrist Helen Morrison. Her aim was not just to learn more about him but also to acquire his brain after his execution for scientific study.

3

In 2004, Dr. Helen Morrison published *My Life among the Serial Killers*. A board-certified forensic psychiatrist, Morrison had by this time edited, authored, and coauthored four academic books and over one hundred articles. Besides child and adolescent psychiatry, she had a firm interest in serial killers, claiming to have interviewed eighty such offenders.

Morrison's method involved hours of interviews, so that she could see through a killer trying to mimic human emotional behavior. She typically continued to interview them even after their trials were over. From her experiences, she formed a theory that serial killers do not possess a concrete personality but only a chameleonic façade. They can keep up a charming persona for only so long, because they use it merely as a tool for manipulation. Behind the charm is a bestial state, lacking in humanity and full of rage. They dissociate well and can thus avoid moral questions, but if they reached the stage through psychiatric help where they could grasp the enormity of their acts and empathize with victims, they would commit suicide.

Morrison argues that because serial killers cannot fully appreciate what they're doing and cannot simply stop their behavior, they should be considered legally insane. What she calls an inability to control compulsions is associated with impulsivity. She devoted three chapters to her relationship with Gacy and details their discussions as they prepared for his trial. Gacy's first defense attorney, Sam Amirante, called her after reading an article in which she had claimed that most serial killers are never caught and that their reasons for killing are complex. She'd described them as Jekyll–Hyde dichotomies, disorganized when they kill but able to pull it together for their daily business.

Amirante explained that Gacy had first denied any involvement with what the police were finding under his house, but then had admitted to everything. Just as quickly, he'd recanted his confession. Morrison met Gacy in Cermak State Hospital at the Cook County Jail, in the area for mental health detainees called 3 North. At the time, Gacy had been incarcerated for nearly a year and was engaged in writing notes for his life story. He'd completed several jigsaw puzzles and had glued them to the wall. His cell was compulsively neat and clean, but Morrison had already decided that while he was organized in the small things, "he wasn't able to organize the big things like what went on inside his head."[3]

As Morrison entered, Gacy took charge, directing her where to sit. She noticed. But she also found him to be pleasant and fastidious, despite his obvious grandiose narcissism and the condescending attitude evident in everything he said. Morrison soon decided that Gacy was not a psychopath, because, as she put it, "a psychopath can plot and carry out complex schemes. Secondly, psychopaths have a structured personality that doctors can pinpoint, utilize and work with. . . . The psychopath has problems with the superego, where guilt and conscience reside . . . he's not scattered the way a serial killer is."[4] In her opinion, contrary to what most of her colleagues believed, a psychopath could be cured but a serial killer could not.

Gacy insisted to Morrison that he was innocent of any crime and believed he was being framed. Yet he also set up conditions for amnesia by claiming that he'd been taking massive amounts of illegal valium. He talked a lot—excessively—but she found that beneath it all was evidence of what had propelled him into rape and murder: anger and aggression. He seemed to be primarily angry at his father, a man whom he said had viewed him as "dumb and stupid" but whom he'd nevertheless tried to please. He never could.

In 1967, when Gacy was twenty-six, he'd been convicted of sexual assault on a teenage boy, whom he'd manipulated into a sexual encounter. During the investigation, police had discovered that this was no isolated incident. Despite Gacy's claim that the sex had always been consensual, it was clear that he'd been raping and strangling these boys into unconsciousness. This helped to end his first marriage and send him to prison. Upon his early release, a psychiatrist predicted that he was now safe.

Gacy told Morrison that there were two people inside his body, as well as fifteen distinct characters. The sex drive, "when it breaks in," was its own person, Jack Hanley. Supposedly, Jack "controlled" him, sometimes for an entire day. He asked Morrison, "How the hell do I get him out?"[5] She noticed that he did not display the classic symptoms of someone with multiple personality disorder, although his shifting moods indicated a lack of integration.

Morrison also interviewed a surviving victim, who'd been lured to Gacy's home with the promise of marijuana. Once inside, he said that Gacy had quickly attacked, knocking him out with chloroform and tying him up. When he revived, he found Gacy shoving dildos into his rectum, as well as a fireplace poker. But Gacy had not killed him. Instead, he'd dumped the young man into a weed-strewn lot. The victim had ended up in the hospital. He told the police about what Gacy had done to him, but no one had acted on his complaint. Morrison thought she'd gained little from the interview, but in one with Gacy's sister, she learned something important: Gacy had once sustained a head injury and had experienced several spells of blacking out. However, no physiological workup had shown that Gacy had ever suffered from a brain injury. That didn't mean it wasn't there; it just wasn't detectable by the machines.

Gacy's mother also agreed to speak to Morrison, telling her that when John was an infant she had given him daily enemas—a potentially significant fact—but later she denied she'd said this. She described John's childhood sleepwalking episodes and affirmed that she and her son had been quite close. Morrison thought this woman seemed to suffer from delusions at times.

Morrison also went driving around Bughouse Square to get a sense of Gacy's movements when he went hunting for boys. It was a three-acre park, renowned for how it once had attracted intellectual activity, but it had become seedy, a place to purchase drugs or solicit male prostitutes. Gacy apparently had worked out several approaches. Sometimes he'd posed as a cop to force them to accompany him, and sometimes as an affable guy just looking for company for the evening. He often offered alcohol or drugs.

The trial was Morrison's first experience as an expert witness in a criminal proceeding. She had read everything Amirante had about Gacy, including all the investigation reports that had been turned over to him, and had spent about sixty hours with the defendant. She felt certain she could show that he was a disturbed man, abnormal in his thinking, who was legally insane.

Her turn on the stand came last, on a Saturday morning.[6] By this time, most of the other mental health experts had stated or agreed that Gacy had experienced an irresistible impulse on thirty-three different occasions: under the influence of drugs and alcohol, his thinking processes had receded, rendering him unable to control his behavior. Morrison stated that Gacy was not just legally insane but also medically insane (i.e., psychotic). Others before her had diagnosed Gacy as having a paranoid form of schizophrenia but did not agree that this made him legally insane (i.e., unable to appreciate the wrongfulness of his actions). Morrison believed he had a complex network of mental illness, including "splitting," where the ego detaches from reality. She thought this was why he could not remember killing anyone. He also had a penchant for "projection," or casting his anger onto another person. She used Freudian concepts to explain this, and added that some symptoms are "autonomic," or beyond our control. Gacy's aggression, Morrison said, could rapidly shift into gear. Because he did not have the emotional structure to appropriately guide his anger, one minute he could entertain kids with a genuine sweetness, but then flash in an instant into rage. In addition, he did not see others as separate from himself, and his emotional life was primitive, like that of an infant. He'd developed an alter ego to handle things as an adult. "It was Bad Jack, not Gacy, who killed."[7]

On cross-examination, Morrison held her ground, believing that even though Gacy had interrupted the murder of Rob Piest to take a phone call, he still had not known what he was doing. She insisted that he'd been unable to control himself during his violent episodes. Although it was clear to other evaluators that Gacy was aware that his acts were against the law (and he'd previously served time for sexual assault), Morrison confidently stated that even if a police officer were standing at his elbow he would have committed his infamous rope trick, rapes, and murder. Nothing could have influenced him to stop.

However, along with the other defense psychiatrists, Morrison was unable to address a key issue: If Gacy had all these "irresistible impulses," why had he dug graves in advance? And if his memory for what he did was so blurred, how could he have drawn a map of his burial zone? In addition, when he realized he'd killed people, why hadn't he sought help for his problem? How could he allow thirty-three bodies to pile up?

Morrison states that she wanted to maintain a "research relationship" with him, because there was something to be gained for science. She asked Gacy to write down details from his dreams. Since he liked keeping track of every detail of his day, it should have been an easy task for him, but he did not send her any dream journals. He did send letters, mostly filled with mundane details of prison life. He also did numerous paintings of subjects like himself in his clown suit, Disney's seven dwarves, and different types of landscapes, earning about $10,000 from sales in two years. He sent some to Morrison, and when she looked at them she believed she could see Gacy's inner life in the depictions, especially his anger and depression.

Upon Gacy's execution in 1994, his family allowed Morrison to attend the autopsy and take his brain. She was certain she would find something that physically set him apart from normal people. However, the pathologist who worked with her found nothing abnormal in its structure. Undeterred, she has kept the organ preserved in the hope that future scientific developments will confirm her beliefs. Her effort to locate a neurological cause for extreme violence was on the forefront of a growing trend to identify neurological or chemical causes for violence. Since the early nineteenth century, psychiatrists have attempted to find a way to associate violence with some abnormal aspect of the brain. "I'm firmly convinced," Morrison wrote, "that there is something in the genes that leads a person to become a serial killer. In other words, he is a serial killer before he is born."[8]

Unlike most criminologists and forensic psychiatrists and psychologists, Morrison separates serial killers from psychopaths. She states that psychopaths are human, while serial killers are not. In other words, they're not sufficiently organized in their personality structure to qualify fully as psychopaths, even though her descriptions of their traits and behaviors align with those on Robert Hare's Psychopathy Checklist-Revised.[9]

After studying many up close, Morrison offers what serial killers share in common: besides not having motives or personality structures, they tend to be hypochondriacs and addicted to acts that result in the deaths of others. They are not psychopaths or mentally retarded. They haven't all been abused. They cannot be rehabilitated, in part because they're mentally primitive. Their crimes are not sexually motivated because they aren't mature enough. They are psychologically incomplete and they're uncontrollably addicted to killing. They pop up in all societies and historical eras.

Perhaps most controversial is Morrison's statement that serial killers lack a motive, even though many have admitted to motives that range from lust to anger to thrill to revenge. Some even espouse a mission, such as to rid the world of prostitutes. "What makes a serial killer?" Morrison queried during an interview in 2004. "After all these years, I still don't know. We try to give them motives, but they don't have any. They just do it."[10]

Not all clinical professionals who study violence accept this claim, and the next case presented helped the police to figure out a killer's psychological makeup, motive, and MO before he ever even met the man.

CHAPTER 13

Andrei Chikatilo and Alexander Bukhanovsky

1

Since the end of the 1970s, more serial killers have been identified in the United States than anywhere in the world, and case analysis took a back seat to focusing on the relationship of crime trends to specific social conditions. What was wrong in America that so many repetitive killers emerged? But then news in 1990 from the dismantled U.S.S.R featured the arrest of a man who'd been wanted for years for the murder and mutilation of more than fifty women and children. This was more than any victim total from an American killer. However, the FBI's behavioral analysis method had played a crucial role in linking the crimes and apprehending the killer, so the "bourgeois problem" had helped a country in denial recognize its own criminal products. Even so, a psychiatric analysis based on a long period of attention to behavioral details created the portrait of this killer. No one knew him quite like Dr. Alexander Olimpiyevich Bukhanovsky. His deep acquaintance with the killer derived not from reading a detailed self-analysis or watching post-conviction behavior, but was the result of an investment of time focusing on every angle of what this person had done. The FBI's Behavioral Science Unit was doing the same thing, but none had extensive psychological training and none had the time to devote like this to a single perpetrator. Unpaid but keenly interested, Bukhanovsky discussed the case with Rostov's chief investigator, Viktor Burakov, and read every crime scene document.

On girls and women, the offender usually damaged sexual organs or the abdomen. On boys, he'd mutilated the genitals and anus—and in one case, he'd apparently chewed out a tongue. He'd stabbed several victims in the eyes. The Russian investigation relied on archaic technology, which had made it difficult to organize an effective investigation. In fact, they were prohibited from publicizing the murders as a way to get much-needed public assistance.[1]

2

The case began when a man gathering firewood in a *lesopolosa*, a strip of trees planted to prevent erosion, discovered a set of decomposing remains. He reported them to the *militsia*, the authorities. The body wore no identifying clothing, but the length of hair strands and tiny holes in the ears for earrings suggested a female. A close inspection revealed stab wounds, including into the eye sockets and pelvis. The remains were soon identified as those of a missing thirteen-year-old, Lyubov Biryuk. Despite a thorough search, nothing was found that could help to identify the killer. The autopsy report showed that Lyubov's killer had attacked her from behind, stabbing her at least twenty-two times.

A railroad worker walking a track twenty miles away came across another set of remains of a nude adult female, face down, with the legs pulled apart. Like Lyubov, there were multiple stab wounds and lacerated eye sockets. Soon, two more victims turned up.

Viktor Burakov, from the criminology laboratory serving the Rostov police, became chief of the task force. With no definite leads, his unit examined older unsolved cases but also linked the killer to a ten-year-old girl who'd recently gone missing on her way to a music lesson. Four months later, the girl's body turned up in a field, stabbed a dozen times. Burakov realized he was looking for a vicious, sexually motivated serial killer who appeared to be escalating in viciousness.

Then, in another wooded area near Rostov-on-Don, a busy port city in southern Russia, a set of bones turned up in a gully. An examination linked them to the *lesopolosa* killer, as he was now called. In short order, the body of a young boy was discovered near Rostov's airport. Left in a thicket, he'd been stabbed in the eyes.

This new development was confusing. Basic knowledge about serial sex killers in the mid-1980s was that they had a preferred victim type, but this offender had killed all different types of victims: grown women, young girls, and boys. It seemed possible that there was more than one killer, but the perverse ritual contradicted this. Then things grew worse.

The mutilated remains of a young woman turned up in yet another wooded area. Her nipples had been removed with some jagged instrument—possibly chewed off—and her abdomen had been cut open. In addition, one eye socket was stabbed. Another victim, found shortly thereafter, bore similar wounds, although her eyes had been spared. Still, some of her internal organs were missing.

Then, early in 1984, another boy was stabbed in the neck multiple times and his genitals were missing. The killer had anally violated him and defecated nearby. However, in this victim, the medical examiner found semen in the anus, which revealed that the killer was a secretor with type AB blood.

That year, many more victims turned up in wooded areas, and a few of them were found not far from where previous bodies had been dumped. Investigators acquired one more piece of evidence: a size thirteen shoeprint. Traces of semen were lifted from the clothing of two victims, and witnesses had seen one of them following a tall, hollow-cheeked older man wearing glasses.

By the end of that summer, with twenty-four apparently linked victims, the killer shifted again. In one case, he removed the upper lip, in another the nose; he also left items in a victim's mouth or placed them inside the stomach he'd sliced open. Of more concern, he had stepped up his pace. Victims were popping up now at the rate of one or two a month.

The task force now numbered some two hundred men and women. One undercover officer watched a man in the Rostov bus station talking with a female adolescent, and when she left him to get on the bus, he walked over to another young woman. The officer approached him and asked his name. He said it was Andrei Chikatilo, adding that he managed a machinery supply company and was on a business trip. Why was he talking with young women? He'd once been a teacher, he said, and missed talking to young people. The officer let him go, but an agent followed him. When Chikatilo solicited a prostitute, he found himself under arrest. A search of his briefcase revealed a jar of Vaseline, a sharp kitchen knife, a piece of rope, and a dirty towel. These were hardly the items one expected to find for a business trip, so he was detained. Yet when Chikatilo proved to have type A blood, not the type AB found in the semen samples from the victims, he was released.

Looking for another approach, Burakov gathered a group of local psychiatrists and explained his case. They offered a few hunches, but came to no consensus. Some believed there was more than one offender. However, Dr. Alexander Bukhanovsky was a specialist in sexual pathology, and he agreed to look at the crime scene photos and autopsy reports to produce a "prospective portrait."

3

At one point, Bukhanovsky had been a suspect and he'd been followed to ascertain his whereabouts during certain periods of time. His father, a Polish Jew, lived in America. Bukhanovsky had been an outstanding student, served his two-year military stint, and gone on to medical school, specializing in the genetic conditions associated with schizophrenia. He was tall, imposing, and confident, prepared to be a pioneer in his field. In 1980, despite the fact that he could be sued, he was one of the first psychiatrists in the Soviet Union to study sexual deviance, specifically homosexuality and transsexuality. He'd even assisted several people with sex change transitions.[2] Later he would found the science of criminal psychiatry in Russia, but in 1984, when he entered the case, he was a member of the Department of Psychiatry at Rostov State Medical University.

When Burakov offered a few basics facts about the investigation and the likelihood of a sexual deviant as the offender, Bukhanovsky invited him into his office. Burakov already knew that Bukhanovsky was a maverick who might be open to trying something new. In addition, Bukhanovsky had a fifteen-year-old daughter, so the mangled bodies of young women concerned him on a personal level.

After two weeks, Bukhanovsky had produced a brief report that ran to about seven pages. There was one killer, he believed, who worked alone. He was a sexual deviate, but not homosexual, as the police believed. The offender suffered from sexual inadequacy and possibly from functional schizophrenia. It was possible that he stabbed the eyes of his victims because he superstitiously believed he left an image on them, as the last person they had seen as they died. He brutalized their corpses in frustration, as well as to arouse himself. A sadist, he had difficulty achieving orgasm unless he used cruelty. It was likely he'd had a difficult childhood. From the way the killings had escalated, it appeared that he was prompted by his need, and possibly by depression. Only killing in a savage frenzy gave him relief. Bukhanovsky believed that weather conditions might trigger him, or he might suffer from headaches. A social loner, he was not retarded, but could make a plan and follow it. In other words, he was a predator. He knew what he was doing. It was possible that he'd looked for medical information about his condition in a library or gone to a clinic, so the police could check such places for new leads.[3]

While this information was not as specific as he'd hoped, Burakov recognized that Soviet officials in their distant offices held wrongheaded notions about the kinds of suspects his task force should be strong-arming for confessions. (When all was said and done, he would reckon they had gained five false confessions and triggered a number of suicides.) Burakov kept in touch with Bukhanovsky as the case progressed, and they became working colleagues. Bukhanovsky found himself fascinated with the offender's compulsions and perversions.

4

Over the next ten months, only one body turned up—a young woman killed near Moscow. Burakov looked at the photos and decided that she was linked to his group. He also learned that three young boys had been raped and killed in that area, which made him wonder if the killer had moved, but then another murder occurred in the Ukraine. In a tree grove near a bus depot, an eighteen-year-old girl lay dead. She'd been cut up, and her mouth was stuffed with leaves. In addition, when she was identified, investigators learned that she had been homeless and thus vulnerable to being led away with the promise of food or alcohol. However, this time, there was more evidence. Red and blue threads were found under her fingernails, and police swabs picked up sweat that was consistent with type AB blood. Between her fingers was a strand of gray hair. This killer was apparently older than they'd realized.

Then the Ministry of Health admitted to an error in typing blood from saliva and sweat. There were rare "paradoxical" cases, the report stated, in which specimens were not consistent with the blood type. In other words, any of the suspects who'd been eliminated based on his blood type could still be the killer.

Officials in Moscow appointed a special investigator, Issa Kostoyev, to take over the *lesopolosa* murder case. Kostoyev dismissed Burakov's efforts. He thought they'd already met the killer but had not realized it. He had Richard von Krafft-Ebing's book about sexual deviance translated into Russian, and used items from *Crimes and Criminals in Western Culture* to better understand crimes that involved victim dismemberment and disfiguration.

Burakov continued to place his trust in Bukhanovsky, eventually allowing him to see the entire file so he could provide more details. Bukhanovsky spent months in 1987 without financial compensation, this time turning out a full sixty-five pages. He gathered weather data from the times of the crimes to assist his interpretation, and noted that the killer most often struck on a Tuesday or Thursday. He labeled the unknown suspect "Killer X." Seeing more photos and having read what he was able to find about criminal behavior, he had changed his mind about a few items and had added many, many more.

X, he reiterated, was in control of his actions; thus, he was not psychotic. He appeared to be narcissistic, which meant he probably considered himself superior to the investigators. However, his intelligence level, aside from his street smarts, was about average. He was heterosexual, so boys were merely a "vicarious surrogate." He seemed to need to watch people die, so he lured them into isolated areas. There, he probably would bludgeon them in the head to render them helpless. Once they were unconscious, he'd undress them. Even this part aroused him. But it was the stabbing behavior that most excited him. It was a symbolic way of sexually penetrating them, cutting shallow at first, and then going deeper and deeper. When he was ready, he would masturbate on or next to the bodies. He would remove organs to feel more in possession of the victims, and it was possible he consumed those that were missing.

Bukhanovsky found an interesting correlation: before most of the murders, the barometer had dropped. He surmised that this pressure might be his trigger, especially if it coincided with other stressors at home or work.

While Bukhanovsky remained vague about the offender's height and occupation, he now thought X's age was between forty-five and fifty, the age at which sexual perversions were most developed. (The strand of gray hair affirmed this.) The killer was conflicted and probably kept to himself, nurturing his rich fantasy life. Bukhanovsky could not tell if the man was married or had fathered children, but if he was married, his sexual relations would be abnormal. In addition, his wife did not intrude on his private time; he was able to keep his secrets. Although his killing habits were compulsive, if he sensed a threat of discovery, he could stop for a while. However, he would not cease altogether until he died or was arrested. Bukhanovsky thought there were several explanations for the sudden decrease in bodies. The offender might be hiding them more carefully, or he was ill, was traveling, or had been arrested for something.[4]

In April 1989, another body turned up, and it soon became clear that the *lesopolosa* killer was still active. The victim had been a sixteen-year-old boy and he'd been stabbed repeatedly, as well as mutilated in the crotch area. Then there were five more boys and a woman. Thus, Burakov had thirty-two unsolved, linked murders.

With limited resources, he devised a new strategy. He stationed undercover officers in the most likely train stations and in the woods nearby. Two victims had been found near a train station in Donleskhoz, but before Burakov's plan was enacted, the killer assaulted a retarded adolescent in this area, removing part of his tongue and his testicles. It was difficult for Burakov to realize how close they'd been to this incident, so he carefully examined every report his officers had made. Among them was one about Andrei Romanovich Chikatilo. He'd been at the Donleskhoz train station on November 6. When Burakov read it, his heart pounded. He remembered this name. The man had been picked up before in a train station. In this report, a witness said that Chikatilo had emerged from the woods with a red smear on his face. He'd immediately washed his hands. In his fifties, Chikatilo had gray hair—like the strand found on one victim. Since the blood-typing data were now useless, Chikatilo became a significant suspect.

Burakov learned that Chikatilo was married with two children. More interesting, he'd been fired from his teaching post after being accused of molesting a student. So, he had a deviant sexual history. He'd spent three months in jail for a petty offense, and during that time, no bodies had been found. In addition, his travel records coincided with murders in other areas suspected to be linked to the *lesopolosa* killer—including in Moscow.

However, the circumstantial evidence was weak. Burakov knew they'd need more to make a case, but when he made his report, Kostoyev ordered Chikatilo's arrest. On November 20, 1990, three officers approached Chikatilo and brought him in. By law, this gave Kostoyev ten days in which to extract a confession. During this time, a medical examination indicated that Chikatilo's semen had a weak B antibody, making it appear in semen and saliva that his A blood type was AB. (This would be a controversial finding, with criticism of the typing methods used in the Soviet Union, rather than the emergence of a true anomaly.)[5]

Nine days elapsed, and Kostoyev tried his best to get Chikatilo to confess to being the notorious serial killer. Burakov thought they should bring in Dr. Bukhanovsky, and Kostoyev finally acceded. The account he later gave indicates little about what occurred, but the account in which Bukhanovsky cooperated provides details from the unique session.[6] (Kostoyev would claim that Bukhanovsky had exaggerated his role in getting Chikatilo's confession.)

5

While talking with Kostoyev, Chikatilo asked to speak with a psychiatric professional, because he believed something was wrong with him. If he was granted this, he said, he'd confess. Kostoyev had little choice but to try this approach. He told Burakov to call in his psychiatrist.

Bukhanovsky agreed to question Chikatilo, but for his own scientific purposes, not for court. He was soon in a closed interrogation room with him. With a rush of excitement, the psychiatrist realized that Chikatilo nearly matched the man he'd gotten to know from crime scene data: ordinary, solitary, and nonthreatening. He sensed that the suspected offender wanted to talk with someone about his difficulties, so he introduced himself, and described the hours he'd spent thinking about Chikatilo and getting to know what had driven him. It seemed to him that this middle-aged, drooping, defeated man knew he had serious problems and was genuinely curious about what an educated mental health professional would reveal. Bukhanovsky read from his report and asked questions designed to let the prisoner vent. Chikatilo listened intently to the detailed excerpts. Whenever he commented, Bukhanovsky thought he displayed no remorse, only self-pity.

Finally, after several hours, Chikatilo agreed to confess to the officials, and what he told his interrogators was far more deviant than what they'd imagined. In fact, they did not even realize the extent of his activities, or that he'd begun killing in 1978, not 1984. Writing a biographical essay for Kostoyev, he said, "I gave myself to my work, my studies, my family, my children, my grandchildren, and there was nothing else in my life. But when I found myself in a different setting, I became a different person, uncontrollable, as if some evil force controlled me against my will and I could not resist."[7]

He'd begun in 1978 by killing a little girl inside a shack that he'd rented for privacy. He'd fantasized as he'd watched kids playing, and then one day, an opportunity arrived. He encountered a girl near his shack, so he invited her inside to rape her. (Initially, he said that he'd accidentally killed her while raping her near the river, but evidence on the body forced the truth.) When he failed to achieve an erection, he admitted, he substituted a knife. After she died, he tossed her body into the river.

Chikatilo then grew obsessed with this crime, and his fantasies became more violent. In 1981, as he attacked a girl he'd found begging for money or food, he bit off her nipple and swallowed it. To his surprise, this had made him ejaculate. To try to relive it, he'd taken her sexual organs away with him.

He was able to recount vivid details of each of the *lesopolosa* murders, and he described the different ways in which he'd followed people. He had learned their routes and habits, selecting people who seemed fairly easy. A few had been victims of opportunity; he'd seen them and had acted on impulse. His impotence, coupled with his wife's constant nagging, had made him enraged. If a female target ridiculed him, so much the worse for her. After a few of these sexual murders, he'd soon realized that violence and blood were key to his arousal.

To explain his brutality with the young male victims, Chikatilo said he'd envisioned them as war captives, and he'd be the hero for catching and torturing them. He would not reveal his motive for cutting off tongues and penises. With some of the women, Chikatilo would remove the uterus and place his semen inside. Sometimes he chewed on them as he walked away from the body, feeling an "animal satisfaction."

To assist the police, Chikatilo sketched a few of the crime scenes. He also added more victims than they'd realized: fifty-six in all. He claimed there was something wrong with him and he was sent for psychiatric testing. The psychiatrists administered a battery of standard assessments, such as the Rorschach Inkblot Test and the Minnesota Multiphasic Personality Inventory. He also underwent several different types of physiological examinations and daily clinical interviews. In addition, the doctors used the interrogation records to try to figure out his history and look for signs of genetic insanity in his family.[8]

Chikatilo had been born in the Ukraine in 1936 with a misshapen head from water on the brain. His father was in a prison camp in Russia, so his mother raised him and his younger sister on her own. He was exposed to a culture in which famine had been a significant factor. Millions had died, and stories had grown up about people engaging in cannibalism just to survive. In an interview, Chikatilo said his mother had revealed that his own brother had fallen victim to starving people. True or not, the possibility had scared him. But it had also aroused erotic feelings. Cannibalism became part of his fantasies.

Other children mocked young Andrei for his awkwardness, so he'd nurtured images of torturing them. His first sexual encounter had involved a struggle with a ten-year-old friend of his sister. Although he'd tried to repeat it, he had a difficult time getting girls interested in him. This made him angry. He disliked being humiliated.

When he returned from military service with the hope of getting married and raising a family, he suffered from erectile dysfunction. A girl he'd dated spread this rumor, and when he discovered how she'd publicly humiliated him, he envisioned tearing her to pieces. His sister took pity on him and arranged a marriage, but his new wife was scornful, especially when she learned he had to ejaculate outside her and push his semen in by hand. They had two children, but their sex life was otherwise nonexistent. After Chikatilo achieved a teaching certification, he found a job that he enjoyed. However, he developed an attraction to young girls. One day he molested one of his students, so he was summarily fired—yet another humiliation. He took solace in his fantasies.

It wasn't long before he committed his first murder, the girl he'd thrown into the river. Chikatilo believed he had an illness or mental defect that caused his uncontrollable desires. He asked for a specialist in sexual deviance and was sent to Moscow's Serbsky Institute. Neurologists there examined him and determined that he'd had brain damage since birth; it had adversely affected his ability to control his bladder and seminal emissions, and it implied that he also could not control other impulses. However, this part of the report received little attention as psychiatrists for the prosecution declared that Chikatilo was sane: he knew what he was doing, he had chosen to do it, and he could have stopped. He was also competent to stand trial.

Chikatilo went to trial on April 14, 1992, placed inside a large iron cage reserved for extreme offenders. The judge prohibited his lawyer from calling his own psychiatric experts who could speak about Chikatilo's long history of sexual problems; he could only cross-examine the prosecution's experts. Thus, it seemed clear which way the case would go. No one expected anything different. This man was a confessed killer and a lot of victims had suffered, as had their families. On October 14, Andrei Chikatilo was found guilty of five counts of molestation and fifty-two counts of murder. The judge sentenced him to be executed, and this took place less than two years later, on February 15, 1994.[9]

6

Since 1991, Alexander Bukhanovsky has directed the Phoenix Research Center for Treatment and Rehabilitation in Rostov-on-Don, Russia, the country's first private psychiatric center. Since his involvement in Chikatilo's case, Bukhanovsky has created a novel but controversial method of finding and treating compulsive serial offenders. Rostov seemingly had attracted a high number of them, with twenty-nine identified between 1984 and 1999. One rapist said that the psychiatrist had a way of inspiring him to talk about things he did not even know were inside his head. Bukhanovsky conducted brain scans, noting structural abnormalities in the frontal lobes. The goal with this approach is to one day cure people during the early phases of orgasmic conditioning, to channel their fantasies away from violence.

However, Bukhanovsky's treatments have raised ethical questions: as long as he is working with a criminal who seems earnest about stopping his behavior, he won't turn in the person to the police. These offenders must trust him, he says, in order to come for treatment. "Maybe I'm wrong to do this," he stated in 1999, "but it is in the interest of science."[10]

Bukhanovsky also continued to write profiles for the police, who had radically revised their notions about Western profiling procedures, and he organized an international symposium on serial killers in Russia. In 2005, he was invited to the FBI's international symposium on serial murder, offering his feedback for revisions to their earlier work on serial killers.

Despite the emergence of Bundy, Gacy, and Chikatilo, the world was in for yet another gruesome surprise. Bundy had been a necrophile, Gacy had kept bodies in his home, and Chikatilo was a cannibal, but Jeffrey Dahmer turned out to have all three habits, and then some.

CHAPTER 14

Jeffrey Dahmer
and Roy Ratcliff

1

When the police entered apartment 213 in the Oxford Apartments building in a crime-ridden area of Milwaukee, Wisconsin, they were stunned. Officers had been here only weeks earlier, but apparently they'd dismissed the noxious odor of decomposition that often permeated the low-rise building. Neighbors had complained about this smell for years, along with the sound of a power saw and some heavy thumps. However, little assistance had been forthcoming until a man wearing handcuffs ran from the place and insisted to police he'd nearly been killed.

It was late on July 22, 1991, and the quiet tenant who'd pointed a knife at the heart of this escapee was about to become world famous. After minor resistance, he was placed under arrest. Around his one-bedroom apartment, investigators found piles of Polaroid photos of men, mostly dead and mutilated. Lifting the lid of a boxlike freezer, they saw three frozen male heads and a torso. The refrigerator (devoid of food) held a box with another one, as well as human intestines, a piece of muscle, chunks of skin, and a frozen heart in three pieces. Investigators collected several skulls painted gray, as well as three bleached skulls, a scalp with hair attached, numerous bones, a bloodstained kettle containing hands and male genitalia, a bloodstained camera, a photographic diary of murdered men and boys, and parts of skeletons. Three decomposing torsos were stored in a fifty-five-gallon barrel full of acid, and in cupboards and drawers were chloroform, bleach, electric saws, an electric drill, rope, and formaldehyde. According to the photos, Dahmer had dismembered victims on a narrow art deco table in the living room, although a mattress on the floor was stained with blood. In all, horrified investigators found the remains of eleven different men scattered about this cramped, fly-infested abattoir.[1]

Recently fired from his job as a candy worker, Dahmer began a confession that would eventually take up 160 pages. Since 1978, he admitted, he had murdered and dismembered seventeen men. His first had occurred when he was just eighteen. He went on for hours, and his motives were just as shocking as the scene in his apartment. He'd tried out many things, from cannibalism to brain surgery to necrophilia. He'd also designed an altar, which he wanted to create from skulls and bones. This meant killing a number of men.

A shy, lonely child, Dahmer had long fantasized about having power over another person, especially a sexual slave, so when his parents abandoned the family home in Medina, Ohio, in 1978, going their separate ways, Dahmer, now eighteen, continued to live at the house and he exploited the sudden privacy. While out driving, he spotted an attractive young hitchhiker named Steve Hicks, so he offered an afternoon of drinking and getting high. Hicks accepted and got into the car. He stayed a few hours, but when Dahmer made a pass, Hicks rebuffed him and tried to leave, so Dahmer picked up a barbell and slammed it into his head. The unconscious body inspired an erotic rush, bringing up images from Dahmer's fantasies of dead bodies, so he strangled Hicks. This experience further aroused him, as did cutting the body into pieces for disposal, so he masturbated several times during the task. Ultimately, he buried the pieces in the woodsy backyard. (A search of the former Dahmer property turned up human bone and tooth fragments, confirming his story.)[2]

Dahmer eventually moved in with his grandmother, but despite being this close to someone who would be shocked by what he was doing, he felt compelled to experience another dead body. Reading about the funeral of a young man, he attended and made plans to go to the cemetery later and dig up the body. Thwarted, he turned to picking up men who were eager to get high or have a sexual encounter. He would entice, drug, and strangle them; have sex with their corpses; and dismember them—even in his grandmother's basement! Twice she'd complained to his father, Lionel, about the disgusting odors in the trash, but Dahmer always managed to talk his way out of discovery.

He told Lionel that he experimented with chemicals on chicken parts from a grocery store and on a dead raccoon he'd found on the street. Lionel searched the house but found nothing unusual except a smelly liquid near the garbage cans that he thought was ordinary meat juice. "I allowed myself to believe Jeff," Lionel mused in his bleak memoir, *A Father's Story*, "to accept all his answers regardless of how implausible they might seem. . . . More than anything, I allowed myself to believe that there was a line in Jeff, a line he wouldn't cross. . . . My life became an exercise in avoidance and denial."[3]

For example, Lionel found a stolen store mannequin in Jeff's closet and allowed him to dismiss it as an impulsive "prank"; similarly, the .357

Magnum under Jeff's bed was a "target pistol." While Lionel admitted he was unaware of his son's substance abuse problem (although his wife once found the boy drunk and passed out at the age of fourteen), he did notice that Jeffrey often seemed vacant—"enclosed"—as if thinking about nothing. When Jeff was charged with child molestation, Lionel believed the lie that Jeff had not known the boy was a child and that he'd "touched" the boy by accident. On another occasion in the grandmother's basement, Lionel asked Jeff about a foot-square sealed box. Jeff had resisted opening it. During the ensuing stand-off, Lionel relented after Jeff said he would show his father the following day. Just as Jeff had claimed, when he opened it the next day, it contained only pornographic magazines. Lionel learned later that had he opened the box the day before, he'd have seen the head of a recently murdered young man.

Dahmer killed one man during a drunken tryst in a hotel. Not sure what else to do, he went out and bought a suitcase large enough for a body, placed the corpse inside, and rolled the suitcase through the lobby. He took his victim back to his grandmother's house to dismember. Finally, fearing discovery, Dahmer persuaded his father that he should have his own apartment. There, his addiction escalated.

In an effort to create zombies, for example, Dahmer drilled holes into the skulls of unconscious men and injected either acid or boiling water. He wanted to prevent the person he'd picked up from remembering that he lived elsewhere or from having a desire to leave. One victim actually survived for two days after this treatment, but in the end, the experiment failed. Still, Dahmer had other ideas. He removed skin from his victims' faces to preserve as masks, but he discovered that they deteriorated too fast to be of much use. Thus, he persuaded his father to purchase the freezer. Regarding the bone altar, Dahmer reportedly believed that it would supernaturally improve his social and financial status.

At times Dahmer seemed careless. He'd leave the apartment with a living victim inside, and sometimes they escaped. In addition, outsiders who might notice the smell were allowed in. However, he probably felt empowered when police officers who questioned him on several occasions accepted his lies.[4] It was almost too easy.

Between 1987 and 1991, Dahmer had murdered and dismembered sixteen of his victims. He had taken numerous photos, alive and dead, and with parts in various arrangements, as well as with corpses standing in stiffened rigor. "They helped him to 'preserve' his guests, acted as a tonic to his fantasy, and enhanced his feeling of closeness."[5]

Not surprising to anyone, Dahmer's attorney decided to go with an insanity defense. There was no way to say that he had not done these things, but what better example of delusional psychosis might there be? (Even serial killer John Wayne Gacy, who'd buried over two dozen men in the crawl space under his house, said, "If Jeffrey Dahmer isn't insane, I'd hate like hell to see the guy who is.")

2

By this time, the *Diagnostic and Statistical Manual of Mental Disorders* had gone into its third edition in 1980 (DSM-III), with a revision in 1987 (DSM-III-R), and talks were under way for the next edition, the DSM-IV. The push was for greater inclusiveness of psychiatric conditions, but the move away from the previous criteria for a psychopath toward personality disorder, antisocial type, made the concept too diffuse for many researchers. Other countries continued to rely on the Hare Psychopathy Checklist, while American psychiatrists and psychologists focused on the antisocial personality. The word "sociopath" had been in vogue for some time, which added to the terminological confusion. For the DSM-III, controversy arose over the decision to delete "neurosis," which represented a push away from "unscientific" psychoanalytic jargon, so a compromise was reached to include it in parentheses.

A new feature of the DSM-III was its multiaxial organization, with symptom-based disorders versus personality disorders, along with axes for medical conditions and stressors. This manual now included 265 mental illnesses (292 in the revised version), based on distinctly defined categories.[6] However, there was much overlap among the personality disorders, which created diagnostic confusion.[7]

Before Dahmer's trial in 1992, the judge granted court-appointed psychiatrist George Palermo permission to perform a computerized axial tomography (CAT) scan on Dahmer's brain as an adjunct to psychological testing and a chromosome analysis. Palermo spent about fourteen hours with Dahmer and made this observation: "He generally provided direct and full answers to questions. . . . He was emotionally tranquil and at ease as he recounted the many memories pertinent to his offenses. He gave the impression of being happy to finally be able to unburden his conscience of his horrendous crimes."[8]

With Palermo and other interviewers, Dahmer was articulate and willing to provide details. He would meticulously describe such things as removing the arm of a corpse, tasting the muscle fiber of a bicep, or gaining sexual gratification from body parts. Although he insisted he'd wanted to stop, this admission seemed disingenuous to many. Robert K. Ressler, who had been a member of the FBI's Behavioral Science

Unit, interviewed Dahmer for several hours. He had the impression that Dahmer was proud of his acts and pleased with all the attention he was getting. To his mind, the man was just evil.[9]

Dahmer changed his plea to guilty but insane a week before the trial began, leaving the jury to determine the appropriate sentence—prison or a psychiatric facility. His attorney, Gerald Boyle, wanted them to view Dahmer as clearly insane, so he opened with the statement, "Jeffrey Dahmer wants a body. A body. That's his fantasy. A body." It seemed to him incomprehensible that anyone could view this desire, along with Dahmer's ability to live day after day in close quarters with stinking human remains, as anything but psychotic.

At issue was not whether Dahmer was ill, but how well he could control his actions. For the defense, Dr. Fred Berlin, who was director of the Sexual Disorder Clinic at Johns Hopkins University, testified that Dahmer suffered from necrophilia, an erotic attraction to corpses. The most common motive for this disorder was the attempt to gain possession of an unresisting or nonrejecting partner. Because Dahmer could not choose his form of sexual attraction and because it was so compelling that he would kill to acquire a corpse, Berlin stated that Dahmer had been unable to conform his conduct according to the law. He might have known it was wrong, but he had a compulsion, a "cancer of the mind." However, Berlin had spent only about five hours with Dahmer and admitted that Dahmer had become an adept liar.

Dr. Judith Becker, professor of psychiatry and psychology at the University of Arizona, described several incidents from Dahmer's childhood that she believed had distorted his sense of reality and of right and wrong. Another psychiatrist echoed her, but no one submitted truly compelling testimony that Dahmer had been devoid of choice in what he did to his victims. That he'd been a lonely, neglected child who indulged in substance abuse and who believed he was responsible for his parents' endless disputes was not contested, but that this had been instrumental in developing an uncontrollable condition seemed far-fetched to many.

The mental health experts for the court viewed his behavior quite differently. In court (and in later writings), Palermo said that Dahmer was the type of hostile, aggressive person—a sexual sadist—who had developed repetitive negative behaviors to fend off injuries to his ego. He believed that Dahmer lived in terror of being alone and that, while disturbed, he was not psychotic. He was also not a necrophile. He believed that the bodies had simultaneously attracted and repelled him, similar to his self-ambivalence. By destroying beautiful males, he could get rid of his emotional turmoil over his attraction to men. "His hostility-out was a counterpart to his hostility-in.["10] If he had not committed murder, Palermo believed, he might have committed suicide. Thus, his necro-sadism was both self-assertion and self-preservation. He killed to keep victims silent.

Dr. Samuel Friedman, also court appointed, agreed that Dahmer had been a lonely person looking for company in an inappropriate manner. His luring and killing had been too strategic to be considered psychotic, although he did suffer from a mental disease. Friedman administered the Minnesota Multiphasic Personality Inventory (MMPI) to him, finding that Dahmer came up high on the scales for Psychopathic Deviate and Schizophrenia. People with this type have odd and peculiar thoughts and behavior; they're often mistrustful and needy, and they lack empathy. They tend to conflate sexuality with aggression and have difficulty controlling their anger. Dahmer was alienated from others and from himself, felt depressed and hopeless, and was paranoid.[11]

For the prosecution, Dr. Fred Fosdel stated that Dahmer was cruel, cunning, and calculating. He had targeted vulnerable young men, had lied to them, and was unconcerned with their terror and suffering. While he practiced necrophilia, this was not his dominant sexual preference. Affirming this, Dr. Park Dietz, a forensic psychiatrist from UCLA, went even further. He denied that Dahmer was suffering from any known mental illness or that he was a sadist. He also stated that having a paraphilia is merely a motive; it does not imply an inability to control one's behavior. The evidence proved, he said, that Dahmer had prepared for each murder. He became intoxicated to reduce his inhibitions, which was done by choice and which contradicted any claim that his crimes were impulsive. Dahmer's clarity of mind in lying to police and the care he took to avoid detection and arrest indicated that despite a peculiar paraphilia and compulsive sex drive, Dahmer was not a disorganized individual. He had known what he was doing, had known it was illegal and immoral, and had chosen to do it anyway.[12]

During all this psychiatric testimony, the jury learned about how Dahmer had kept a private pet cemetery as a child, using his chemistry set on animal pelts, and that he began to compulsively masturbate to images of animal dissection. Also, by the age of fourteen, Dahmer was already pondering the use of a corpse for sex. He would ride around in a car with a friend who enjoyed hitting dogs, and he viewed his first murder the way many other men thought of their first sexual conquest. In fact, before he killed Stephen Hicks, he'd gone out to bludgeon a jogger into unconsciousness with a baseball bat so he could rape him, but the jogger had not shown up that day. Dahmer's father suggested that a neighbor had molested him when he was eight, but Dahmer denied it. He could achieve an erection, he'd said, only if his sexual partner was unconscious, and he found the heat arising from a dismembered body arousing. He needed that sense of complete control but did not wish to reciprocate by subjecting himself to others' desires. He claimed to have eaten body parts because he believed the victims would return to life through him. So that he could continue to have sex with them, he left his victims lying around for as long as possible (sometimes he showered with them in the tub), and when he finally had to dispose of them, he felt a loss. There were times when he felt evil, but the feeling subsided when he would drink and get another victim under his control. Then he felt alive. The prosecutor would later sum this up: "He was the engineer of a rolling train."[13]

On February 15, 1992, Dahmer was found guilty of fifteen counts of first-degree murder and sentenced to fifteen terms of life imprisonment. In May that year in an Ohio court, he received a sixteenth term for the murder of Stephen Hicks, his first victim. The remains of the seventeenth victim were never found.

3

A solar eclipse occurred on May 10, 1994, the day John Wayne Gacy was executed. To many, it seemed to be a celestial condemnation of another event not far away—the baptism into the Christian faith of Jeffrey Dahmer. Months earlier, he'd sought out a minister who would assist him to affirm his new faith, and Roy Ratcliff had responded.

Ratcliff was the minister of a Wisconsin congregation in the Church of Christ. A graduate of Oklahoma Christian University, to this point he'd had no experience counseling prisoners. He ended up becoming Dahmer's religious mentor by default, and he learned by experience what being up close and personal with a serial killer was like. While he had no direct experience counseling prisoners, he did have some training in counseling, rather than being an investigator or reporter, his narrative is included in this book. In fact, he did see Dahmer in ways that others missed, because as they met once a week over the course of seven months, Dahmer seemingly grew to trust Ratcliff as a friend. While Ratcliff's naïveté is present—and even admitted—this was still a privileged access to an extreme offender by someone with psychological perspective. Ratcliff wrote about his experience in *Dark Journey, Deep Grace.*

Dahmer had grown up in the Church of Christ. He'd attended regularly until he was five, but during his parents' personal troubles religion took a back seat. However, it remained important to his father who, while a scientist, was also a firm Creationist. For a brief time when Dahmer lived with his grandmother, he'd tried to resume his association with a church, but had found it too boring. Only after he was sentenced to life in prison did Dahmer seek to reengage with the church of his childhood.

A woman in Virginia, Mary Mott, had sent Dahmer a twelve-part correspondence course on Bible study. He accepted it and sent the lessons to her to grade. He then petitioned to be rebaptized and asked Mott to assist. "I want to accept the Lord," he told her in a note. "Would you please try to find someone to bring a baptistery tank to the prison?" She thought he had done well on the lessons, so she made some calls.

Ratcliff accepted the task, asking Dahmer to discuss the matter with him first. They met for an hour in a small room in the prison, and Dahmer admitted that he'd been nervous that the church would prohibit him from being a member. Ratcliff, who noted with surprise the small size of Dahmer's hands—the instruments of death—reassured him that grace was afforded to all sinners. Dahmer stated that he wanted to be cleansed of his sins. Ratcliff listened to him and grew convinced that Dahmer had made a true spiritual conversion, so he agreed to perform the ritual. He was unable to find someone to donate a baptistery tub for full immersion, but the chaplain suggested the infirmary's whirlpool as a viable substitute.

On Tuesday, May 10, 1994, at the Columbia Correctional Institution, Ratcliff performed the sacred ceremony. Accompanied by the prison chaplain and two guards, they walked down a long corridor to the prison infirmary.[14] Apparently, Dahmer was under the impression that the baptism would not be valid unless Ratcliff mentioned *only* the name of Jesus, but Ratcliff convinced him to allow the use of the more generic formula that included the Father and Holy Spirit. Dahmer changed into a baptismal robe, and they entered the pool together.

Dahmer did admit remorse and a desire to follow the path of righteousness, so Ratcliff had a duty to recognize this. By church doctrine, no sin is greater than any other, including murder. Ratcliff was aware that prisoners will often fake a spiritual transformation to gain some privileges, yet the tenets of his faith allowed for anyone to be washed clean and spiritually renewed in the eyes of God. "After his arrest," Ratcliff wrote, "a veil was lifted. He began to see order and design in the universe. He began to see the case for God."[15]

Ratcliff admitted that he could not be absolutely certain what was in Dahmer's heart, but from what he saw in Dahmer's eyes and body language, he was convinced of his sincerity. "I listened to the tone of his voice and observed his mannerisms and I am convinced he was totally sincere in his desire."[16] Strangely, he didn't recognize how odd it was that Dahmer refused to allow Mary Mott to visit him. She was the one who'd sent him a Bible and the study course. She wanted to visit him to see for

herself the miraculous change in him, but since she was not a church official, Dahmer would have had to place her on his official visitor's list. This
he refused to do, as it "was too complicated" and would displace someone else. His decision seemed strikingly indifferent toward, even dismis-
sive of, the person who had supposedly changed his life for the better, but
Ratcliff made no comment.

He stated that, over the course of the next several months, he became
better acquainted with Dahmer as a "brother in faith." He described how
Dahmer preferred the King James translation and how he "revered the Bible
as God's Word."[17] They met weekly to discuss Bible verses and theology, and
Ratcliff caught a glimpse of Dahmer's stubborn side. He'd get an idea in his
head and not yield, even though Ratcliff clearly had more knowledge on the
subject. "He was also influenced deeply toward the pre-millennial viewpoint
of the second coming of Christ and the once-saved-always-saved viewpoint
of the televangelists. But he was very open to Bible study and studied on his
own as much as he could. He also read everything that was sent to him."[18]
Ratcliff stated that their meeting was often the highlight of his week.

Most mental health experts who studied Dahmer would agree that he
was primed for a religious conversion. After all, he'd built a shrine from
the parts of his victims and viewed this altar-in-progress as a way to gain
greater powers. To study the Bible and then ask for a regular visit would
have surprised no one who knew him.

There was no indication from the discussions that Ratcliff includes in
his book that Dahmer had arrived at any profound self-insight. (In fact,
he complained that none of the psychiatrists who interviewed him offered
him any answers about his motives, although it's clear that they had done
so in court.) The only time he seemed to actually address his crimes was
when he told Ratcliff that he was annoyed about people sending him pornography that featured disgusting poses of naked women. In this context,
he admitted that before each assault he'd primed himself with pornography. Ratcliff, clearly uncomfortable, suggested to Dahmer that he report
this violation of the mail system to prison officials. (Dahmer had to have
known he had this option; it seemed more likely that talking with Ratcliff
about "the mail" was his way of opening a door into a sensitive topic, but
Ratcliff failed to see the subtle opportunity.)

The appearance of the religious lessons was this: Dahmer had killed
seventeen young men and had enjoyed sexually violating their corpses.
He'd taken their lives and deprived their families of their sons and brothers. But with baptism, Dahmer learned he could erase this from his soul
and conscience and still get to heaven. No one asked the question that
offers a proving ground: Were he to become free again, postbaptism,

would he really be reformed or would he indulge again in his desire for the dead? Ratcliff avoided this issue. For him, the point appeared to be whether Dahmer was spiritually clean, not profoundly repentant.

In fact, Dahmer showed the same selfishness. He complained how an attorney had funneled his meager prison wages to benefit relatives of victims, whining that this had made his life more difficult. Ratcliff seemed to agree, likewise viewing the attorney as a bully: "Is the point of prison to torment him over and over again?"[19] Dahmer also mentioned that other inmates were making it difficult for him to live according to the tenets of his new faith. Ratcliff failed to recognize this "poor me" attitude. He did not see the possibility that Dahmer was just a psychopath who wanted his life to be organized around *his* needs.

At no time does Ratcliff state that Dahmer clearly expressed remorse over the way he'd tormented victims (the lone survivor had described four hours of psychological torture). His recognition of doing wrong remained vague and general: "Although it took bad things to bring me to the position I'm in, I don't think I would have any kind of faith in God without them."[20] He did mention feeling badly about his victims' families but in the same breath expressed anger over their attorneys' theft of his prison salary. Ratcliff offers only vague and idealistic notions about the newly baptized soul, so it's not clear how (or if) Dahmer made a life-changing shift. In light of the heinousness of his crimes, Ratcliff might have illuminated Dahmer's change a little more if he'd shown how Dahmer now viewed those acts from a spiritual perspective. Perhaps Dahmer should have been full of self-loathing, and should have been eager to discuss it with a spiritual mentor; perhaps he should have been contemplating suicide, as Morrison suggests (Chapter 12). Yet with Dahmer, apparently, Ratcliff got mostly distance. Dahmer kept him at arm's length with intellectual discussion and argument.

However, Ratcliff believed they grew closer, especially when they prayed together. "When you pray with someone about his family, and he lets you into his life and allows you to see his concerns and feel his worries, you get closer to his heart. You begin to feel friendship."[21]

Ratcliff saw Dahmer the day before Thanksgiving. He led the prayer and talked animatedly about the Bible. He also gave Ratcliff a Thanksgiving card, in which he'd expressed gratitude for their sessions. It was the first time Ratcliff seemed to realize they'd become friends—the first time in seven months. Dahmer's card included a line, "Thank you for your friendship."[22] Apparently, he'd never stated this before to Ratcliff. Nor had he ever told his father about his spiritual renewal, or thanked him for materials he'd sent on Creationism. Dahmer seemed singularly ungrateful to people unless they were able to do something for him in his most immediate circumstances. Ratcliff doesn't comment, but it's evident in what he leaves out.

4

On November 28, 1994, Christopher Scarver murdered Jeffrey Dahmer and another inmate at the Columbia Correctional Institute. They had been mopping the shower and toilet area when Scarver used a bar from the weights to bash in Dahmer's skull—an odd poetic justice, in light of the way Dahmer had done this to his first victim, Stephen Hicks. Dahmer died quickly thereafter.

Despite Dahmer's request that in the event of his death there be no funeral service, Lionel Dahmer conducted a private memorial service for the family. Ratcliff conducted it on December 2, 1994. Lionel spoke about his positive memories of his son, but few others had much to say, so Ratcliff summarized the point of the service. Although he had never recorded such a conversation, he said that Dahmer had confessed great remorse for his crimes and wished he could do something for the victims' families. "He turned to God," Ratcliff said, "because there was no one else to turn to, but he showed great courage in his daring to ask the question, 'Is heaven for me too?' I think many people are resentful of him for asking that question. But he dared to ask, and he dared to believe the answer."[23]

At the postmortem, Dr. Robert Huntington removed Dahmer's brain and preserved it under lock and key in formaldehyde at the University of Wisconsin Medical School. Several researchers requested brain tissue samples and hair follicles, but Huntington insisted on a court order, even from Dahmer's mother, Joyce Flint.[24] She hoped to donate his brain to science, based on a conversation she'd had with Georgetown neurologist Jonathan Pincus, but Dahmer had expressly wished to be cremated, so Lionel Dahmer blocked the request. (Dahmer also had insisted on no funeral, open casket, headstone, or grave marker.)

A few weeks after Dahmer's body was finally cremated (with his ashes shared between his parents), there was a hearing about the disposition of his brain. On October 3, 1995, before the Honorable Daniel S. George, Flint's attorney, Robert Fennig, presented his case. He said that Dr. Pincus had the funds to transport, store, and examine the brain. In a fax, Pincus had written that the opportunity to study the brain of an offender like Jeffrey Dahmer "represents an unparalleled chance to possibly determine what neurological factors could have contributed to his bizarre criminal behavior." Dr. Huntington, who had also hoped for such an opportunity, warned that this brain "had to be studied carefully" to guard against premature conclusions. He offered some parameters for how such a study should be carried out.

Lionel Dahmer opposed the entire enterprise, wishing only to honor his son's request.

The judge saw merit in both sides. He was concerned, however, that Dr. Pincus had been vague about just how he would examine Dahmer's brain. "The court is looking at a balancing kind of test there in terms of the potential good or bad that could come from the research. . . . What sort of comparisons are going to be made? . . . I am extremely concerned over the propriety of the handling of this issue and the avoidance of exploitation."[25] He decided that Fennig should bring to the court a more detailed analytical proposal from Dr. Pincus, as well as have Dr. Pincus give testimony by phone.

There is no record of another such hearing, and no mention in Pincus's book aside from a conversation with Flint. Only two months later, on December 12, Judge George ordered Dahmer's brain to be cremated, as per his wishes.

After Dahmer's death, Ratcliff learned that the notorious inmate had misled a number of women into believing he loved them, by sending each the same poetry and the same types of letters. Clearly, the entire time Dahmer was professing his newfound life in Christ, he was dishonestly manipulating these women. Ratcliff dismissed it as their misunderstanding. He seemed unable to see Dahmer's truly dark, nasty side. He even admitted, "I will never know why Jeff developed these relationships, and how they fit into the puzzle of Jeffrey Dahmer."[26] Nevertheless, he started up a prison-based ministry to continue his work with others.

In his book, Ratcliff added a final chapter addressing the question of Dahmer's sanity. "I never saw anything in him to indicate to me that he was off track, mentally," he said. "As far as I can tell, Jeff was as sane as anyone."[27] He presented himself as normal, was able to engage in a conversation, could look Ratcliff in the eye, and seemed to be fully aware of his situation. Only once did Dahmer show how he had compartmentalized his murders, when they were discussing the book of Hebrews. He had told Ratcliff, "When I was committing my crimes, I felt that as long as I could hide them away so no one could see what I'd done, I wouldn't have to deal with my crimes or think about them. I could go about acting like a normal person and feel like a normal person."[28] Ratcliff's conclusion was that anyone who leaves God out of his or her life is capable of doing what Dahmer did.

While the issue of Dahmer's sanity set mental health professionals against one another, no case has been quite as controversial on this legal issue as the family massacre committed by a woman, Andrea Yates.

CHAPTER 15

Andrea Yates and Phillip Resnick

1

A 911 call in Houston, Texas, on the morning of June 20, 2001, opened a stunning case of family mass murder. Andrea Pia Yates, thirty-six, had drowned all five of her children. She had then turned herself in to await justice in a Texas county infamous for its support of the death penalty. Her defense attorneys quickly learned about one of the most renowned experts in child murder, Dr. Phillip Resnick. He agreed to reduce his typical fees so they could invite him to examine the severely depressed defendant. Although Resnick did not befriend her in the manner of some of the cases that precede this one, he felt real concern and spent a great deal of time on her peculiar case. He also included his interns in the process.

Resnick is an adjunct professor at Case Western Reserve University (CWRU) School of Law and director of the Division of Forensic Psychiatry at the CWRU School of Medicine, as well as director of the Court Psychiatric Clinic at the Justice Center in Cleveland, Ohio. Practicing psychiatry for over forty years, he has specialized in forensics for most of this time and is a past president of the American Academy of Psychiatry and the Law.

In 1969, while Resnick was still a resident in psychiatry, he treated two women who had murdered their own children. He then reviewed the literature on this subject from as far back as 1751 (getting a grant to have papers in thirteen languages translated) and published what would become a seminal article on the phenomenon of child murder by parents. He included 131 cases (eighty-eight mothers and forty-three fathers), observing two basic types: the killing of an unwanted neonate and the killing of a child with a clear place in the family. He coined the term "neonaticide" for the former and defined "filicide" as taking place at least twenty-four hours after birth. Among the cases, he described a man who had drilled a hole through his son's heart, a woman who thought her child was shrinking, and a woman who tried taking her daughter with her off a cliff. Neither was killed, but the mother realized that her daughter would have terrible scars if she survived, so she tried choking the girl. When this did not work, she picked up a rock and bludgeoned her to death. During therapy sessions, she described unexpressed anger she felt toward her own mother. Using the known cases, Resnick designed a classification system according to motive: (1) altruistic, (2) acutely psychotic, (3) unwanted child, (4) accidental, and (5) spouse revenge. He also explored the psychodynamics of filicide as displaced aggression and offered some warning signs.[1]

In a later report, Resnick showed that the filicide rate had risen dramatically. Between 1976 and 1985, 384 filicides were reported on average every year, with young children at the greatest risk. The older they were, the more likely it was that the father would be the fatal parent. Resnick noted a relief of tension accompanying many incidents and added that while assessing murder in response to a command hallucination, the treating physician should always consider the possibility of malingering. Resnick described a study of twenty women who were found to be not guilty by reason of insanity. Most of them had been suicidal, delusional, or both, and they had tended to view the deceased child as defective, in need of saving from a terrible future fate, or demonically possessed. Few had attempted to conceal their crime.[2]

Early in his education, Resnick had attended law courses and national meetings, thereby teaching himself medical forensics. It was not until 1979 that the National Institute of Mental Health offered funding for forensic fellowships, so he started one to assist students to specialize in this area. "I view my identity as a teacher," he said in an interview. "That's a very important part of who I am. It's very gratifying for me."[3]

Those who know Resnick describe his strong and compassionate mentoring style, and he agrees that this is a firm part of his educational program:

> I currently have three fellows each year. I began this in 1979 with one fellow each year for the first ten years or so, before it expanded. That person would accompany me to just about everything I did. So I developed a personal mentoring relationship. Even with three fellows, I come to care about each of them. I want each of them to succeed. I take each fellow on at least one out-of-town trip, so in the Andrea Yates case, I took two fellows with me who sat in on the evaluations. At least two observed my courtroom testimony so that they got to experience it from the beginning to the end—meeting the attorney, gathering background information, seeing the evaluation, writing the report, and seeing it through with testimony.

One intern remarked on Resnick's drive for consistency and accuracy: "First, he teaches you to write reports with complete medical certainty. Then he cross-examines you to make sure you've thought your opinion through and are confident of it."[4]

Recognized as a national leader in forensic psychiatry, Resnick testified before Congress after the controversial not guilty by reason of insanity (NGRI) verdict in the case of John Hinckley Jr., who'd shot President Ronald Reagan in 1981. He has served on a number of forensic task forces and been on the editorial boards of several prominent forensic journals. As a result, he has been involved in many nationally publicized cases, such as those of William Kennedy Smith, Timothy McVeigh, Theodore Kaczynski, and Susan Smith (a mother who'd also drowned her children, albeit by car). He is meticulous, prepared, and thoroughly versed in both the psychological and legal angles of any case he accepts. "I found a niche," he once said, "for my ability to be articulate, analytical and logical."[5]

Yates's defense team, George Parnham and Wendell Odom, asked him to make an assessment. "I received a call from one of the two defense attorneys," he said, "and at the time they had had several recommendations that I be the one to do this, because I had written on child murder. When I'm called by either a prosecutor or defense attorney, what I agree to do is evaluate the case and then I may or may not be helpful. So, there's no problem in taking a case. It doesn't mean that I'm committed to testifying in favor of the person employing me. It just means that I'm willing to review the case, and I'm paid for my time in reviewing the case, whether I'm helpful or not. In a case of child murder, that's my interest and this case was also getting national attention. It was not a hard call to agree to see her."

First, he learned the facts.

2

Yates was married and had five young children, three of whom she was homeschooling. On the fatal morning, she waited for Rusty, her husband, to leave for work. Aware that her mother-in-law would be there in an hour, she knew there was no time to waste. She entered the bathroom and turned on the water to fill up the tub. Starting with Paul, the three-year-old named for a biblical figure, Yates held him under the water. After a brief struggle, he succumbed. Yates would later say that she had viewed herself as a bad mother for having led them astray. Their souls, she believed, were in danger of being claimed by Satan. She thought the age of accountability was around ten, and they would have to die before then. Otherwise, she envisioned a terrible fate for at least four of them: one would be hit by a truck, one would become a serial killer, one would become a prostitute, and one would die a tragic death. Their disobedience also meant that Satan was present in her home. If she killed them, she believed, the state would execute her, which would cast the devil from the world.

After she laid out Paul on a double bed and pulled a sheet over his body, Yates drowned Luke, John, and Mary. Seven-year-old Noah, the oldest, walked in and saw what she was doing to Mary, so he ran. Yates chased him down. He struggled, proving difficult to kill, but she managed it. She left him lying in feces-polluted water while she placed Mary on the bed with her other three brothers, with John's arm wrapped around her. Then, exhausted, Yates called 911 to tell a dispatcher to send an ambulance. She also wanted the police. When this task was done, she called Rusty. It was the children, she said. Panicked, he drove home and arrived just after the police.

The central issue was whether Yates had killed her children while in a state of psychosis or had done it merely to escape a life that had become a burden. That is, had she experienced a psychotic break or was she a cold-blooded mass murderer?

At Houston Police Department headquarters, where Yates was placed in a cell, a police officer prepared to record her statement. She stared straight ahead, the pupils of her eyes pinprick size, as she slowly mumbled that she was aware of her rights. From these signs, she looked like she might be on drugs or have a brain hemorrhage.

"Who killed your children?" the officer asked.

"I killed my children." Her face was blank.

"Why did you kill your children?"

"Because I'm a bad mother."[6]

For about seventeen minutes, they pressed her for details of exactly what she had done that morning. She tried to respond, but she could barely speak. The entire interview was recorded on video.

The police charged Yates with intentionally causing the deaths of three of the children with a deadly weapon (water). Through an attorney, she pleaded NGRI, but right away her competency to be tried came under question. On the videotape, she said that Satan was visiting her there in her cell. He'd been speaking to her. She insisted that she did not need an attorney and she would not enter a plea of not guilty, and then asked that her hair be cut into the shape of a crown. She explained that 666, the number of the Antichrist, had been imprinted on her scalp, so she needed to shave her head to make it visible. In addition, she thought that hidden cameras in her home, as well as in her mother-in-law's glasses, had been monitoring the quality of her child care.[7] She had not killed herself that morning, she explained, because only the state could kill Satan, and this had to be done to prevent him from completing a prophecy about a catastrophe. The mental health professionals who evaluated her thought she was one of the sickest people they had ever seen.

One psychiatrist asked Andrea what she thought was going to happen to her children. She mumbled that God would "take them up." He reversed the question and asked what might have happened if they were still alive. She said she thought they would have continued to stumble, which would ensure that they'd go to hell.

Puzzled, he asked what they had done that was so bad. She responded that they didn't treat Rusty's mother with respect, clarifying this with "They didn't do things God likes." It was her fault, she insisted, for neglecting them.[8]

Resnick visited about three weeks after the incident, and while Yates was now on medication, she was still in bad shape. "She was very sad," he recalled, "and she wasn't showing much emotion, so I would not describe her in my first meeting as highly likable or engaging, but she obviously was severely ill, so in that sense, my heart went out to her. I knew that somewhere down the line, she was going to come to the nonpsychotic realization that she had needlessly killed her children . . . as she did. And then of course she went through the terrible agony, crying and moaning, so that I felt sympathetic toward her." He thought she suffered from a schizoaffective disorder.

Resnick, an expert on malingering, also considered this angle, but believed that there was no evidence for it. "In every case, I certainly consider malingering, and in the Yates case it was never a suspicion, because we have a well-documented psychiatric history, we have the absence of a rational motive, and we have a woman who loved her children very much."

He also went to the Yates home where the homicides had occurred. "Rusty drove me out there, rather than the attorney. He showed me around the house and showed me the bus that was still in their backyard, that they had lived in before they bought the home. There were pictures drawn by the kids still on the walls. He showed me the bathtub where they were drowned and the master bedroom, where the kids had been laid out on the bed, so it was moving to relive it with him, since it was so personal for him. I found him to be like a typical engineer, not much emotion, kind of methodical, hyperlogical, although when he talked about the kids, he did show some emotion. He had a matter-of-fact quality as he told me his story."

As the defense team put together a case, they insisted on a full competency hearing to determine if Yates was able to assist adequately in her own defense. They pieced together her life story to try to determine at what point it had occurred to her to kill her children, and why.

3

In high school, Andrea Kennedy had been an accomplished student, class valedictorian, and captain of her swim team. She went on to graduate from the School of Nursing at the University of Texas, finding a good job at a cancer center. In 1993, she married Russell Yates, an engineer at NASA. A year later, they had their first child, and shortly thereafter Andrea experienced auditory hallucinations of a male voice telling her to use a kitchen knife to kill the child. However, she kept her frightening secrets to herself, aiming at being a "supermom." She gave birth to four more children in quick succession, and people who knew her said that she was a terrific mother. However, of her four siblings, one had bipolar disorder and two others had suffered from depression.

Rusty followed the teachings of a preacher named Michael Woroniecki, a self-proclaimed "prophet" who was so belligerent in public about sinners going to hell that he was often in trouble. Rusty purchased a thirty-eight-foot touring bus from the man and had his family live in it. When Yates had more children, her family pressured Rusty to move them into a regular home. He did so, but Andrea had come under the preacher's spell. As she read letters from him and his wife, and referred to the Bible verses they quoted to her, she feared that she was a poor mother and thus doomed to go to hell. The more she read of Woroniecki's ramblings, the more worried she grew. She was especially focused on Luke 17:2: "It would be better for him if a millstone were hung around his neck and he were thrown into the sea than that he should cause one of these little ones to stumble."

In 1999, shortly after the birth of her fourth child, Yates sank into a serious state of depression. She overdosed on drugs, so Rusty rushed her into treatment. She took an antidepressant, Zoloft, but when the insurance coverage ended, she was discharged. Then Rusty came home one day to discover her in the bathroom, terrified and pressing a knife to her throat. She intended to kill herself to prevent hurting someone else. Once again, he got her hospitalized. Another doctor prescribed the antipsychotic Haldol, and she improved. Doctors warned her against having another child, as she would certainly have more problems with depression, but soon she had another child, Mary. She seemed to be all right, but a few months later, Yates's father died and she was so overcome with stress that she stopped eating or caring for the children. Rusty's mother pitched in, but Yates began to read the Bible compulsively, and at one point she filled the bathtub for no apparent reason. Again, she was treated, wavering between selective mutism and fits of screaming, but she was then taken off the antipsychotic medication and put back into her husband's care. The discharging physician warned him not to leave her alone with the children. On the morning of the murders, he thought she would be all right for the brief period before his mother arrived. But it was the very opportunity she'd been waiting for.[9]

4

Resnick brought his interns to observe his interview with Yates.[10] They met in a conference room at the Harris County jail, and Resnick gently asked Yates to tell him what she had done on the morning she killed her family. Still within her delusion, she described with little show of emotion what had occurred. Resnick knew that an insanity case would be difficult to win in Texas, but he also knew that if he believed that Yates had truly been unable to appreciate what she had done, due to a mental disease, he would do his part. She would need an advocate.

He explained:

> In Texas, the insanity standard is a narrow standard. There's actually research showing that the test, whether it's a little broader or narrower, does not make a lot of statistical difference. However, Houston, which is in Harris County, is a very conservative county. They put more people on death row—if they were a state, they would be third after Texas and Virginia. So, it's a very conservative area, and then the crime was somewhat heinous, with five children dying, so I knew it would be an uphill fight. I told that to the defense attorneys, not just because of the narrow insanity defense but because of public attitudes.

On September 18, jury selection began for the competency proceeding. Yates's attorneys provided extensive documentation on her considerable history of mental illness. There was little doubt that she'd had a number of reactive episodes of near-psychotic depression. Their experts insisted she was not ready for a trial, while the prosecution experts intended to say she was competent. Because Yates had been on medication throughout the summer, her mental state had improved. She was aware of her surroundings and could hold a coherent conversation, but she experienced difficulty remembering things and still had delusions about Satan. Her intelligence had tested above average and, most important for competency, she seemed to understand her situation.

Dr. Lauren Marangell testified about the way the brain changes during different psychological states such as those through which Yates had gone. She had mapped Yates's psychotic episodes since 1999 and had concluded that, with continued treatment, Yates would eventually be competent. However, she was not presently competent to fully participate in her defense.

The prosecutor questioned Dr. Steve Rubenzer, who had administered several competency examinations to Yates, as well as the Minnesota Multiphasic Personality Inventory (MMPI). He believed that her comprehension had improved and that she passed the state's competency requirements. However, he believed that Yates had a serious mental illness, that she was not malingering, and that her psychotic features were in only partial remission. She apparently did believe that Satan still inhabited her and expected that with a death warrant Governor George W. Bush (who was not even the governor of Texas any longer) would destroy him.

On September 24, the jury deemed Yates competent to stand trial.[11]

That November, Resnick returned to question Yates again, this time in preparation for her trial. "By that time," he said, "she was no longer psychotic, whereas in the first interview, she was still psychotic and still thought that what she had done was right for her children. In the second interview, she was wracked with guilt and felt terrible about what she had done." No longer did she believe her apocalyptic visions about saving the world from Satan, and without this deific decree, she was bereft. She recalled how Noah had shouted, "I'm sorry, Mommy!" and how she'd placed each of her other children on the bed.

Resnick had interviewed many people who knew Yates, collected numerous reports, and talked with the prison psychiatrists. He'd even read letters that Yates had written to family members. His task was to work within the Texas definition of "insanity," aware that the "appreciation of wrongfulness" can mean different things under the influence of a psychotic delusion. He explained:

> The Texas law uses the word, "know," rather than "appreciate." "Appreciate" allows a little more wiggle room of "emotionally understand" as well as "intellectually understand." One thing I had the attorneys do was research Texas law on whether the word "wrongfulness" had been interpreted in case law as being restricted to legal wrongfulness or could it allow her to believe that what she did was morally right? Fourteen state jurisdictions have addressed that issue, the last time I researched it; eight favored limiting it to legal wrongfulness and six allowed moral wrongfulness. Rather than addressing that issue head-on, Texas said, "That's not

the question—the question is just whether the person thought that what they were doing was right." So Texas begged the issue. When I testified, I conceded that she knew that what she was doing was against the law, but rather than say, "In my opinion, she knew that what she was doing was morally right," I chose to phrase it, "She knew that what she was doing was right for her children, even though she knew it was against the law."

Among the issues was how much Yates's religious notions had influenced her delusional state. Resnick said:

I had a lot of press asking, "Do all Texas home-schooling religious people kill their children?" The way I would phrase it is this: religion was the trellis along which the delusions grew, so that if someone becomes delusional and they're deeply religious, it's not surprising that the delusions would involve religious themes. So the religion didn't make her psychotic, but when she became psychotic, the psychotic themes had to do with religion. She was raised Catholic initially, and Woroniecki had a powerful influence on Rusty, so she was pulled in and did read that literature, which talked about Satan being a very real, day-to-day figure in her life. So, yes, I do believe that her perceptions of religion were strongly influenced by Woroniecki, and that became some of the framework. Then she became psychotic, and that's what she built her psychotic thinking around.

Another issue that always crops up with a high-profile insanity case is the political climate. Resnick pointed out:

When there's so much press, prosecutors tend to feel under the gun. They have to look like they're tough, so they're less willing to plea bargain. They have to posture themselves to be demanding. I don't think this should have been a death penalty indictment, because of her obvious mental illness, and when it came down to the trial, although the prosecutors were vigorous in fighting against the insanity defense, when it came to the penalty phase, they presented no new witnesses, and in effect said to the jury, do what you think is right. In the appeal to the Texas Court of Criminal Appeals, one of the arguments was that the real reason they had indicted for the death penalty was to select a jury which was death qualified, so they would be even more conservative. Evidence for this was the lack of effort they made in the penalty phase.

5

Prosecutors Joe Owmby and Kaylynn Williford went for the death penalty on three counts of first-degree murder (holding the other two for a later trial, if needed). Because Yates pleaded NGRI, her team had to prove it with a preponderance of evidence. Yet to make her able to assist, she had been treated with powerful antipsychotic medications. The woman the jury saw was, in many significant ways, not the same woman who had killed her children, although she still believed she should die for her crimes. Yates was therefore at a serious disadvantage. In addition, under Texas law, the jury could not be told the consequences of acquitting her.[12]

Her trial, held in 2002, became a battlefield for experts in mental illness. Yates's defense team presented her history of depression, delusions, suicide attempts, and uneven success in treatment. They offered research about how postpartum mood swings can evoke psychotic episodes. Yet the primary legal issue—her mental state at the time of the crime—overshadowed her prior years of psychological decline. The prosecution played her 911 call, as well as her initial confession. The jury also viewed home videos of the Yates children, laughing and playing. Pairs of pajamas showed just how small and defenseless these children had been.

Nine psychiatrists and two psychologists testified for the defense. Six of these professionals had seen Yates within hours or days of the killings. Resnick was the defense team's key expert. He explained that Yates had long suffered from psychotic delusions, as evidenced in four hospitalizations, and had believed that she had been right to kill her children. In her mind, it had been an altruistic act, even if irrational. "There is no rational explanation to drown five children as a devoted mother unless you believe it's in their interest," he testified. Yates thought that killing them was tantamount to saving them from Satan, and she had willingly sacrificed her own soul for theirs. He acknowledged that she knew that her actions were *legally* wrong, but she had believed they were *morally* right. Nothing she did could be construed as trying to hide her activities, because she believed a camera was monitoring her. The homicides had been difficult for her emotionally, but she believed they had to be done.

The prosecution called only one witness, Dr. Park Dietz, an equally renowned forensic psychiatrist and a persuasive expert, albeit with no experience in treating postpartum depression. He had taped his November 2001 interview with Yates, showing in her own words that at the time of the killings she'd believed that Satan possessed and directed her; she'd admitted to Dietz that she was determined to do whatever Satan said. Dietz testified that "the fact that she regards it as coming from Satan is the first indication of her knowing that this is wrong. . . . She doesn't think this is a good idea that comes from God."[13]

Yates had also told him that by killing her children before they did something truly terrible, she was ensuring their salvation. They would be safe only in heaven. Whenever Dietz asked her whether she knew that her acts were wrong, she always admitted that she did. In fact, she said, it had all been planned. She'd been looking for the right opportunity for at least a month. She also accepted the consequences. She believed that God would not approve of her act, which even more clearly indicated to Dietz that she knew it was wrong, and he interpreted the act of covering the bodies with a sheet as evidence of guilt. He later said that he was entitled to apply logic to the thinking of a mentally ill person because Yates had seemed psychologically ready to engage in killing her children.[14] According to Dietz, the fact that she had not comforted or reassured them in death (a misrepresentation, since he acknowledged that she had described putting Mary into John's arms for protection)[15] indicated that she had not been bestowing love and protection. Ordinarily when a person keeps a criminal plan secret, Dietz told the jury, he or she knows it's wrong. He acknowledged that Yates was mentally ill, but he believed that her most extreme symptoms had occurred *after* she was arrested.[16]

Dietz also had learned that Yates was an avid viewer of the television show *Law and Order*, for which he consulted, and he stated that an episode of that show in which a mother drowns her child in a bathtub and then fakes insanity had inspired the murders. His observation gave Yates's actions the quality of premeditation (i.e., he made sense of something that otherwise made little sense).

After closing arguments, the jury convicted Yates of first-degree murder. However, instead of the death penalty, they gave her life in prison. There, she attempted to starve herself to death and was hospitalized.

Three years later, there was a surprising development. On January 6, 2005, an appeals court overturned Yates's conviction. While her attorneys had appealed on numerous legal grounds, the item that stood out involved part of Dietz's testimony. The episode of *Law and Order* that he'd cited, which had featured a mother drowning her children and beating the rap with an insanity defense, in fact had not existed: no such episode had been written or aired, so it had been a false statement. (He'd attempted to correct it, but had been assured it would not be an issue.) Since the prosecutor had drawn a connection to it via Yates's known interest in the program, implying that she'd gotten the idea to malinger a mental illness in order to get away with killing her children, the First Appeals Court decided that Dietz's status as an expert might have unduly influenced the jury. If so, the false statement had precipitated a miscarriage of justice.

Yates went back to a much less publicized trial, and Resnick convinced a second jury that she had been unable to recognize that her actions were wrong. He pointed out that Dietz had seen Yates after she had been on medication for five months, so when she answered his questions, she could not have exhibited her original state of mind. Dietz was present as well, but this time the outcome was different: Yates was found NGRI. "She had changed by then," Resnick recalled. "She was much less thin, and she had more relatedness in terms of connecting with people, so she looked very different. When she first went to prison, her suicide efforts occurred there. She was eventually transferred to a psychiatric hospital." He was aware that this jury had not been "death qualified," so its members had possibly been more liberal.

Asked if he thought Yates might one day get out, Resnick responded affirmatively. "I do, but I think that, politically, it will be hard for the judge to let her out. Often the presiding judge, who is elected, doesn't want to take the heat. Will she get out in 15 or 20 years? I think, yes, but not in the next five or eight years."

In an article, Resnick summarized the difficulty he thought Yates would face in the future: "Women who have killed their children while they were psychotic find it difficult to forgive themselves even after society has forgiven them."[17]

Another notion about evil entered into the next case, wherein a psychiatrist developed a scale to measure different degrees of evil. He came face-to-face with the worst type in his encounter with serial killer Tommy Lynn Sells.

CHAPTER 16

Tommy Lynn Sells and Michael Stone

1

The use of the word "evil" to describe an offender is understandably controversial, especially by a twenty-first-century psychiatrist. Most such professionals prefer a more clinical descriptor, believing that "evil" makes laypeople think of Satan. On a jury, for example, someone pondering the case of Jeffrey Dahmer, Carl Panzram, or Richard Speck might make a moral judgment that filters the clinical assessment, assigning to "evil" defendants an extreme punishment. However, this issue does not deter forensic psychiatrist Michael Stone, a professor of clinical psychiatry at Columbia University College of Physicians and Surgeons in Manhattan. He has spoken to many offenders at Creedmoor and Mid-Hudson Psychiatric Centers, where he consults. Stone is formerly the host of a Discovery series, *Most Evil*; is the author of ten books, including *The Anatomy of Evil*; and has invented a Scale of Evil, based loosely on Dante's *Inferno*. The categories derive from his own responses to a rising level of malice and sadism found in many criminal acts. In fact, he has examined the concept of evil from numerous angles, including philosophy, theology, psychology, neurology, and medicine. Thus, a Scale of Evil that places these acts in perspective seems appropriate. "We're talking about people who commit breathtaking acts," he stated, "who do so repeatedly, who know what they're doing, and [who] are doing it in peacetime, under no threat to themselves." It was time, he believed, to give their behavior "the proper appellation."[1]

Stone may possess the world's largest collection of true crime biographies, as well as an impressive array of antique medical and psychiatric texts in his hand-carved floor-to-ceiling bookshelves. He has penned an exhaustive history of psychiatry, *Healing the Mind*, and from his immense volume of research, he devised criteria for the different degrees of evil. He explained:

I used my responses to different murders and other violent crimes I read about as my yardstick. I tried to rank the various crimes and criminals according to how horrific and shocking they were, and according to the level of suffering that their acts imposed on the victims. After reading about one hundred biographies of criminals, I ended up with twenty-two categories. I anchored the scale to a "zero" point, where there was no evil at all: that was for "justified homicide," category number one. Then came crimes of passion, the first level of evil, category number 2. At the opposite end, level number 22, was murder after prolonged torture of the most heinous type—or even torture of that sort without murder. Now that I've read almost 700 such books and have interviewed violent criminals in many more places, I still use the same scale, although I've found a few [offenders] who are difficult to place in a precise way.[2]

One of Stone's mentors was the psychoanalyst Otto Kernberg, a former director at the Menninger Clinic who had crystallized the complexities of narcissism and the organization of a borderline personality. He developed a framework for coordinating personality disorders along dimensions of severity and pioneered the defense mechanism of the "split-self," which occurs when someone cannot fully integrate disparate emotions like love and hate. Perhaps most relevant to the notion of evil is Kernberg's description of pathological or malignant narcissism.

Stone points out that the scale's focus is on murderers, although he also includes serial rape and extreme cruelty that precipitated a suicide. "The common trait that runs through almost all of the categories from number 9 through number 22 is the element of malice."[3] Those people who are truly evil are also extremely narcissistic, as well as callous, manipulative, and lacking in remorse (i.e., classic psychopaths). "Armed with those dreadful qualities," said Stone, "a person is capable of just about anything."[4]

Lest anyone think the science is lacking, Stone researched recent social science findings as well as the latest data about the violent brain. He recognizes that there is no single causal factor, no "common route," by which people become evil. There's no "evil gene," although heredity can be a factor. So might a major mental illness, a low arousal rate, a brain disorder or injury, a form of autism called Asperger's syndrome, a violent role model, substance abuse, impaired judgment, neural immaturity, or seething unresolved resentment. Each person appears to have his or her own pathway, and the same constellation of factors that precipitate violent aggression in one person may have a very different effect on another. "If we wanted to narrow our focus to single out the personality configuration that is connected with particular closeness to our concept of evil," Stone writes, "it would be at the place where psychopathy, sadistic personality, and schizoid/autistic-spectrum disorders all come together."[5] When one adds the adrenaline rush that certain people get from committing evil, you have the mechanisms of addiction. That is, a person who harms others and enjoys it will most likely do it again—with more intensity.

"As for the childhood development of narcissistic/psychopathic killers," Stone added, "many had been treated with either brutality or neglect (or both) by their parents—which seems to have some explanatory value. But more intriguing are the ones brought up in normal families, especially the *adoptees* in normal families (like serial killer Gerald Stano or Lawrence Bittaker—the latter with whom I correspond). Clearly, there is a strong genetic component to psychopathy, such that some psychopaths, even though never abused or neglected, go on to commit horrific crimes—thanks in part to their congenital deficiency in compassion."

Although Stone did not create the scale to assist the criminal justice system, he can see applications:

> In states that use the death penalty, for example, I would want to see that punishment reserved for the truly depraved torturers and not for crimes of passion where the killer happens to kill several people at once, as in the case of Coy Wayne Wesbrook who killed his ex-wife when she invited him for a "reconciliation." She was giving sex to two men at once, and two others in the front room were making fun of Wayne. Being a good Texan, Wayne went to his truck, got his rifle, and blew all five away. Because there were so many bodies, even Texas couldn't look the other way, so they put him on Death Row—and then gave him a stay of execution. My point: capital punishment is currently used rather indiscriminately and should be thought of only for the most heinous crimes—and then only where the evidence is at the level of 100% proof.

Some offenders stand out for their brutality, for example David Parker Ray, who devised a fiendish torture chamber he called his "Toy Box," but a few have been surprising. "I was surprised by Tommy Lynn Sells, on death row in Texas. I assumed I'd hate him and want to pull the switch on him myself. But when I interviewed him, I was struck by his candor and openness about his dreadful childhood and about the terrible crimes he committed. He was willing to explain to me how his crimes gave him a temporary surcease from the rageful and vengeful feelings he had stored up over the years because of his maltreatment. So I ended up with some respect and sympathy for him."

2

Tommy Lynn Sells wore a tombstone tattoo on his arm with the name of his dead twin sister on it. She had died during infancy from spinal meningitis, while he had survived. He was never certain who his father had been. The child of an unwed mother, Sells had developed a sense of insecurity, as he was shunted to his aunt's home to live. By the time he was seven, he was drinking alcohol. By age ten, he'd moved on to marijuana, and by thirteen he was on his own, abandoned by his family. Within a few days, he'd taken out his fear and rage on a woman he didn't know, pistol-whipping her. He then started to drift. He was only a week past his fifteenth birthday when he committed his first murder in 1979. Sells had entered a home in Mississippi to rob it when the homeowner caught him, so he shot the man. From there, it was easier to do it again, and Sells claimed to have killed several more men over the next few years, often during scuffles.[6] (Since his initial confession, he has added a story that his first murder occurred after he saw a man giving oral sex to a boy, and he flashed back to an image of being sexually abused himself, so he retrieved a weapon and killed this man in a blind rage.)[7]

In 1981, Sells found his mother and sisters again in Little Rock, Arkansas. However, when he tried a sexual move on his mother in the shower, she kicked him out. Sells signed himself into a psychiatric clinic, but no one there offered a treatment plan for his existential lament: "I don't know who I am." Still, they noticed how angry he seemed, and the results of diagnostic testing indicated that he felt unloved. He disliked himself and how he seemed to be the reason for the trouble at home. The psychiatrist recommended regular therapy sessions, which would amount to a form of anger management. Sells agreed, but he went to only five before he left the clinic.[8]

Thus, he continued to drink and to kill; he also tried heroin. When he was nineteen, Sells entered the home of Thomas Gill and beat his wife and four-year-old daughter to death. Only when he stole a car did he get caught. He went to prison for a brief stint, and, once free again, he used a baseball bat to kill a young woman and her son.

Sells drifted around the country, possibly killing people he didn't remember. He claimed he woke up from a blackout with someone else's blood on his clothes, and he was near where a young woman's skeletal remains were found years later. Sells's aggression soon became more sadistic. One man who picked him up in Illinois and kindly brought him home for a meal ended up shot in the head, with his penis severed off. His heavily pregnant wife and his son were beaten to death with a baseball bat, which made the woman spontaneously give birth. Sells battered the newborn infant as well, and then stuffed the bat into its mother's vagina.

Many of his victims were hitchhikers or transients, but among them were parents and their young children. He received a few short prison sentences, and each time he was released he took up where he'd left off and continued killing people. He also married several times and had two children.

It was a ten-year-old girl in Del Rio, Texas, who ended Sells's reign of cross-country terror. At 4:00 A.M. on December 31, 1999, he climbed through a window to enter the double-wide trailer of an acquaintance, Terry Harris, while Harris was away. He'd seen Harris's thirteen-year-old daughter, Kaylene, at a store and found her enticing. Once inside the trailer, he made his way to her bedroom. There, he assaulted and killed her, stabbing her sixteen times, and then slit the throat of Krystal Surles, a friend spending the night on the top bunk. She had witnessed the whole thing and begged for her life. Sells was merciless, but when he slipped from the house, Krystal managed to run to a neighbor and get help. Despite her critical injury, she fought to live. She was determined to get justice for Kaylene. As best as she could from her hospital bed, she described Sells to authorities, and when he was arrested a few days later, she identified him. Later she testified at his trial, finally putting him away for good. He received a death sentence.⁹

Nevertheless, a psychologist for the defense indicated that Sells had an abnormal electroencephalogram (EEG) that suggested that the executive part of his brain did not communicate well with the primitive parts; thus, he had no means to thwart his aggression. This could have resulted from the high fever he'd suffered as a baby when he had spinal meningitis, or from his constant and varied substance abuse.¹⁰

Sells quickly offered a lengthy and detailed confession about all the murders he'd committed over the past two decades.¹¹ Not all of the murders were corroborated, in part because the remains could not be located. The estimate of his murders ranges from thirteen to seventy, and one confession freed a mother who'd been convicted of killing her own son. However, killers who seek notoriety often falsely claim a high number of victims, so as of this writing, Sells's confession is the only link to the majority of his crimes.¹²

3

Stone was angry about some of the things he'd read before he met Sells:

> I felt like killing him when I first encountered Tommy, for all the terrible things he'd done, but when I began interviewing him, speaking

by phone-to-phone through the glass partition that separates death-row prisoners from persons addressing them, I said, "Well, Tommy, I guess they got these three inches of glass here, so I don't kill you and you don't kill me!" He laughingly replied, with his Texan twang, "You got that raght!" That was his first bit of candor that "broke the ice" for me and gave me a more positive feeling toward him, which I hadn't at all anticipated.

As Stone interviewed Sells and then engaged in a more personal correspondence with him, he found the killer to remain remarkably candid. To Stone, Sells described his childhood and the violations he'd endured before he'd begun to hit back. He also admitted to the adrenaline rush he'd experienced whenever he slit someone's throat and "saw the blood rushing out."[13] Usually, a murder had the effect of dampening his hunger for violence, but it always returned. For him, murder was a fix, like heroin to a drug habit. Stone finds this description to be consistent with brain research on repetitive violence.

Sells, he says, is among the 30 percent of serial offenders whose parents were substance abusers. Sells also described a man he'd lived with for a while when he was eight who had sexually abused him. Supposedly, his mother seduced him, too (and he claimed that his grandmother and brothers did as well). A poor student and the subject of teasing and bullying in grade school, Sells had learned to act out violently. (Stone says that this is how Sells "leveled out the playing field.")[14] Unsurprisingly, Sells felt detached from people, as well as angry and vengeful. Yet Stone spotted a small measure of humanity in him. "In some people," he writes, "evil can co-exist with a few human qualities one would scarcely imagine were there underneath."[15] Sells repeated his story to Stone about how he'd witnessed a neighbor forcing a boy into oral sex, which had brought back apparently repressed memories of this being done to him. He self-diagnosed this as the trigger that had launched his killing spree. However, as Stone pointed out, "This may be a self-serving memory of dubious authenticity."

Although he was not nervous about talking with Sells, having already spent a considerable amount of time with extreme offenders, Stone wrote about a dream he had directly after their interview. In the dream, he's the tenth person in line to congratulate Hitler about a reelection. As he approaches, he thinks about killing the man, and since Dr. Kernberg (who had actually seen Hitler in person) is present, Stone asks him if killing Hitler would be considered murder. Kernberg reassures him that such an act would be morally permissible. To Stone, this dream revealed his ambivalence about Sells, represented in the figure of Hitler: the offender's "split-self"—half human, half demon—had inspired a split-self in Stone, "half-homicidally contemptuous, half compassionate."[16]

Sells is a typical complainer, blaming others and stating he's being treated poorly. He doesn't sleep well, he says in letters posted on the Internet, and he hates prison food. He feels sorry for himself, believing there was no evidence to condemn him to death row. When questioned about murders he has claimed to commit, he can be cagey, acting as if he recalls few details, which could be his way to fish for them. The interview he gave to a reporter for the television show 20/20 is a case in point. He prompts interviewers to lead the way before he provides details (e.g., "Well, if we're on the same page here, I would assume I went in the bedroom and killed someone").[17] When confronted with his inconsistencies, he just says it's hard to talk about; he does not like admitting to these things. Then he might say he wants to provide closure, make amends, or get rid of his demons. Referring to the final murder, he can't explain to anyone why he entered a home to kill a child without bringing his own weapon.

One thing about Tommy Lynn Sells, when comparing several sources that present his confessions in his own words, is that it's difficult to know when he actually means what he says. For example, when Stone asked Sells if he'd like to kill his mother, Sells reacted as if such an idea was unthinkable. "Anyone touch a hair of her head, he wouldn't last a minute; you only got one mum."[18] And yet he has accused her of foul things and blamed her for all his problems.

In letters to Stone, Sells jokes about the fact that Texas hasn't killed him yet and mentions that his lawyers believe they can get him a life sentence. He claims he doesn't care, but he then declares that he has "one right left," which is the right to die. He has decided to drop his "appels" and he "bets the ass of the next petite women that walks by" that he'll get what he wants. He asks Stone to contact him ASAP "if you want to see me be kill." Clearly, he considers Stone among his important correspondents.

When Stone responds, he's sympathetic and admits that he cannot know what it must be like to spend one's life in a Texas prison cell. He hints that remorse could be a key factor in pushing for execution, such that dying might seem like the right thing to do. He admits to liking Tommy and appreciating his honesty. "If you don't want any more appeals, I'd respect your decision—even though, to tell the truth, I'd miss you."

Sells's return response was quick, as well as lengthy. He insists that a brief talk together was insufficient for Stone to really get to know him; he invites a longer conversation so that "someone as yourself" could present a different picture of Tommy Lynn Sells than the news media had done. He admits that dropping his appeals has more to do with losing a girlfriend than with boredom or justice for victims. "Life starts and stops with her." He then raises the problems from his childhood and says it is "hard not to cry." He mentions the years of sexual abuse he had endured from a neighbor and from his brothers, his mother "traiding me off," and his mother and grandmother both forcing him into sexual acts. He suggests that Stone can help him to "pice together all this broken glass in my head."

Stone offers sympathy and reiterates his respect.[19]

Of all the offenders he'd interviewed for *Most Evil*, Tommy Lynn Sells seemed to Stone to be the most forthright:

> He emerges as a person with what I call "islands of humanity." He has some measure of remorse. He says that if he allowed himself to have full remorse, he'd have to kill himself. I've often said that if you could get a psychopath to really feel badly about what he's done, he'd have to kill himself. So this was a confirmation that if you could treat one successfully, you'd know, because you'd have a dead person. Many of them insulate themselves.

Although Stone realizes that not all of the claims that Sells made about his terrible childhood have been corroborated, he thinks the enduring anger and resentment affirm at least some of them. When asked about why Sells would murder an entire family who were only kind to him, since Sells claims he's just looking for one person to give him a break, Stone said, "He doesn't seem to see that people were in fact kind to him."

Yet the mitigating factors are not sufficient to diminish the heinousness of what Sells freely did to people. No amount of personal charm affects the way Stone places offenders into his categories. Despite Sells's "islands of humanity," he ends up on level 22 on the Scale of Evil—the lowest ring in the Inferno—keeping company with the likes of Ed Kemper, Jim Jones, Dennis Rader, and John Wayne Gacy. He's a sadistic tormenter who killed people for no particular reason except that they crossed his path the wrong way. He often tormented victims by making them witness what was in store for them.

During the first decade of the twenty-first century, Stone wrote in *The Anatomy of Evil*, the role of brain disorders has gained considerable attention as a way to explain certain types of impulsive or extreme violence. "In the last few years, neuroscience has had a great deal to tell us about what is missing or malfunctioning in the brains of antisocial persons, especially those with the added characteristics that qualify them as psychopaths."[20] Although the pathways to evil acts are diverse, Stone says, focused research has isolated a few specific factors, and it seems likely from the many clinicians around the world joining this work that one day we may develop treatments for some of these contributing conditions.

CHAPTER 17

The Most Intimate Approach

1

While some professionals have tried to get personally acquainted for privileged access to the secrets of extreme violence, others believe we should sidestep the lies, manipulations, subterfuges, and blind spots and go right to the brain itself for the most truthful revelations. Toward this end, the brains of certain notorious criminals have been collected and preserved in the hope that science will one day penetrate their truths.

It's not the first time in history that the physical brain has been valued. Cesare Lombroso and his colleagues spent plenty of time looking at the organ of thought for its relation to criminal insanity, while in France, elite members of the Society of Mutual Autopsy pledged their postmortem brains to one another for study, to let biology prove their superiority.

During the same period in the nineteenth century, serial killer and self-proclaimed genius Edward Rulloff anticipated that there would be keen interest in his corpse. He was right. Many people tried to claim it, but Dr. George Burr was the victor, acquiring it for the Geneva Medical College. Dumping the body, he kept the skull and brain, hoping that measurements of the cranium or gray matter would reveal something about Rulloff's criminal disposition. Weighing over fifty-nine ounces, Rulloff's brain was heavier than most adult male brains, but it resisted all attempts to gain significant information. Eventually Burt Green Wilder, a former Civil War surgeon, acquired it for his collection of brains at Cornell University. He hoped to learn through comparisons if differences in size, shape, chemistry, or weight accounted for certain behaviors or personality traits. At its peak, the collection had over 600 specimens, but even in its considerably diminished form today, it includes Rulloff's brain, pickled in formalin.[1]

We've seen in earlier chapters that psychiatrists tried to or did acquire the postmortem brains of John Wayne Gacy, Jeffrey Dahmer, and Richard Speck, and this same practice has gone on in England with the likes of notorious killers Fred West, Michael Ryan, and Harold Shipman (a doctor with between 215 and 250 victims).[2] Mass murderer Charles Whitman seemed to think his intense inner turmoil was from a brain abnormality, and in the suicide note he wrote in 1966 before climbing the tower in Austin, Texas, to start shooting strangers, he asked for an autopsy. It turned out that a glioblastoma multiforme tumor the size of a walnut impacted the hypothalamus, extending into the temporal lobe and compressing the amygdaloid nucleus. A study of the brain of Thomas Hamilton, who slaughtered sixteen children in Dunblane, Scotland, in 1996, showed evidence of a serious thyroid disorder that has been associated with mental confusion and impulsive violence. Still, no one could prove there was a causal relationship between his physical condition and what he did. Or, at least, not yet.

In the late 1980s, brain scans were used for analyzing the metabolic states of aggressive people, and by the late 1990s, scans were performed on violent offenders to see if there were structural differences or internal damage. While head injuries had been reported in many cases, from what we know at this stage, a head injury is neither a necessary nor sufficient condition for provoking aggressive violence. It seems to have been a contributing factor in certain cases, but the causal mechanism is difficult to pinpoint.

2

Dr. Adrian Raine currently teaches and does research at the University of Pennsylvania. His primary interest is neurocriminology, in which he uses techniques from neurology to probe the causes and treatment of criminal behavior. In 1999, he published the results of a study—a first—that he'd focused exclusively on the brains of murderers. With positron emission tomography (PET), he compared the structure of forty-one murderers against forty-one matched controls and found brain deficits in most of the violent individuals—specifically in the limbic system (emotional center), the corpus callosum, the left angular gyrus, and areas of the prefrontal cortex: anterior medial prefrontal, orbitofrontal, and superior frontal. This is where executive decisions are made and inappropriate behavior is inhibited. Abnormalities may allow people to be impulsive, fearless, less responsive to aversive stimulation, and less able to process emotional information or make socially correct decisions about aggression toward others.

Raine also found a difference between "predatory" and "affective" murderers. The predatory killers' prefrontal cortex was closer to normal, which indicated that they could regulate their behavior toward their personal ends. However, both groups showed higher functioning than controls in the right subcortex, or the amygdala-hippocampal complex. Raine's team speculated that this might predispose them toward a more aggressive temperament. (Most of the murderers did not think there was anything wrong with them; they attributed the cause of their violence to external cues, such as poverty, abuse, or poor parenting.)

If the prefrontal cortex fails to function as an inhibitory agent in affective killers, Raine found, increased desire and reduced control may facilitate seeking what the neurons reward. For those who grow fascinated with certain types of violence, and have that fascination repeatedly rewarded in fantasies and activities, it feels better to act out than to inhibit the impulse. The person grows bolder in pursuit of it, and may have a reduced ability to follow social rules or make moral decisions.[3]

In 2008, Raine and his colleagues published a survey of the results of different types of brain imaging on a large population of inmates diagnosed with antisocial personality disorder (APD). They reviewed prison records worldwide and concluded that around 50 percent of incarcerated offenders had been diagnosed with APD, linking it closely to violence. They then discussed the use of PET, single photon emission computed tomography (SPECT), functional magnetic resonance imaging (fMRI), and anatomical functional magnetic resonance imaging (aMRI) as the most widely used approaches to scan the brain. In other words, they examined blood flow patterns and the anatomical structure of gray matter. In some studies, substance abuse and addiction appeared to have been factors.

The researchers concluded that there are visible structural and functional impairments in antisocial, psychopathic, and repeatedly violent individuals. By now, they had narrowed down the areas of the prefrontal cortex to the orbitofrontal and dorsolateral prefrontal cortex, as well as the superior temporal gyrus, the amygdala-hippocampal complex, and the anterior cingulate cortex. These people would have an impaired ability to respond to the threat of punishment, make clear moral judgments, and grasp the emotional implications of their behaviors. However, the researchers stated that using these results in a legal context should be undertaken cautiously, as the interpretation of brain scans is not yet definitive and the causal relationship still unclear. (That is, does the impairment cause the behavior, or does a lifestyle of aggressive behavior restructure the brain?) The future hope, the authors say, is that "a better understanding of the neurobiological basis to antisocial aggressive behavior can facilitate the development of a new generation of biosocial treatment and prevention programs."[4] Carefully designed longitudinal studies are necessary.

Defense teams have already incorporated brain scan studies into their courtroom strategies. In the early 1980s, a computerized tomography (CT) scan was used to defend John Hinckley Jr. to help prove his insanity when he shot President Ronald Reagan in 1981. Since then, others have used every possible means to claim that science has demonstrated that the brains of aggressors are structurally and/or functionally different from those of normal people. It's difficult to say how much mitigation these claims actually achieve, but the authors forecast an increased role in the courtroom and in policy legislation in the future. At present, there is a gap between the questions the legal system needs answered and the questions that science *can* answer.[5] (Scan results on adolescent brains have already influenced the decision to stop capital punishment for juvenile offenders.)

One case of a serial killer that relied on brain scan technology was that of Stephen Stanko. He killed two people and attempted to murder a third before he was caught. During his trial, the prosecutor said Stanko was a man without any remorse for his actions, a psychopath who knew what he was doing. The defense attorney, William Diggs, hoped to prove that Stanko had no control, thanks to a brain defect, and therefore should be considered insane at the time he'd killed. Diggs hired Dr. Thomas H. Sachy, founder of Georgia Pain and Behavioral Medicine, to scan Stanko's brain with a PET scan. On the witness stand, Sachy testified that the scan showed decreased function in the medial orbital frontal lobes. He explained that one region of the brain directly above the eyes and behind the eyebrows did not function normally—"this area of the brain that essentially makes us human." By this, he meant that Stanko was deficient in the areas that are implicated in feeling compassion and was unable to perceive the moral landscape the way normal people do. The jury listened but convicted Stanko. However, the day is coming when this research will have a greater impact.[6]

Another intriguing development is in the area of neurotransmitters and addiction. Recent research from Vanderbilt University, which used thirty volunteers who were not substance abusers but who scored high for anti-social impulsivity and other psychopathic traits, suggests that the brains of psychopaths may be wired to keep seeking a reward, no matter what the potential cost. That is, it's not that they aren't aware of consequences; it's that the potential reward—especially in their brain—outweighs them. These people may have a hyperreactive dopamine reward system, or an abundance of dopamine in the brain. Other research shows that people in need of constant stimulation do have more dopamine, and as a result they can develop a dangerous addiction.

Addiction is the inability to appropriately manage a desire for a specific behavior. Regarding dopamine's role, the brain choreographs the body's information-processing system, directing its diverse neurotransmitters. Among those most implicated is dopamine, because it floods the system during novel or exciting situations, triggering the brain's reward system. Thus, we approach with anticipation those behaviors and situations that may feel good, and pending a continued pleasurable experience, dopamine fuels an edgy high that spurs us to seek it again. It provides a biological investment in life's unpredictable twists and the thrill of being alive.

Yet the brain adapts, and dopamine levels increase or decrease accordingly. When they diminish, the person seeks new avenues of stimulation and reward. In addition, research indicates that those people with fewer dopamine receptors in the brain are more prone to craving stimulation, which might be what makes them vulnerable to addiction or compulsive pleasure seeking. They might have too much unprocessed dopamine. For those who find their reward in psychopathic aggression, it feels better in the brain and body to act out than to inhibit the impulse. In addition, the longer a reward is delayed, the more the brain produces these hormones, and frustration can have a facilitating effect. People who scored high on the Psychopathic Personality Inventory (PPI) were found to release four times as much dopamine as normal controls in response to the administration of amphetamine. In addition, when told they would receive money, the dopamine reward center, the nucleus accumbens, was more active in those with high PPI scores.

Dysfunctional reward and craving could clearly be implicated in recidivism, sadism, lust murder, substance abuse, risky behavior, and extreme forms of fantasy-based violence. Psychopaths, being self-centered, appear to be drawn toward self-enriching rewards. Devoid of the inhibitions framed by compassion and social rules, their lack of a conscience linked with dopamine's reward mechanism may clarify their repetitive and diverse criminality.[7]

Additionally, research indicates that a gene for monoamine oxidase-A (MAOA), an enzyme that breaks down neurotransmitters like serotonin and dopamine, has gained the reputation of being the "violence gene." When this enzyme fails, leaving the neurotransmitters to build up in areas where they should be absent, it can produce negative emotions and behaviors like irritability, hyperactivity, and aggression. Genes have not been shown to directly code for violent behavior, so adding genetic information to brain-imaging data—"imaging genomics"—is the next step for identifying a baseline of genetic variation within specified brain areas. For example, mice lacking the gene for MAOA are excessively aggressive.

Using MRI and DNA analysis, 142 healthy males and females with no known history of violence were shown pictures of angry and fearful faces. Researchers found that those with low-expressing MAOA (MAOA-L) were more impulsive, with brain activity in males differing from normal more than in females. For males, the MAOA-L genotype is associated with amygdala hyperresponsiveness during emotional arousal, coupled with diminished reactivity of regulatory prefrontal regions. MAOA-L males also show changes in orbitofrontal volume, amygdala and hippocampus hyperreactivity during aversive recall, and impaired cingulate activation during cognitive inhibition. MAOA-L males who had been abused or neglected were more likely to become antisocial as teenagers and adults.

One more potential biological marker involves neuronal nitric oxide synthase (nNOS). The gaseous nitric oxide it produces affects different behaviors, from reproduction to social interaction. An imbalance can cause social withdrawal and an increased propensity to act out aggressively.[8]

As we see consistent results at the neural level, especially when we can't find behavioral clues, we gain the possibility of reading an emerging neural signature that could grow more distinct with adverse environmental circumstances. In other words, risk assessment with this neural component could be more accurate than with only behavioral signals.[9]

3

Another intriguing development is Brain Fingerprinting. Psychiatrist Lawrence Farwell developed this technology, for which he claims a 99.9 percent accuracy rate, in his Brain Wave Science and the Human Brain Research Laboratory in Fairfield, Missouri. The idea is this: the brain is central to all human activities, so it records all of our experiences—even crimes. No matter how we might try to lie, distort, or forget about it, the brain retains a memory. Brain Fingerprinting records distinct patterns, called "event-related potentials," which are measures of the brain's electrical activity as it corresponds to events in the environment. By averaging the distinct patterns of electrical activity, a singular waveform arises that can be dissected into components related to cognitive functions. Those related to Brain Fingerprinting are the P300 and the memory- and encoding-related multifaceted electroencephalographic response, or MERMER*. The P300 is a positive charge that peaks between 300 and 800 milliseconds in response to meaningful or noteworthy stimuli. Dr. Farwell found that the P300 was one aspect of the MERMER, a more complex brain wave response that peaks at 800–1,200 milliseconds.

Farwell created a headband with sensors to monitor a suspect's brain activity while he or she looked at pictures and words devised from the crime scene. Some would be relevant to the crime and some irrelevant. If the suspect's brain recognized the relevant stimuli, it would respond with MERMERs, which meant that the person had a memory of the crime. Like a fingerprint at a scene, it did not necessarily prove murder, but it added an indicator of guilt, because innocent people would display no such response. If, on the other hand, the suspect offered an alibi for the time of the crime, scenes from *this* scenario should elicit MERMERs. If the device is truly reliable, it negates the need for confessions and adds a compelling dimension to assessments of malingering and to the accuracy of a criminal autobiography.[10]

In 1999, this technology was instrumental in eliciting a confession from fifty-three-year-old inmate James B. Grinder. He was the most likely suspect in a rape and murder from 1984 in Macon County, Missouri. Julie Helton's badly beaten body was discovered in a field four days after she went missing. Her hands had been bound in front of her with baling twine, and she'd been raped and stabbed to death. There were two sets of footprints in the snow—the victim's, and prints leading to and away from the scene that implicated an adult male. The body was moved to the morgue, where the postmortem showed bruises and scrapes, as well as blunt-force trauma and deep stab wounds to the neck. Her right hand showed defensive wounds, affirmed by broken fingernails, which suggested that she'd fought to save herself.

There had been insufficient evidence in 1984 to take Grinder, a wood-cutter from Arkansas, to trial, although he was arrested later for another incident. The sheriff read about Brain Fingerprinting, and at his behest Farwell tested his device on Grinder's brain. The test itself was divided into blocks of twenty-four stimuli, each of which was presented three separate times. Grinder sat in a chair in front of the screen, wearing the sensor-equipped helmet that measured areas in the parietal, frontal, and central areas of his brain. He participated in seven tests with five different sets of probes, and his responses were graphed and calculated so that results for "relevant" stimuli could be mathematically compared against results for "irrelevant" stimuli.

After forty-five minutes, the computer analysis showed "information present" for probe stimuli, with a computed statistical confidence level of 99.9 percent accuracy. Thus, Grinder had quite specific concealed knowledge about the crime. Farwell told reporters that Grinder's brain held critical detailed information that only the killer would have, stored fifteen years earlier when he'd committed the murder of Julie Helton.

Apparently disturbed by the experience, Grinder pled guilty to first-degree murder and received a sentence of life in prison without the possibility of parole. He was transported to Arkansas, where he also confessed to the long-unsolved murders of three young girls. Their skeletal remains were found in 1986, although they had gone missing ten years earlier. Two were thirteen, and one was fourteen.

At the time of the girls' disappearance, the police had believed their best suspect was James B. Grinder, seen with the girls that day. Grinder admitted he'd noticed them hitchhiking and had picked them up, but said he'd dropped them off at an interstate exit. In reality, according to his later confession, he'd purchased alcohol and had taken them to Brock Cemetery, where he'd raped, strangled, and stabbed two of them. He'd then taken the remaining girl to another location, where he'd raped and bludgeoned her to death. For his plea, he was sentenced to life in prison.

Brain research is becoming more important in present cases like Stanko's, and in looking back to cold cases like those committed by Grinder. It can also be taken even further to help reexamine a past case already closed because it might provide a better explanation or even correct errors.

4

In early January 1956, the body of seventeen-year-old Ann Kneilands was discovered in a golf course near Glasgow, Scotland. She'd been sexually assaulted and battered around the head. A suspect was twenty-nine-year-old Peter Manuel, but his father provided an alibi. Nine months later, someone entered William Watt's home, killing Watt's wife, sister-in-law, and niece. Watt was on a fishing expedition, but he'd been close enough to have committed the crime, so the police detained him. Peter Manuel was brought in during this period on burglary charges. He saw Watt and said that he could prove that the man was innocent. (Some accounts say he persuaded police that Watt was guilty.) The information Manuel gave convinced Watt's attorney that Manuel himself was either the killer or an accomplice. However, there was no evidence with which to charge him. Watt was released for the same reason, but he remained under suspicion. Then another adolescent girl, Isabelle Cooke, vanished, and three days later the three members of the Peter Smart family were murdered during an apparent burglary.

When a five-pound note, traceable to the Smarts' home, was spent, the police arrested Peter Manuel. They nearly arrested his father as well, because stolen items were found in his home. Manuel at first denied everything, but under pressure from his mother he admitted to the murders and said that after killing the Smarts he'd stayed in their home with the bodies for a week, eating food from their New Year's feast. He also revealed where he had buried Isabelle Cooke. He took police to the field, and when they asked him the whereabouts of her remains, he said, "This is the place. In fact, I think I'm standing on her now." It turned out that he had a record of petty theft and rape, going back to when he was ten years old. He confessed to eighteen murders, but he was tried for only eight.

Manuel had predicted that he'd avoid a conviction by proving in court that he was insane. From the records, it appears that whenever someone from the prosecution team came to question him he was in a twitchy catatonic state. The psychiatrists who examined him concluded that since his symptoms matched no known mental illness and since no organic cause was found, he was probably malingering. (The prison guards agreed; his behavior told them he knew exactly what was going on around him.) Most examiners believed he had the presence of mind to know what he was doing at the time of the crimes, to know it was wrong, and to control it.[11]

Despite the "Beast of Birkenshaw's" impressive comportment in representing himself that May, the jury convicted him of seven of the murders (there was insufficient evidence for one). Lord Cameron, the trial judge, commented in his report, "I saw no sign indicative to a layman of any illness or abnormality beyond callousness, selfishness and treachery in high degree, but I did inform the impression that he was even then laying the foundation of a suggestion that he might in the end of the day be presented not as a criminal, but as one in need of medical care."[12]

In June, Manuel's appeal was denied. On July 11, 1958, at the age of thirty-one, he was hanged. He remained a suspect in the 1957 murder of a cab driver, because a button that appeared to be from his coat was found in the cab.

Recently, psychologist and legal expert Richard Goldberg, from Aberdeen University's law school, decided that Manuel had been wrongly executed. Goldberg is the son of a prominent Scottish physician who had witnessed Manuel's medical assessment on February 16, 1958. He had also spoken with the key psychiatrist, Dr. John Gaylor, and recalled Gaylor saying that he'd found evidence of temporal lobe epilepsy, which would mitigate Manuel's offense, especially when added to the diagnosis of psychopathy. Thus, Manuel would have been eligible for a finding of diminished capacity and for treatment.

While Goldberg had no opportunity to get to know the offender on a personal basis, he undertook to study the files held in the National Archives in Edinburgh that were released under the Freedom of Information Act: the killer's recorded confessions, his writings, the various psychiatric interviews, written descriptions of Manuel's behavior, and medical records.

"Dr Gaylor was ready to give evidence of this to the High Court when Manuel dismissed his counsel, Harald Leslie," said Goldberg, "so this fantastic evidence about the epilepsy was never heard before the court."[13] Goldberg believed that the government's agenda had been to execute him, and that the medical records that demonstrate a collusion and cover-up are still sealed.

However, the available records do offer the results of Gaylor's examinations, as he wrote them. While temporal lobe epilepsy might have been present, especially in light of several incidents in Manuel's life in which he received a blow to the head that had knocked him out, Gaylor stated that nothing had shown up on electroencephalograms (EEGs). Manuel had mentioned to him a few periods of memory failure, but had insisted that his accidents had not otherwise affected him.

In a recorded interview, Manuel discussed the murder of the Smart family. He sounded composed as he denied that there was a solid case against him. Yet in his notebooks was a sketch showing where he'd buried Isabelle Cooke, a murder for which he'd demonstrated no remorse.

The question that Goldberg raises is whether the combination of epilepsy and psychopathy was substantially influential to determine that Manuel did not have full awareness or control of his criminal acts. In the 1950s, when Manuel was tried, psychopathy alone was not a mitigating factor. The 1946 decision in *Carraher v. HM Advocate* stated that psychopathy was no basis for claiming diminished responsibility.

It should be noted that *several* psychiatrists had examined Manuel, not just one, and Gaylor had administered several EEGs, none of which revealed an abnormality. According to his notes after observing Manuel's odd behavior in his cell, Gaylor stated, "Taking his history, quite apart from the EEG findings, the periods of amnesia, and automatic behavior do not conform to the classical description of epileptic automatism, nor in my experience have I seen an epileptic with such automatisms as the Accused alleges he suffers from."[14] While this does not necessarily prove that Manuel had no brain impairment, it also does not support a claim that he did.

Although it's possible that the records were falsified to suit the supposed conspiracy, it's just as possible that Goldberg's father misunderstood or misremembered his conversation with Gaylor, or even that Gaylor's supposed concern stemmed from Manuel's inexplicable catatonia and not from the EEG results. However, if some records are still sealed and there is reason to believe that they contradict those that are available,

Goldberg's demand that the public be granted access seems reasonable. Today's reading of an EEG might deduce something more than EEG readings were able to do half a century ago. This is all Goldberg asks.

As yet, there is no proof either way, but the point for the thesis of privileged access is that, with a better understanding of neurological conditions, we can review cases even of deceased offenders to learn more about their development into violent individuals.

Now, let's look at what a century of privileged access by trained professionals to extreme offenders has revealed.

CHAPTER 18

The Collective Findings

1

Most interviewers know the dangers of personal bias. If they must work at getting information from virtual strangers, they must be friendly and at least act as if they care. Sometimes they do care. Roy Ratcliff, for example, said that his meeting with the notorious Jeffrey Dahmer was the high point of his week and the card from him a treasured possession. But crossing over the clinical line toward friendship, even a shallow one, means the potential for compromise for those seeking accurate information. When you like someone, you're inclined to interpret words or behavior more benignly than they might deserve.

In addition, it can be difficult to accept being "friends" with someone who has done terrible things to others unless you can assure yourself that you're connecting with a glimmer of humanity with which you can identify. Who, after all, can truly befriend a monster, even one with an affable personality like Bundy's? It's easier to believe that there are mitigating factors for the offender's behavior, like abuse, brain damage, neurochemical disturbances, or justified rage. Speck, Kürten, Starkweather, Manuel, and Panzram all complained of headaches. Couldn't something in their heads, and thus outside their control, be a significant factor in what they did?

Another issue, perhaps the central one for a study like this, is whether a relationship of any type can improve one's chances of getting at the truth. The FBI agents from the Behavioral Science Unit learned during their prison interviews that self-reports from killers and psychopaths did not necessarily enlighten. Psychopaths, playing the victim card, often exaggerated or fabricated their personal stories and blamed others for what they'd done. Panzram and Sells both stated that they'd have been different if only they'd been treated kindly, and yet they usually repaid kindness with irresponsibility or brutality. Psychopaths also liked to brag, the agents found, while psychotic individuals like Mullin often did not make much sense. In addition, some had reasons to keep their activities secret: Speck played out amnesia with Ziporyn, Chloe Davis deflected her questioners, and Gacy hid behind "Jack Hanley."

In addition to issues with the offenders, professionals themselves can have blind spots. Wertham had an ax to grind about the insanity defense, so for him, Fish was the perfect opportunity to challenge it. Some professionals enter with a theory intact, hoping the offender will confirm it. Dobson guided Bundy toward a succinct statement that he could use in his stand against pornography, and Brussel had ideas about DeSalvo long before they met. He'd decided that he would assist on the defense only if DeSalvo turned out to be schizophrenic. It's not hard to understand that if one really wants the opportunity to join a high-profile case in a privileged manner, he will see what he wants to see. In addition, DeSalvo was interested in Brussel's prediction that he'd have a "problem," possibly because he hoped for some mitigating factor to help him avoid prison. Thus, he'd have reason to use the clever tactics he'd relied on previously to get the psychiatrist (and Brussel's independent examiner) on his side. It seems that Brussel's pride in predicting from the crimes who the offender would be influenced how he perceived DeSalvo's character. In addition, Brussel had recently fallen from favor with the New York police, so he had reason to prove himself on a case with extensive visibility. Thus, his objectivity in this case is questionable.

De River, too, made comments throughout his report about Chloe Davis, to the effect that each time she stated or did something that confirmed his ideas, he asked readers to note it. He cherry-picked to confirm his diagnosis when he should have performed a full and proper investigation. Thus, he ignored or didn't observe whatever failed to confirm what he believed. Nevertheless, he must be credited with offering some of the most detailed early case histories about sex offenders, rivaled only by Krafft-Ebing's earlier tome.

Let's also address Ziporyn's belief that, due to his special relationship with Richard Speck, he was the only "objective" interpreter of Speck's behavior, while other professionals who spoke with the mass murderer suffered from "interpreter's bias." His claim is almost laughable, since his own bias is visible throughout his book: he spent a great deal of energy trying to convince Speck that he wasn't responsible and to teach him the type of behavior he should demonstrate if he truly felt remorse. As we know, Speck later proved Ziporyn's notions to be not just false but also naïve.

In any event, each professional in these pages had to decide how he or she would maintain a relationship, and for what purpose. Lacassagne got the ball rolling by thinking an autobiography would elicit insight as well as contribute to future knowledge via comparisons with others. Resnick used the Yates case to teach interns, while Berg and Bukhanovsky both spotted an opportunity to focus on a rare type of sadist, and they were correct to believe that the details assisted our understanding of compulsive, remorseless sex offenders. Those clinicians with a psychoanalytic bent revealed as much about the history of psychiatry as about the offender, and those who began to see the value of detailed neurological studies have helped move this research in its most productive directions. Will neurological research, even some version of brain fingerprinting, one day replace the clinical interview or confession analysis? Probably not, since neurochemical activity cannot reveal the specific personal details of the erotic conditioning of puberty, the dopamine rush, the depth of subjective experiences, or the complex array of developmental issues. It may explain addiction, aggression, compulsion, and the effect of head injury or structural brain deficit, but it will not tell us why fifteen-year-old Ed Kemper decided on a specific afternoon to shoot and kill his grandparents. Thorough case histories, whether as a subset of one or grouped for trend analysis, play no small part in our understanding, although neurobiology appears to be the most productive and verifiable direction thus far for assessing potential causes.

Clinicians, whether psychiatrists or counselors, who overtly elicit offender assistance for science have a better platform for keeping the relationship clinical. Berg told Kürten exactly what he was doing, and the offender agreed to participate. Not that he wasn't still manipulative, but Berg never capitulated to the obligations of a friendship. In addition, he had no personal theory to defend. While Berg added little to the theories of sadism to that point, he did learn something important about how a serial killer might operate: Kürten had changed his weapon, MO, and victim type, according to his circumstances, his decision to deflect the investigation, and his experimentation. This study, had it gained more recognition, might have helped prevent stereotypes about serial killers that are still entrenched today. Bukhanovsky, too, had to ponder a killer with several victim types, MOs, and deviances, and he was working from his own pattern, with no agenda for where it would lead except for his own research. Carlisle responded to Bundy's need for attention, but used him as only one of several subjects for developing a theory based on the data he'd collected. Stone did perhaps the most comprehensive study, reading hundreds of accounts of serial and mass murderers to devise his Scale of Evil. Thus, while a friendship with Sells could skew his opinion about Sells, this would not adversely affect the larger picture he has organized.

Yet no matter how objective someone tries to be, whenever there are two or more people, each with his or her own perceptions and agendas, the potential for misjudgment and inaccuracy is part of the process. However, over time, we've managed to clarify a few things.

2

From the earliest criminal autobiographies to the latest neurobiological research, these bold or compassionate professionals have probed more deeply than most into the minds of murderers. They relied on knowledge and ideas from their time periods, and their clinical curiosity offered unique benefits. Since the early 1800s, the psychomedical field has focused on making sense of dangerous aggression. Initially, psychiatrists believed that mental illness had a biological cause, and as it was passed to successive generations, it degenerated into more primitive forms. These notions endured for decades, expressed in theories about skull formations, body odors, and body types, until a new generation of experts challenged the etiology and theoretical vagueness. During the early twentieth century, alienists and neurologists both competed with psychogenic theories that shifted focus to the mind, particularly the subconscious.

Case histories helped psychotherapists understand and anticipate what they were dealing with. They testified in court about motives and mitigations, offering forms of psychological logic that helped juries understand why someone like Speck would kill eight nurses or Fish could be so cruel and peculiar. Freud's legacy dominated in one form or another in the diagnostic manuals until proven neurological research challenged claims about unconscious conflicts. During the 1950s, medications made inroads into the treatment of major mental illness, and within two decades a more science-based form of biological psychiatry emerged. Today, there is much more involvement in studying specific areas of, or chemicals in, offender brains, and the professionals like Morrison who preserved a serial killer's brain for future study were thinking ahead. While brains had been dissected and/or scanned for well over a century, given the progress of the past decade, those preserved brains might one day reveal something not yet known.

Many offenders have described a feeling that some force overwhelmed them when they went out to kill. Some may have been malingering multiple personalities, but from certain accounts we know that Manuel, Bundy, Vacher, Kürten, Sells, Chikatilo, and Dahmer all seemed to change dramatically when the killing urge took over, and some described an "entity" that possessed them. They could have been experiencing a disturbance in their brains.

In 2006, an article was published in *Nature* about how Swiss neuroscientists had stimulated the brain of a twenty-two-year-old woman, lacking a history of psychiatric disorders or delusions. During their examination of the patient prior to her surgery for epilepsy, they stimulated the left junction of her temporoparietal lobe. From a supine position, she reported an impression of someone standing close behind her—a young person, possibly male, posing in a way that mirrored her own position. But no one was there. The doctors urged her to sit. She did so, wrapping her arms around her knees. They stimulated her brain once again, and this time she said the shadow had wrapped his arms around her, just like she had her arms around her knees. She didn't like the feeling. The scientists thought this was simply a projected sense of her own body image, but it did not feel that way to her; the shadow felt like a distinct other. Then, for another test, she held a card in her right hand, and after stimulation of her brain, she reported an impression: "He wants to take the card," she said. "He doesn't want me to read." The researchers concluded that the perceptions may have been "due to a disturbance in the multi-sensory processing of body and self at the temporoparietal junction."[1]

The brain still has mysteries to unlock, and from what we've seen thus far, it's likely we'll discover much more in the future about how it participates in violence and what this suggests for treatment. Until then, case analyses of motive and behavior still provide the best guide for comprehension, comparison, prediction, and treatment of excessively violent individuals like those we've examined.

A century of privileged access to extreme offenders offers the field of forensic psychology and psychiatry some significant items:

- Awareness that offenders can have helpful insight about their behaviors.
- Greater clarity about the nature and behaviors of a psychopath.
- The ability to better assess future dangerousness.
- Greater understanding of the role of perceptions of abuse, betrayal, and bullying in the formation of aggressive revenge.
- Knowledge that even educated and experienced professionals can be hoodwinked, especially when their agenda is obvious.
- Awareness that making distinctions among types of crimes assists us to learn more about the development of different types of offenders.
- Awareness that females can be as brutal and aggressive as males.
- Knowledge that accomplishment, good looks, and friendliness do not disqualify someone from being a predatory or deviant killer.
- Learning that a theory is only a step along the way, not the final truth.
- Awareness that evil intent can coexist with mental illness.

- Ways (and the need) to demonstrate that a killer's perception of his or her life does not necessarily correspond to fact.
- Clarity on how legal issues can interfere with clinical assessments.
- Awareness that professionals who invest the time to listen and study an offender from diverse sources and circumstances can gain greater comprehension of subtleties in deviance and psychological development.
- Awareness that to devise an accurate rendering, professionals must see past sensational data in press coverage and avoid the lure of high-profile fame.
- Clarity about personal involvement: when a case triggers personal issues, the professional must sort it out; subjective issues cannot be wholly extracted, but personal awareness helps avoid biased observations.
- Recognition that theories are important as a guide but should not limit, mutate, or revise the data.

I'll end now where I began, with Karl Berg's study of Peter Kürten. The dust jacket flap of this old book indicates that the material was intended for the eyes of professionals: "Professor Berg's study will be found to be of great value to the psychologist, the psychiatrist, the pathologist, the penologist, and higher police officer." I hope the same will be said of this book, but in addition, I hope I will inspire a far wider range of professionals and laypeople to see the value of what the pioneers were doing. Even when flawed, these studies are unique in the field of forensic psychiatry, psychology, and criminology, and thus they merit respect for their boldness and intent.

Notes

Chapter 1

1. Katherine Ramsland, *The Human Predator* (New York: Berkley, 2005), 57–58.
2. H. Payne and R. Luthe, "Isaac Ray and Forensic Psychiatry in the United States," *Forensic Science International* 15, no. 2 (1980): 115–27.
3. Stephen Kern, *A Cultural History of Causality: Science, Murder Novels, and Systems of Thought* (Princeton, N.J.: Princeton University Press, 2004), 1–26.
4. Michael H. Stone, *Healing the Mind: A History of Psychiatry from Antiquity to the Present* (London: Norton, 1997), 87–103.
5. Edward Shorter, *A History of Psychiatry* (New York: John Wiley, 1997), 145.
6. Harry Oosterhuis, *Stepchildren of Nature: Krafft-Ebing, Psychiatry, and the Making of Sexual Identity* (Chicago: University of Chicago Press, 2000), 75–76.
7. Oosterhuis, *Stepchildren of Nature*, 25–55.
8. Cesare Lombroso, *L'uomo delinquente* (Milan: Hoepli, 1876), 86.
9. David G. Horn, *The Criminal Body: Lombroso and the Anatomy of Deviance* (New York: Routledge, 2003).
10. "Criminals Who Revel in Torture Are Fit Subjects for the Surgeon," *Washington Post*, March 24, 1907.

Chapter 2

1. "Guilty of Eight Murders," *New York Times*, October 13, 1897, p. 7; Alister Kershaw, *Murder in France* (London: Constable, 1955); and "French Ripper Guillotined," *New York Times*, January 1, 1898, p. 7.
2. Jurgen Thorwald, *The Century of the Detective* (New York: Harcourt, Brace & World, 1964), 126–32; and Colin Wilson and Damon Wilson, *Written in Blood: A History of Forensic Detection* (New York: Carroll and Graf, 2003), 178–80.
3. Alexandre Lacassagne, "Les Transformations du droit pénal et les progrès de la medicine légale, de 1810 á 1912," *Archives d'anthropologie criminelle* 28 (1913): 364.
4. Philippe Artières, "What Criminals Think about Criminology," in *Criminals and Their Scientists: The History of Criminology in International Perspective*, ed. Peter Becker and Richard F. Wetzell (Cambridge: Cambridge University Press, 2006), 363–75.
5. Artières, "What Criminals Think," 317.
6. "Parisian News and Gossip," *New York Times*, October 24, 1897, p. 13.

7. Alexandre Lacassagne, "Vacher l'eventreur," *Archives d'anthropologie criminelle* 13, no. 78 (1898): 632–95.

8. Richard von Krafft-Ebing, *Psychopathia Sexualis with Especial Reference to the Antipathic Sexual Instinct: A Medico-Forensic*, rev. ed. (Philadelphia: Physicians and Surgeons, 1928), case 18, 87–89.

Chapter 3

1. Karl Berg, *The Sadist*, trans. Olga Illner and George Godwin (London: William Heinemann Medical, 1945; originally published as *Der Sadist*, Berlin: Julius Springer Verlag, 1932), 55.

2. Ibid., 96.

3. Ibid., 118.

4. Ibid., 80.

5. Ibid., 123.

6. Ibid., 124.

7. Ibid., 101.

8. Ibid., 102.

9. Ibid., 110.

10. Ibid., 111.

11. Ibid.

Chapter 4

1. Edward Shorter, *A History of Psychiatry* (New York: John Wiley, 1997), 155–58.

2. Karl Menninger, *The Vital Balance* (New York: Viking, 1963), 33.

3. Thomas Gaddis and James O. Long, *Killer: A Journal of Murder* (New York: Macmillan, 1970), 11.

4. Ibid., 12.

5. Ibid.

6. Stephen D. Singer, "Applying Social Learning Theory to Childhood and Adolescent Firesetting: Can It Lead to Serial Murder?" *International Journal of Offender Therapy and Comparative Criminology* 48, no. 4 (2004): 468.

7. Gaddis and Long, *Killer*, 238.

8. Brian King, *Lustmord* (Burbank, Calif.: Bloat, 1996), 209.

9. David K. Frasier, *Murder Cases of the Twentieth Century* (Jefferson, N.C.: McFarland, 1996), 354–56.

10. Ibid., 354.

11. "Panzram Goes to Gallows Cursing Race, Including Himself," (Kansas City, KS) *Sunday Star*, September 7, 1930.

12. Karl Menninger and Jean Lyle, "The Psychology of Crime," *Kansas Magazine*, 1933, 61.

13. Gaddis and Long, *Killer*, 252.

14. Ibid., 281.

15. Karl Menninger, *Man against Himself* (New York: Harcourt, Brace, 1938), 181.
16. Richard Swallow, "The Strange Story of the World's Worst Murderer," (Topeka, KS) *Daily Capital*, January 1933.
17. Menninger, *Man against Himself*, 178.
18. Ibid., 180.
19. Ibid.
20. Duncan Cartwright, "The Narcissistic Exoskeleton: The Defensive Organization of the Rage-Type Murderer," *Bulletin of the Menninger Clinic* 66, no. 1 (Winter 2002): 1–18.

Chapter 5

1. Fredric Wertham, *The Show of Violence* (New York: Doubleday, 1949), 8.
2. Ibid., 10.
3. Ibid., 66–67.
4. John Borowski, *Albert Fish* (Waterfront Productions, 2007); various articles, *New York Times*, June 5, 1928–January 17, 1936; and Harold Schechter, *Deranged: The Shocking True Story of America's Most Fiendish Killer* (New York: Pocket, 1990).
5. Wertham, *The Show of Violence*, 69.
6. Ibid., 72.
7. Ibid., 74.
8. Ibid.
9. Ibid., 93.
10. Ibid., 76.
11. Ibid., 86.
12. Harold Schechter, *The Serial Killer Files* (New York: Ballantine, 2003), 244.
13. Arthur Garrison, "The Catathymic Crisis: An Explanation for Serial Killers," *Journal of Police and Criminal Psychology* 11, no. 1 (1996): 5–12.
14. Fredric Wertham, "Why Do They Commit Murder?" *New York Times*, August 8, 1954, p. SM8.

Chapter 6

1. Paul Lieberman, "The Black Dahlia Fiasco," *Los Angeles Times*, October 30, 2008.
2. "Three Little Girls," *Time*, July 12, 1937; and Larry Harnish, "Three Girls Found Slain in Hills: Felon Hunted in Fiendish Crimes," *Daily Mirror*, May 5, 2007.
3. J. Paul de River, "Foreword," in *The Sexual Criminal* (Springfield, Ill.: Charles C. Thomas, 1949; reprinted by Bloat Books, 2000), xiv.
4. "Woman, 3 Children Beaten to Death," *New York Times*, April 5, 1940, p. 24.
5. Ibid.
6. Ibid.
7. "Girl's Death Story Prevails on Coast," *New York Times*, April 7, 1940, p. 46.

8. Brian King, "The Strange Case of Dr. de River," in *The Sexual Criminal* (Springfield, Ill.: Charles C. Thomas, 1949; reprinted by Bloat Books, 2000), xxxii–xxxix; and Michelle McKee, "The Strange Case of Chloe Davis," http://criminalconduct .blogspot.com/2007/06 (accessed September 20, 2009).

9. De River, *The Sexual Criminal*, 34.

10. Ibid., 45.

11. Ibid., 35.

Chapter 7

1. Edward Shorter, *A History of Psychiatry* (New York: John Wiley, 1997), 298.

2. James Melvin Reinhardt, *The Murderous Trail of Charles Starkweather* (Springfield, Ill.: Charles C. Thomas, 1960), 27.

3. Ibid., 101.

4. Ibid., 100.

5. Ibid.; and Michael Newton, *Wasteland: The Savage Odyssey of Charles Starkweather and Caril Ann Fugate* (New York: Pocket, 1998).

6. Reinhardt, *The Murderous Trail*, 133.

7. Ibid., 3.

8. Ibid., 4.

9. Daniel Lachance, "Executing Charles Starkweather," *Punishment and Society* 11 (2009): 346.

10. James M. Reinhardt, "Crime in a Discordant Culture," *Journal of Criminal Law and Criminology* 41, no. 1 (May–June 1950): 32.

11. Ibid., 48.

12. Ibid., 81.

13. Ibid., 14.

14. Ibid., 64.

Chapter 8

1. Portions of this chapter appeared in a different format in my article, Katherine Ramsland, "James A. Brussel: 'The Sherlock Holmes of the Couch,'" *Forensic Examiner* 22 (Spring 2009): http://www.theforensicexaminer.com/archive/ spring09/22/ (accessed August 5, 2010).

2. Michael Stone, *Healing the Mind* (London: Norton, 1997), 201.

3. James Brussel, *Casebook of a Forensic Psychiatrist* (New York: Dell, 1968), 17.

4. Gerold Frank, "Foreword," in *Casebook of a Forensic Psychiatrist* (New York: Dell, 1968), 9–12.

5. Edward Shorter, *A History of Psychiatry* (New York: John Wiley, 1997), 299.

6. Stone, *Healing the Mind*, 201.

7. Brussel, *Casebook*, 49.

8. Ibid.

9. Ibid., 16.

10. Malcolm Gladwell, "Dangerous Minds," *New Yorker*, November 12, 2007; and H. P. Jeffers, *Who Killed Precious?* (New York: Dell, 1991), 36–38.
11. Gerold Frank, *The Boston Strangler* (New York: New American Library, 1966).
12. Brussel, *Casebook*, 161.
13. Ibid., 166.
14. James E. Starrs and Katherine Ramsland, *A Voice for the Dead* (New York: Putnam, 2005), 189–243.
15. Ibid., 173.
16. Brussel, *Casebook*, 178.
17. Ibid., 181.
18. Ibid., 177.
19. Susan Kelly, *The Boston Stranglers* (New York: Pinnacle, 1995; updated ed., 2002), 130.

Chapter 9

1. "LSD," *Time*, June 17, 1966.
2. Jack Altman and Marvin Ziporyn, *Born to Raise Hell: The Untold Story of Richard Speck* (New York: Grove Press, 1967), 193.
3. Ibid., 101.
4. Ibid., 214.
5. Bob Greene, "The Voice of Richard Speck," *Chicago Tribune*, December 8, 1978.
6. John Douglas and Mark Olshaker, *Mindhunter: Inside the FBI's Elite Serial Crime Unit* (New York: Scribner, 1995), 127–31.
7. Robert K. Ressler and Tom Shachtman, *Whoever Fights Monsters* (New York: St. Martin's Press, 1992), 71.
8. The film is shown on a documentary, *Richard Speck*, produced by the A&E Network in 2001; it is also described in "Nary a Speck of Decency," *Time*, May 27, 1996.
9. Jan E. Leestma, *Forensic Neuropathology* (Boca Raton, Fla.: CRC Press, 2008), 691–92.

Chapter 10

1. Donald T. Lunde, *Murder and Madness* (San Francisco: San Francisco Book Co., 1976), viii, 47.
2. Jay Shore, "Psychiatrist Claims Frazier Is Insane," *Santa Cruz (Calif.) Sentinel*, December 3, 1971.
3. Lunde, *Murder and Madness*, 49–52.
4. Ibid., 46.
5. Ibid., 48.
6. Michael H. Stone, *Healing the Mind* (London: Norton, 1997), 204.
7. Lunde, *Murder and Madness*, 64.
8. Ibid., 80.
9. Ibid., 81.

10. Sharon Yamanaka, "Serial Murders in Santa Cruz County," www.santacruzpl .org/history/crime (accessed August 12, 2003).

11. David K. Frasier, *Murder Cases of the Twentieth Century* (Jefferson, N.C.: McFarland, 1996).

12. Margaret Cheney, *Why: The Serial Killer in America* (Saratoga, Calif.: R&E Publishing, 1992), 128.

13. "The Santa Cruz Murders," *Mugshots* (Court TV, 1996).

14. Ibid.

15. Margaret Cheney, *The Co-ed Killer* (New York: Walker, 1976); and Ward Damio, *Urge to Kill* (New York: Pinnacle, 1974).

16. Lunde, *Murder and Madness*, 53.

17. Ibid., 89–90.

18. Ibid., 54.

19. Ibid.

20. Ibid., 53.

21. Edward Shorter, *A History of Psychiatry* (New York: John Wiley, 1997), 301–2.

Chapter 11

1. Stephen G. Michaud and Hugh Aynesworth, *The Only Living Witness* (New York: Signet, 1983), 81–84.

2. Ibid., 305.

3. Unless otherwise noted, comments from Dr. Al Carlisle are from a phone and email interview with the author, May 15, 2010.

4. Ann Rule, *The Stranger beside Me* (New York: Norton, 1980; updated ed., 1989), 209.

5. Al C. Carlisle, "The Divided Self: Toward an Understanding of the Dark Side of the Serial Killer," *American Journal of Criminal Justice* 17, no. 2 (1993): 109.

6. Carlisle, "The Divided Self," 106–19.

7. Ellsworth Lapham Fersche, ed., *Thinking about the Insanity Defense* (New York: iUniverse, 2005), 134–44.

8. Rule, *The Stranger beside Me*, 25.

9. Ted Bundy Multiagency Investigative Team, *Ted Bundy Multiagency Investigative Team Report* (Washington, D.C.: U.S. Department of Justice, 1992), 4.

10. Ibid.

11. Vernon Geberth, *Practical Homicide Investigation*, 4th ed. (Boca Raton, Fla.: CRC Press, 2006), 801.

12. James Dobson, *Life on the Edge* (Dallas, Tex.: Word Publishing, 1995), 194.

13. Ibid., 196.

14. Ibid., 197.

15. Ibid., 195.

16. Ibid.

17. Ibid., 196.

18. Ibid.

19. Ibid., 197.

20. Ibid.

21. Ibid., 199.

22. Geberth, *Practical Homicide Investigation*, 495.

Chapter 12

1. Author's interview by phone with Robert Ressler, June 25, 2004.

2. Terry Sullivan and Peter Maiken, *Killer Clown* (New York: Grosset & Dunlap, 1983), 176.

3. Helen Morrison and Harold Goldberg, *My Life among the Serial Killers* (New York: HarperCollins, 2004), 73.

4. Ibid., 71.

5. Ibid., 93.

6. Sullivan and Maiken, *Killer Clown*, 354.

7. Morrison and Goldberg, *My Life*, 110.

8. Ibid., 256.

9. Ibid., 273.

10. Sharon Cohen, "Doctor Hunts for Motive in Brain of a Serial Killer," Associated Press, May 8, 2004.

Chapter 13

1. Serge Schmemann, "'Citizen Ch': Russia Opens Files on Serial Killings," *New York Times*, April 4, 1992.

2. Richard Lourie, *Hunting the Devil: The Pursuit, Capture and Confession of the Most Savage Serial Killer in History* (New York: HarperCollins, 1993), 120.

3. Robert Cullen, *The Killer Department: Detective Viktor Burakov's Eight-Year Hunt for the Most Savage Serial Killer in Russian History* (New York: Pantheon Books, 1993), 90–92.

4. Ibid., 125–30.

5. Lourie, *Hunting the Devil*, 87–88.

6. Ibid., 206–7; and Cullen, *The Killer Department*, 192–93.

7. Schmemann, "'Citizen Ch,'" 3.

8. Cullen, *The Killer Department*, 211.

9. Mikhail Krivich and Ol'gert Ol'gin, *Comrade Chikatilo: The Psychopathology of Russia's Notorious Serial Killer* (Fort Lee, N.J.: Barricade Books, 1993); and Lourie, *Hunting the Devil*, 245.

10. Owen Matthews, "A Crime-Fighting MD and the Twisted Citizens of the Capital of Serial Crime: City of the Dead," *Newsweek*, January 25, 1999.

Chapter 14

1. Jeffrey Jenzen, George Palermo, T. Johnson, K. C. Ho, K. A. Stormo, and J. Teggatz, "Destructive Hostility: The Jeffrey Dahmer Case," *American Journal of*

Forensic Medicine and Pathology 15, no. 4 (1994): 285; and Alex Prud'homme and Ken Myers, "The Little Flat of Horrors," *Time*, August 5, 1991.

2. Alex Prud'homme and Mary Cronin, "Milwaukee Murders: Did They All Have to Die?" *Time*, August 12, 1991.

3. Lionel Dahmer, *A Father's Story* (New York: William Morrow, 1994); and David S. Nichols, "Tell Me a Story: MMPI Responses and Personal Biography in the Case of a Serial Killer," *Journal of Personality Assessment* 86, no. 3 (2006): 244.

4. Anne E. Schwartz, *The Man Who Could Not Kill Enough* (New York: Carol Publishing, 1992).

5. Nichols, "Tell Me a Story," 244.

6. R. Mayes and A. V. Horwitz, "DSM-III and the Revolution in the Classification of Mental Illness," *Journal of Historical Behavioral Science* 41, no. 3 (2005): 249–67.

7. Michael H. Stone, *Healing the Mind* (London: Norton, 1997), 302.

8. George Palermo, "Narcissism, Sadism and Loneliness: The Case of Serial Killer Jeffrey Dahmer," in *Serial Murder and the Psychology of Violent Crime*, ed. Richard Kocsis (Totowa, N.J.: Humana Press, 2008), 92.

9. Robert K. Ressler, *I Have Lived in the Monster* (New York: St. Martin's Press, 1997), 116.

10. Jenzen et al., "Destructive Hostility," 291.

11. Nichols, "Tell Me a Story," 245–46.

12. Catherine E. Purcell and Bruce A. Arrigo, *The Psychology of Lust Murder: Paraphilia, Sexual Killing, and Serial Homicide* (San Diego, Calif.: Academic Press, 2006), 67–83.

13. Don Davis, *The Jeffrey Dahmer Story* (New York: St. Martin's Press, 1991, rev. ed. 1995), 297.

14. Steven Walters, "Dahmer Is Baptized in Prison Tub," *Milwaukee Sentinel*, May 12, 1994.

15. Roy Ratcliff, "The Baptism of Jeffrey Dahmer," *Christian Woman*, April–May 1995.

16. Walters, "Dahmer Is Baptized."

17. Ratcliff, "The Baptism of Jeffrey Dahmer."

18. Ibid.

19. Roy Ratcliff, *Dark Journey, Deep Grace* (Abilene, Tex.: Leafwood, 2006), 129.

20. Ibid., 126.

21. Ibid., 128.

22. Ibid., 130.

23. Ibid., 9.

24. "Dahmer's Brain Kept for Research," *Milwaukee Journal*, March 17, 1995.

25. State of Wisconsin, motion hearing, case no. 94-PR-175, October 3, 1995.

26. Ratcliff, *Dark Journey*, 135.

27. Ibid., 155.

28. Ibid., 156.

Chapter 15

1. Phillip J. Resnick, "Child Murder by Parents: A Psychiatric Review of Filicide," *American Journal of Psychiatry* 126 (September 3, 1969): 73–82.
2. Phillip Resnick, "Child Murder by Parents," paper presentation at Special Training Services in Las Vegas, Nev., March 11, 2002.
3. All quotes not otherwise cited in this chapter are from a phone interview with Phillip Resnick, January 13, 2010.
4. Kristin Ohlson, "Darkness Visible," *CWRU Magazine*, Winter 2003, 22.
5. Ibid., 23.
6. Suzy Spenser, *Breaking Point* (New York: St. Martin's Press, 2002); and Deborah W. Denno, "Who Is Andrea Yates? A Short Story about Insanity," *Duke Journal of Gender Law & Policy* 10, no. 1 (2003): 1–60.
7. Phillip Resnick, "The Andrea Yates Case: Insanity on Trial," *Cleveland State Law Review* 55, no. 147 (2007): 147–56.
8. Transcript of Andrea Yates's confession, *Houston Chronicle*, February 21, 2002.
9. Resnick, "The Andrea Yates Case," 147–56; and Timothy Roche, "Andrea Yates: More to the Story," *Time*, March 16, 2002.
10. Ohlson, "Darkness Visible," 20–23.
11. Spenser, *Breaking Point*, 273.
12. Charles Patrick Ewing, "Andrea Yates," in *Insanity: Murder, Madness, and the Law* (New York: Oxford University Press, 2008), 150.
13. Ibid., 152.
14. Denno, "Who Is Andrea Yates?" 45.
15. Ibid., 46.
16. Ibid.
17. Resnick, "The Andrea Yates Case," 155.

Chapter 16

1. Benedict Carey, "For the Worst of Us, the Diagnosis May Be 'Evil,'" *New York Times*, February 8, 2008.
2. Phone and in-person interviews with Michael Stone, March 13 and April 18, 2010.
3. Michael Stone, *The Anatomy of Evil* (Amherst, N.Y.: Prometheus, 2009), 48.
4. Ibid., 47.
5. Ibid., 317.
6. Diane Fanning, *Through the Window* (New York: St. Martin's Press, 2003), 25–26.
7. Tori Rivers, *13 ½: Twelve Jurors, One Judge, and a Half-Assed Chance* (Ramsay, N.J.: Riverbend Press, 2008), 3.
8. Fanning, *Through the Window*, 27–28.
9. "Krystal's Courage," *48 Hours*, November 21 (CBS, 2009).
10. Fanning, *Through the Window*, 128.

11. Fanning and Rivers both provide extensive if inconsistent accounts of his confessions; Rivers offered Sells the opportunity to publish his account in his own words.

12. John MacCormack, "Killer Smile: Tommy Lynn Sells Claims to Have Murdered Dozens, and Texas Rangers Fear He's Telling the Truth," *San Antonio Express-News*, September 13, 2000.

13. Stone, *The Anatomy of Evil*, 230.

14. Ibid.

15. Ibid., 231.

16. Ibid., 232.

17. News transcript, *20/20*, May 26 (ABC, 2005).

18. Stone, *The Anatomy of Evil*, 258.

19. From correspondence between Tommy Lynn Sells and Michael Stone, quoted with permission from Dr. Stone.

20. Stone, *The Anatomy of Evil*, 317.

Chapter 17

1. Richard W. Bailey, *Rogue Scholar: The Sinister Life and Celebrated Death of Edward Rulloff* (Ann Arbor: University of Michigan Press, 2003); and Susan Lang, "A Case for Brains: Cornell's Cerebral Display Gets Refurbished Home," May 5, 2006, http://www.news.cornell.edu/stories/May06/Wilder.brains.ssl.html (accessed August 5, 2010).

2. Lois Rogers, "Secret Tests on Brains of Serial Killers," *(London) Times*, April 4, 2004.

3. Adrian Raine, "Murderous Minds: Can We See the Mark of Cain?" Dana Foundation, April 1, 1999, www.dana.org (accessed March 21, 2010).

4. Yaling Yang, Andrea L. Glenn, and Adrian Raine, "Brain Abnormalities in Antisocial Individuals: Implications for the Law," *Behavioral Sciences and the Law* 26 (2008): 65–83.

5. Ibid., 65–66.

6. Benedict Carey, "Brain Injury Said to Affect Moral Choices," *New York Times*, March 22, 2007; and "Murder on His Mind," *48 Hours*, January 13 (CBS, 2007).

7. Joshua W. Buckholtz, Michael T. Treadway, Ronald L. Cowan, Neil D. Woodward, Stephen D. Benning, Rui Li, M. Sib Ansari, Ronald M. Baldwin, Ashley N. Schwartzman, Evan S. Shelby, Clarence E. Smith, David Cole, Robert M. Kessler, and David H. Zald, "Mesolimbic Dopamine Reward System Hypersensitivity in Individuals with Psychopathic Traits," *Nature Neuroscience* 10 (2010): 1038.

8. Brian C. Trainor, Joanna L. Workman, Ruth Jessen, and Randy J. Nelson, "Impaired Nitric Oxide Synthase Signaling Dissociates Social Investigation and Aggression," *Behavioral Neuroscience* 121, no. 2 (April 2007): 362–69.

9. Andreas Meyer-Lindenberg, Joshua W. Buckholtz, Bhaskar Kolachana, Ahmad R. Hariri, Lukas Pezawas, Giuseppe Blasi, Ashley Wabnitz, Robyn Honea, Beth

Verchinski, Joseph H. Callicott, Michael Egan, Venkata Mattay, and Daniel R. Weinberger, "Neural Mechanisms of Genetic Risk for Impulsivity and Violence in Humans," *Proceedings of the National Academy of Science* 103, no. 16 (2006): 6269–74.

10. Lawrence A. Farwell, "Farwell Fingerprinting Testing," forensic report prepared for Sheriff Robert Dawson, Macon County (Missouri) Sheriff's Office, August 5, 1999; Tom Paulson, "Brain Fingerprinting Touted as Truth Meter," *Seattle Post-Intelligencer*, March 1, 2004; and Beth Dalby, "Brain Fingerprinting Testing Traps Serial Killer in Missouri," *Fairfield (Mo.) Ledger*, www.brainwavescience.com (accessed January 5, 2007).

11. John Gray Wilson, *The Trial of Peter Manuel: The Man Who Talked too Much* (London: Secker and Warburg, 1959); "New Evidence in Psychopath Case," *BBC News*, February 16, 2009; and National Archives of Scotland, "The Mind of a Killer: The Peter Manuel Case," 2009.

12. Iain Lundy, "'Callous' Beast Who Rattled Scotland," Scotsman.com, November 7, 2005, http://heritage.scotsman.com/notoriouscriminalsfeatureseries/Callous-beast-who-rattled-Scotland.2676231.jp (accessed August 5, 2010).

13. Graeme Smith, "Vital Evidence in Manuel Case 'Was Withheld,'" *The Herald*, Scottish ed., May 1, 2008, http://www.heraldscotland.com/vital-evidence-in-manuel-murder-case-was-withheld-1.879632 (accessed August 5, 2010).

14. John Baxter Gaylor, medical report, National Archives of Scotland, reference no. HH60/703/1, February 20, 1958.

Chapter 18

1. S. Arzy, M. Seeck, S. Ortigue, L. Spinelli, and O. Blanke, "Induction of an Illusory Shadow Person," *Nature* 443, no. 21 (2006): 287.

Bibliography

Altman, J., and Marvin Ziporyn. *Born to Raise Hell: The Untold Story of Richard Speck*. New York: Grove Press, 1967.

Artières, P. "What Criminals Think about Criminology." In *Criminals and Their Scientists: The History of Criminology in International Perspective*, ed. Peter Becker and Richard F. Wetzell, 363–75. Cambridge: Cambridge University Press, 2006.

Berg, Karl. *The Sadist: An Account of the Crimes of Serial Killer Peter Kürten: A Study in Sadism*. London: Heinemann, 1945.

Brussel, James. *Casebook of a Crime Psychiatrist*. New York: Grove Press, 1968.

Buckholtz, J. W., Michael T. Treadway, Ronald L. Cowan, Neil D. Woodward, Stephen D. Benning, Rui Li, M. Sib Ansari, Ronald M. Baldwin, Ashley N. Schwartzman, Evan S. Shelby, Clarence E. Smith, David Cole, Robert M. Kessler, and David H. Zald, "Mesolimbic Dopamine Reward System Hypersensitivity in Individuals with Psychopathic Traits," *Nature Neuroscience* 10 (2010): 1038.

Carlisle, Al C. "The Dark Side of the Serial-Killer Personality." In *Serial Killers*, ed. Louis Gerdes. San Diego, CA: Greenhaven Press, 2000.

Cartwright, Duncan. "The Narcissistic Exoskeleton: The Defensive Organization of the Rage-Type Murderer." *Bulletin of the Menninger Clinic* 66, no. 1 (Winter 2002): 1–18.

Cheney, Margaret. *Why: The Serial Killer in America*. Saratoga, CA: R&E Publishers, 1992 (originally *The Co-ed Killer*, New York: Walker Publishing, 1976).

Cleckley, H. *The Mask of Sanity*, 5th ed. St. Louis, MO: Mosby, 1976.

Colaizzi, Janet. *Homicidal Insanity, 1800–1985*. Tuscaloosa: University of Alabama Press, 1989.

Cox, Bill G. *Born Bad*. New York: Pinnacle, 1996.

Cullen, Robert. *The Killer Department: Detective Viktor Burakov's Eight-Year Hunt for the Most Savage Serial Killer in Russian History*. New York: Pantheon Books, 1993.

Dahmer, Lionel. *A Father's Story*. New York: William Morrow, 1994.

Damio, Ward. *Urge to Kill*. New York: Pinnacle, 1974.

Davis, Don. *The Jeffrey Dahmer Story*. New York: St. Martin's Press, 1991, rev. ed. 1995.

DeNevi, Don, and John H. Campbell. *Into the Minds of Madmen: How the FBI Behavioral Science Unit Revolutionized Crime Investigation*. Amherst, N.Y.: Prometheus Books, 2004.

Denno, D. W. "Who Is Andrea Yates? A Short Story about Insanity." *Duke Journal of Gender Law & Policy* 10, no. 1 (2003): 1–60.

De River, J. Paul. *The Sexual Criminal: A Psychoanalytic Study.* Springfield, Ill.: Charles C. Thomas, 1949.

Dobson, James. *Life on the Edge.* Dallas, TX: Word Publishing, 1995.

Douglas, John, and Mark Olshaker. *Mindhunter: Inside the FBI's Elite Serial Crime Unit.* New York: Scribner, 1995.

Fanning, Diane. *Through the Window.* New York: St. Martin's Press, 2003.

Frank, G. *The Boston Strangler.* New York: New American Library, 1966.

Frasier, David K. *Murder Cases of the Twentieth Century.* Jefferson, NC: McFarland, 1996.

Gaddis, Thomas, and James O. Long, *Killer: A Journal of Murder.* New York: Macmillan, 1970.

Garrison, A. "The Catathymic Crisis: An Explanation for Serial Killers." *Journal of Police and Criminal Psychology* 11, no. 1 (1996): 5–12.

Geberth, Vernon J. *Practical Homicide Investigation,* 4th ed. Boca Raton, FL: CRC Press, 2006.

Hickey, Eric. *Serial Murderers and Their Victims,* 3rd ed. Belmont, CA: Wadsworth, 2002.

Horn, David G. *The Criminal Body: Lombroso and the Anatomy of Deviance.* New York: Routledge, 2003.

Jeffers, H. Paul. *Who Killed Precious?* New York: St. Martin's Press, 1991.

Jenzen, Jeffrey, George Palermo, T. Johnson, K. C. Ho, K. A. Stormo, and J. Teggatz. "Destructive Hostility: The Jeffrey Dahmer Case." *American Journal of Forensic Medicine and Pathology* 15, no. 4 (1994): 283–94.

Johnson, Steven. *Mind Wide Open: Your Brain and the Neuroscience of Everyday Life.* New York: Scribner, 2004.

Kelly, Susan. *The Boston Stranglers.* New York: Pinnacle, 1995; updated ed., 2002.

Keppel, Robert D. *The Psychology of Serial Killer Investigations.* San Diego, CA: Academic Press, 2003.

Keppel, Robert D., and William J. Birnes. *The Riverman: Ted Bundy and I Hunt for the Green River Killer.* New York: Pocket, 1995.

King, Brian, ed. *Lustmord: The Writings and Artifacts of Murderers.* Burbank, CA: Bloat Books, 1996.

Krafft-Ebing, Richard von. *Psychopathia Sexualis with Especial Reference to the Antipathic Sexual Instinct: A Medico-Forensic Study,* rev. ed. Philadelphia: Physicians and Surgeons, 1928.

Krivich, Mikhail, and Ol'gert Ol'gin. *Comrade Chikatilo: The Psychopathology of Russia's Notorious Serial Killer.* Fort Lee, NJ: Barricade Books, 1993.

Lester, David. *Serial Killers: The Insatiable Passion.* Philadelphia: Charles Press, 1995.

Lombroso, Cesare. *L'uomo delinquente.* Milan: Hoepli, 1876.

Lourie, Richard. *Hunting the Devil: The Pursuit, Capture and Confession of the Most Savage Serial Killer in History.* New York: HarperCollins, 1993.

Lunde, Donald T. *Murder and Madness.* San Francisco: San Francisco Book Co., 1976.

Lunde, Donald T., and Jefferson Morgan. *The Die Song: A Journey into the Mind of a Mass Murderer*. New York: Norton, 1980.

Menninger, Karl. *Man against Himself*. New York: Harcourt, Brace, 1938.

Michaud, Stephen, and Hugh Aynesworth. *The Only Living Witness: A True Account of Homicidal Insanity*. New York: New American Library, 1983.

Morrison, Helen. *My Life among Serial Killers*. New York: William Morrow, 2004.

Newton, Michael. *Wasteland: The Savage Odyssey of Charles Starkweather and Caril Ann Fugate*. New York: Pocket, 1998.

Niehoff, Debra. *The Biology of Violence*. New York: Free Press, 1999.

Oosterhuis, H. *Stepchildren of Nature: Krafft-Ebing, Psychiatry, and the Making of Sexual Identity*. Chicago: University of Chicago Press, 2000.

Purcell, Catherine E., and Bruce A. Arrigo. *The Psychology of Lust Murder: Paraphilia, Sexual Killing, and Serial Homicide*. San Diego, CA: Academic Press, 2006.

Raine, Adrian, and Jose Sanmartin, eds. *Violence and Psychopathy*. New York: Kluwer Academic, 2001.

Ramsland, Katherine. *The Criminal Mind: A Writer's Guide to Forensic Psychology*. Cincinnati, OH: Writer's Digest Books, 2002.

Ramsland, Katherine. *The Human Predator: A Historical Chronicle of Serial Murder and Forensic Investigation*. New York: Berkley, 2005.

Ratcliff, Roy. *Dark Journey, Deep Grace*. Abilene, TX: Leafwood, 2006.

Ray, Isaac. *A Treatise on the Medical Jurisprudence of Insanity*. London: n.p., 1838.

Reinhardt, James M. "Crime in a Discordant Culture." *Journal of Criminal Law and Criminology* 41, no. 1 (May–June 1950): 32.

Reinhardt, James M. *The Murderous Trail of Charles Starkweather*. Springfield, IL: Charles C. Thomas, 1960.

Resnick, Phillip J. "Child Murder by Parents: A Psychiatric Review of Filicide." *American Journal of Psychiatry* 126 (September 3, 1969): 73–82.

Resnick, Phillip J. "The Andrea Yates Case: Insanity on Trial." *Cleveland State Law Review* 55, no. 147 (2007): 147–56.

Ressler, Robert K. *I Have Lived in the Monster*. New York: St. Martin's Press, 1997.

Ressler, Robert K., and Tom Schachtman. *Whoever Fights Monsters*. New York: St. Martin's Press, 1992.

Rivers, Tori. *13 ½: Twelve Jurors, One Judge, and a Half-Assed Chance*. Ramsey, NJ: Riverbend Press, 2008.

Rule, Ann. *The Stranger beside Me*. New York: Norton, 1980.

Schechter, Harold. *Deranged: The Shocking True Story of America's Most Fiendish Killer*. New York: Pocket, 1990.

Schwartz, Anne E. *The Man Who Could Not Kill Enough*. New York: Carol Publishing, 1992.

Shorter, Edward. *A History of Psychiatry*. New York: John Wiley, 1997.

Spenser, Suzy. *Breaking Point*. New York: St. Martin's Press, 2002.

Starrs, James E., with K. Ramsland. *A Voice for the Dead*. New York: Putnam, 2005.

Stone, Michael H. *Healing the Mind: A History of Psychiatry from Antiquity to the Present*. London: Norton, 1997.

Stone, Michael H. *The Anatomy of Evil*. Amherst, N.Y.: Prometheus, 2009.

Sullivan, Terry, and Peter Maiken. *Killer Clown: The John Wayne Gacy Murders*. New York: Grosset & Dunlap, 1983.

Tanay, Emanuel. *American Legal Injustice*. Lanham, MD: Jason Aronson, 2010.

Vronsky, Peter. *Serial Killers: The Method and Madness of Monsters*. New York: Berkley, 2004.

Wertham, Fredric. *The Show of Violence*. New York: Doubleday, 1949.

Wertham, Fredric. "Why Do They Commit Murder?" *New York Times*, August 8, 1954, p. SM8.

Wilson, J. G. *The Trial of Peter Manuel: The Man Who Talked Too Much*. London: Secker and Warburg, 1959.

Yang, Yaling, Adrian Raine, Todd Lencz, Susan Bihrle, Lori Lacasse, and Patrick Colletti, "Prefrontal White Matter in Pathological Liars." *British Journal of Psychiatry* 187 (2005): 320–25.

Index

About the Author

Katherine Ramsland, Ph.D., holds graduate degrees in forensic psychology, clinical psychology, and philosophy. Currently, she teaches forensic psychology and criminal justice at DeSales University in Pennsylvania. She has published over 900 articles and thirty-eight books, including *The Forensic Psychology of Criminal Minds, Beating the Devil's Game: A History of Forensic Science and Criminal Investigation, The Human Predator: A Historical Chronicle of Serial Murder and Forensic Investigation, Inside the Minds of Serial Killers, Inside the Minds of Healthcare Serial Killers, Inside the Minds of Sexual Predators,* and *Inside the Minds of Mass Murderers.* She has been published in ten languages. Her background in forensic studies positioned her to assist former FBI profiler John Douglas on his book, *The Cases That Haunt Us,* to co-write a book with former FBI profiler, Gregg McCrary, *The Unknown Darkness.* She speaks internationally about forensic psychology, forensic science, and serial murder, and has appeared on numerous documentaries, as well as such programs as *The Today Show, 20/20, Montel Williams, NPR, Larry King Live* and *E! True Hollywood.*